The Splintering of the American Mind

THE SPLINTERING
OF THE
AMERICAN MIND

IDENTITY POLITICS, INEQUALITY, AND
COMMUNITY ON TODAY'S COLLEGE CAMPUSES

WILLIAM EGGINTON

BLOOMSBURY PUBLISHING
NEW YORK · LONDON · OXFORD · NEW DELHI · SYDNEY

BLOOMSBURY PUBLISHING
Bloomsbury Publishing Inc.
1385 Broadway, New York, NY 10018, USA

BLOOMSBURY, BLOOMSBURY PUBLISHING, and the Diana logo are trademarks of
Bloomsbury Publishing Plc

First published in the United States 2018

ISBN: HB: 978-1-63557-133-2
        eBook: 978-1-63557-134-9

Library of Congress Cataloging-in-Publication Data
Names: Egginton, William, 1969- author.
Title: The splintering of the American mind : identity politics, inequality, and community
on today's college campuses / William Egginton.
Description: New York, NY : Bloomsbury Publishing, [2018]
Identifiers: LCCN 2017058793 | ISBN 9781635571332 (hardback) | ISBN 9781635571349 (ebook)
Subjects: LCSH: Multiculturalism—United States. | Group identity—United States. |
Equality—United States. | Education, Higher—United States. |
College students—United States—Attitudes.
Classification: LCC HM1271 .E374 2018 | DDC 305.800973—dc23 LC record available at
https://lccn.loc.gov/2017058793

2 4 6 8 10 9 7 5 3 1

Typeset by Westchester Publishing Services
Printed and bound in the U.S.A. by Berryville Graphics Inc., Berryville, Virginia

To find out more about our authors and books visit www.bloomsbury.com
and sign up for our newsletters.

Bloomsbury books may be purchased for business or promotional use.
For information on bulk purchases please contact Macmillan Corporate and
Premium Sales Department at specialmarkets@macmillan.com.

This book is dedicated to America's youth, that they may receive the education they deserve—not just for their sake, but for ours.

CONTENTS

Introduction

On a balmy afternoon in the spring of 2015 I found myself strolling across
the idyllic campus of the University of California, Santa Barbara, the gentle
breezes wafting in from its gleaming Pacific beaches only slightly marred
by the faint odor from a recent oil spill. The beach where I had just been
walking was abuzz in preparations for a "paddle-out" planned for that
evening to mark the one-year anniversary of the gruesome mass killing
that had terrorized the neighboring community of Isla Vista. On an evening
much like this one the previous June, a young white man, isolated and
resentful, had driven his BMW through town on a killing spree. In a screed
posted just prior to setting off, he claimed this was his revenge on all the
women he desired from afar but could never possess. As I made my way
toward Isla Vista to retrieve my car I couldn't help but reflect on the vaguely
incongruous scene that would take place later that evening, of dozens of
candles bobbing up and down on surfboards to commemorate the victims
of a hate- and desperation-fueled ballistic orgy.

My reverie was due to be interrupted by another incongruity. As I passed
the outer ring of dormitories and administrative buildings that abut the
campus's border with the town, I noticed that the signs around me were
of a similar design and message. Each one displayed a face drawn from a
rainbow coalition of bright young people. Under these portraits were

testimonials mandating how the students should be addressed, what topics were permissible to discuss in their presence, and what sorts of questions one should avoid asking them, all based on the pictured students' race, gender, or sexuality.

In some regards we are living in a most enlightened age, and our universities are beacons of that enlightenment. How can we not admire the social changes that have led our centers of learning to embrace the ethnic, cultural, and sexual differences that so recently in our own national history were open justifications for denigration, discrimination, and even exclusion from those very institutions? Nonetheless, on that walk—from a beach being staged for a paddle-out to the adjacent streets where a dejected social outcast had taken his rage out by killing young students—my admiration for academe's embrace of diversity and difference registered a momentary pall.

Did the curb I was just stepping over, a symbolic and yet totally porous border between town and gown at UCSB, also represent an equally fragile border between two worlds whose mutual distrust, antagonism, and even repulsion are tearing apart the country's social fabric? In one corner a mostly white, sometimes rural, often male America that simmers in despair and resentment at the privilege of university-educated, coastal elites who seem ready to give every group in America a leg up except them. In the other, a cosmopolitan, educated, multicultural America that has every reason to see its embrace of racial and ethnic difference and its defense of minority rights as representing significant progress in human history. Here I was on a campus nestled among the dunes, featuring dorms with multimillion-dollar views of the Pacific, whose students paddled out on surfboards to express their outrage and grief while ensuring that newcomers be well instructed on the etiquette of gender pronouns. Was such a campus not at risk of degenerating into something like the worst caricature of its opponents' opposition research?

In light of America's evident identity crisis, what are our universities doing? Part of what made America a beacon for the world's democracies was the explicit understanding that democracy depended on an enlightened, educated public. In Thomas Jefferson's powerful words, democracy can only flourish "where the press is free, *and every man able to read*," an injunction that implies a much higher bar than bare literacy. Indeed, as he said of the university he founded, "This institution will be based on the illimitable freedom of the human mind. For here we are not afraid to follow truth wherever it may lead, nor to tolerate any error so long as reason is left free to combat it." Has our education system lived up to the courage of these sentiments, or to the requirements of contributing to a truly democratic culture, and have universities continued to lead us by aiming, as Cardinal John Henry Newman insisted in his 1852 blueprint for *The Idea of a University*, at "raising the intellectual tone of society, at cultivating the public mind, at purifying the national taste, [and] at supplying true principles to popular enthusiasm and fixed aims to popular aspiration"?

As they surveyed the decisive damage to our body politic revealed by the corrosive presidential campaign of 2016, some critics blamed the progressive bent of campus life and its infiltration into mainstream politics for the decimation of the Democratic Party and a resurgence of reactionary politics. As Columbia professor of humanities Mark Lilla put it the weekend following the 2016 election, "In recent years American liberalism has slipped into a kind of moral panic about racial, gender and sexual identity that has distorted liberalism's message and prevented it from becoming a unifying force capable of governing." While acknowledging that the "moral energy surrounding identity . . . has had many good effects," he went on to admonish that "the fixation on diversity in our schools and in the press has produced a generation of liberals and progressives narcissistically unaware of conditions outside their self-defined groups, and indifferent to the task of reaching out to Americans in every walk of life." This sentiment was promoted by the left, with Bernie Sanders castigating the Democratic Party for its embrace of identity politics without enough regard for class. Donald Trump capitalized on it as well, with complaints against political correctness that, as reported in the *New York Times Magazine*, "conjured a world of absurdist campus politics, where overprivileged students squabble over gender pronouns and the fine points of racial victimization." To be sure, every accusation of sexism or racism leveled against Trump could be read by his followers as confirmation of the "liberal" press's enthrallment to identity politics.

Is this story true? Are campus identity politics, by feeding into stereotypes and allowing their detractors more easily to dismiss their claims, responsible for the degeneration of political discourse? A tiny sliver of the population has soared to extremes of wealth never seen before while the wages of working families have stagnated and even declined for thirty years; is "identity liberalism" one of the reasons why so many of those families are unable to find common ground with constituencies that have every reason to share their concerns and desires? And are cultural politics, on campus and off, the Pyrrhic victory that lost for the left its economic and political war, or the red herring that has allowed the Republican Party to pull a generation-long bait and switch on America's working class?

As I argue in this book, some colleges in the 1970s, by accepting and accommodating a justifiable intellectual demand for *equal* treatment of minority perspectives, were also encouraging the cultivation of isolated *identities*. And this was happening at the same time as *community*, the underlying theme of both the postwar economic expansion and the civil rights movement itself, was suffering debilitating attacks from both the right and the left. Conservatives undermined community by promoting small-government, free-market fundamentalism; progressives through an ever-expanding embrace of social freedoms and distrust of traditional institutional authority, which they saw as oppressive. In the face of this almost perfect storm, colleges jettisoned the defense of the social contract that the liberal arts had helped formulate, and instead exacerbated the situation by providing intellectual cover and justification for the dissolution of social bonds.

The ability of our universities to counter this cultural and intellectual shift was further compromised by the pressures of the market, ironically the very same economic trends that a resurgent right was championing. State institutions, stripped of state funding, were becoming more and more like slightly discounted private schools, raising tuitions at unprecedented rates to pay for the amenities that allow them to vie for the best students. Private schools, in turn, had no incentive to stop the exorbitant rise of their own tuitions, as they competed against one another for the best (and wealthiest) students with shiny new facilities, and climbed in the coveted *U.S. News and World Report* rankings by winning bidding wars over the professors with the most impressive publication records.

Through all this the left failed to see that while winning the battle over identity, it was losing the war over community. Universities had allowed the liberal tradition, civics, and the American idea of democracy to be painted as the antithesis of identity rather than its very condition of possibility. The irony is that, by focusing our attention on identity yet again, this time to blame identity liberalism for its role in distracting us from questions of economic equality, we are at risk again of ignoring the role our entire education system continues to play in intensifying both inequality and the degeneration of our civic discourse.

With the momentum of the civil rights movement propelling them, young professors from the late sixties through the early eighties began to bring real intellectual heft to courses and programs that gave pride of place for the interpretation of texts or the organization of syllabi to the personal expressions and experiences of minorities and women. In this sense a line can be drawn from the publication of Betty Friedan's *The Feminine Mystique* in 1963, a sociological and psychological study of women's dissatisfaction in family life despite rising standards of living in the 1950s, to that of Sandra M. Gilbert and Susan Gubar's now classic work of feminist literary criticism *The Madwoman in the Attic* in 1979, a revisionist look at English literature of the Victorian age from the perspective of its female characters. Likewise, as intellectuals fresh from the civil rights movement assumed faculty positions at prestigious universities, some, like Cornell University's James Turner, were inspired to create programs that focused on the global experience of blacks. Turner founded the Africana Studies and Research Center, in 1969, in order to teach and research the African diaspora and the experiences of black populations in Africa, the Caribbean, and North America.

For students arriving on college campuses in the 1970s, these new classes and specializations offered intellectual support for the idea that there was political value in maximizing personal expression. In practice this sometimes meant that the core of the liberal arts curriculum, books written mostly by European men, was cast aside or made optional in favor of incorporating works by women, minorities, or writers from non-Western cultures. Colleges also added new majors and minors to the curriculum that focused on gender and ethnic identities; black, women's, and queer studies programs and departments started to proliferate. By 1991 even a left-leaning historian like Arthur M. Schlesinger Jr. would complain,

> the militants of ethnicity contend that a main objective of public educa-tion should be the protection, strengthening, celebration, and perpetu-ation of ethnic origins and identities. Separatism, however, nourishes prejudices, magnifies differences, and stirs antagonisms. The consequent increase in ethnic and racial conflict lies behind the hullabaloo over "multiculturalism" and "political correctness," over the iniquities of the "Eurocentric" curriculum, and over the notion that history and litera-ture should be taught not as intellectual disciplines but as therapies whose function is to raise minority self-esteem.

Whether or not Schlesinger was right to call the turn toward identity in our schools a mode of therapy intended to assuage minority self-esteem, his arguments presaged by almost twenty years the line today that is casting blame for the dominant success of the populist-oligarchical alliance on identity liberalism. Indeed, the current ascendancy of extreme right-wing politics in the United States—in ways not dissimilar to its rise in Europe—is at least partially explainable as a kind of reaction against the perception that "liberal elites" are more interested in coddling identity-based special interest groups than in advancing the cause of economic equality for all, a perception bolstered by data showing that employment gains over the last decade have gone exclusively to the college-educated. The irony is that, while enthusiastically supporting policies and instruction intended to ameliorate entrenched gender- and race-based inequality, our colleges have inadvertently become a potent factor in a new kind of identity poli-tics, and a powerful symbol and instance of inequality themselves.

On their own the new programs were tremendously positive, both for women and blacks as historically oppressed populations, as well as for the advancement of knowledge, since the understanding of texts and historical events was broadened to encompass previously excluded or underappreciated perspectives. They also had some unintended consequences. One of these was the tendency, now ubiquitous on college campuses and beyond, to preface argumentation with a statement of the position of the speaker: "as a black man," "as a woman," or now, indeed, "as a white man." While born of the admirable impulse to recognize the primacy of subjective experience, the generalization of such self-evident caveats has led to a presumption of incommunicability. Balkanization of perspective among students is now the accepted state of affairs, and it is one that encourages and apparently justifies segregation based on race, ethnicity, and now even political passion.

In the narrative that now blames identity politics on the left for the rise to power of a xenophobic, nationalist president, the excesses of the 1980s have only intensified in recent years. Critics point to a campus culture in which activists verbally abuse faculty and students who don't share their views; demand "safe spaces" free from the presence of those who disagree with or are critical of them; occupy administration offices and insist that controversial speakers be disinvited; monitor student and faculty speech in order to call attention to "microaggressions"; and require faculty to include "trigger warnings" to warn prospective students of course content they might find objectionable. In what could seem the acme of absurdity, more than four hundred students and professors signed a letter criticizing University of Virginia president Teresa Sullivan for quoting, of all people, the university's founder, Thomas Jefferson, forcing Sullivan to issue the painfully obvious proviso that "quoting Jefferson (or any historical figure) does not imply an endorsement of all the social structures and beliefs of his time." According to the current narrative, such hypersensitivity on campus bleeds directly into the kind of politics that has the Democratic Party focused on which bathrooms can be used by transgender people while Middle America's jobs get shipped overseas, thus opening the door for a populist demagogue to come to power, threatening the very core of our democratic system.

It is a truism that campus politics are fomented in the humanities classes that are a fundamental part of a liberal arts education. The excesses we are witnessing today, however, are a distortion of the ideal of the liberal arts, an educational institution that laid the cornerstone of modern democracy in the mutual interdependence of liberty *and* equality. Orphaned from that context, race, ethnicity, gender, sexual orientation, and class, rather than factors in the historical denial of specific rights pertaining to *humanity*, are treated as unique substances granting the owner an ineffable perspective from which to speak. But if all perspectives are ineffable, then dialogue devolves into an endless clamor of competing claims: Duke University student David Grasso insisting that he be freed from the obligation to read lesbian author Alison Bechdel's memoir because it offends his Christian values; Brandeis University disinviting a Muslim woman critical of Islam because students objected that her perspective would be offensive to Muslims; college Republicans demanding safe spaces because they voted for Donald Trump.

The irony is that these demands emerged from noble impulses. The drive to stand up for an unpopular belief, to speak out for a minority creed, was essential to the founding of the American community. But without an equal drive to cherish the community in which such dissent takes place, to recognize that my right to self-realization requires mutual respect and toleration, these demands are in a way stillborn, miscreant. How much more powerful would our dissent be if we read and engaged the offending work, if we listened to and argued with this or that offending speaker, and if we all exposed ourselves to those whose votes caved in our comfortable worlds! This book asks us to imagine the sort of community in which those conversations can take place.

Universities and the humanistic debates on their campuses did not create our current predicament by promoting identity politics, cultural relativism, and cultural diversity. On the contrary, the succor and support on campuses for historically maligned and marginalized groups not only have made worlds of difference to those fortunate enough to enter the collegiate world, they have also benefited our understanding of society and the cultures that inform it. At the same time, the inclusion of underrepresented perspectives in higher education inevitably challenged and expanded the American ideal of community. Where that ideal had been based on an implicit sense of a shared ethnic origin in western Europe and on the explicit, often violent exclusion and oppression of entire races and genders, the emerging American community would eventually stretch to contain multiple cultures and ethnicities as well as genders and sexual orientations. And while universities have taken the lead in substantiating and exploring the multiple identities that are seeking self-realization and expression, they have paid less attention to the role of community and how it supports and enables such self-realization.

Like our society, our education system has not been up to the task of redressing the tilting of our democracy away from equality and community, and toward unfettered individual freedom for those with the means to enjoy it. While campus culture wars have played a role in that, we have also failed to sustain and promote equal access to quality public education, from kindergarten through high school. These two trends are intertwined in problematic ways. The confluence of a greater emphasis on identity and individual expression with an increase in income inequality and inequality of access to the very educational opportunities that support and encourage such individual advancement has compounded the problem in ways that affect our society and culture at large.

By the time those who do attend college ever arrive on campus, the tables are steeply stacked, leading to two thirds of Americans never earning a bachelor's degree, the demographic equivalent of an eternity in economic limbo. Some public institutions are still responding to their calling to lift Americans out of poverty. New York's City College, once known as the "Harvard of the proletariat," along with schools like the University of Texas at El Paso and California State University, Bakersfield, still managed to move more than three fourths of their students from the lowest economic quintile into the top three. These community colleges and public universities do yeoman's work trying to reset the playing field and restore opportunity where it is lacking. Excepting these outliers, however, higher education in general aids and abets inequality with its pyramid of privilege, at the top of which sit the schools that have become self-perpetuating enclaves, boutique department stores where the elite go to purchase an education the way one might purchase a luxury automobile. Meanwhile, the social and economic sorting has led to the rise of the statistically most identifiable Trump supporter—the white, high-school-educated male.

———

Have identity politics produced anything of value? Without a doubt! For one thing, the focus on identity on college campuses has contributed greatly to the beneficial awareness of and promotion of cultural, racial, and gender diversity in society at large. But it is also true that the advocacy of identity politics without ensuring that their study be placed in the proper historical and sociological context has in some cases undermined the advances made toward equality. In 1869, when Susan B. Anthony founded the *Revolution*, a newspaper dedicated to defending the rights of women as well as blacks, its masthead read, "The True Republic: Men Their Rights and Nothing More; Women Their Rights and Nothing Less," a succinct reminder that the goal of the movement's advocacy was nothing other than the society-wide equality enshrined in the nation's founding documents. The long title of the Civil Rights Act of 1964, perhaps the crowning legislative achievement of both the Johnson administration and the civil rights movement, includes the key phrases "to enforce the constitutional right to vote" and "to protect constitutional rights in public facilities and public education." These phrases refer to rights implicitly established by the original text of the Constitution and explicitly by the Fifteenth Amendment, which states, "The right of citizens of the United States to vote shall not be denied or abridged by the United States or by any State on account of race, color, or previous condition of servitude."

The words of the amendment were the belated fulfillment of a promise contained and yet hidden in a Constitution forged by political compromise. John Locke, perhaps the single most influential of those thinkers of the prior century on whose shoulders the founders stood as they debated the core principles of their new republic, believed that humans were naturally equal. He defined equality as a state "wherein all the Power and Jurisdiction is reciprocal, no one having more than another: there being nothing more evident, than that Creatures of the same species and rank promiscuously born to all the same advantages of Nature, and the use of the same faculties, should also be equal one amongst another without Subordination or Subjection." For Locke, individuals voluntarily left the state of nature and formed a social contract in order to better defend their natural liberties, which are guaranteed first and foremost by a community's willingness to guarantee that natural equality among its citizens. This idea of the social contract lies at the core of the liberal tradition of political philosophy running from Locke and Jean-Jacques Rousseau through Immanuel Kant and up to contemporary thinkers like John Rawls and Richard Rorty.

These thinkers are fundamental to the American democratic project not because their work comprises a body of doctrines that establishes what Americans believe in, but because they constitute a multigenerational conversation about the very nature of individual liberty and its relation to and dependence on the communities that individuals inhabit. Together they trace a story in which the individual's quest for maximal personal freedom is worked out against the backdrop of a similar guarantee for all others who share his or her community, such that, in Rawls's famous formulation, "Each person is to have an equal right to the most extensive total systems of equal basic liberties compatible with a similar system of liberty for all." In other words, the philosophical tradition upholding personal liberty as its central principle has always considered access to the same liberty on the part of other members of the group. The slow arc of progress toward greater equality for all was thus bent by a philosophical lodestone left by the founders, who, despite the prejudices of their age and indeed their persons, drew from the writings of a specific tradition a set of principles that would outlast and transcend their human foibles. In this way those who fought for greater freedom and equality in the centuries after a slave owner like Jefferson could redeem his fatal failings by realizing the deeper truth of his vision.

In the pragmatist and utilitarian version espoused by my mentor Richard Rorty, liberalism became a philosophy for maximizing happiness and minimizing cruelty for oneself and others. As he once put it, borrowing Judith Shklar's phrasing, a liberal is ultimately one for whom "cruelty is the worst thing we do." The other side of Rorty's philosophy was the belief that a vital ingredient in the "glue" that holds liberal societies together—what Adam Smith called the "fellow-feeling" that binds our interests to those of others—was their "common vocabularies and common hopes . . . stories about future outcomes that compensate for present sacrifices." Stories like these seem to be hard to find these days, when the latest data tells us that the current generation will be the first in American history not to improve on the standard of living of their parents, a statistical burden carried almost exclusively by those who have been sorted into the class of educational have-nots. At the heart of this book is the conviction that the drift of education has spurred inequality, not only because of unequal access and unequal quality, but at a deeper level because education has ceased to cultivate those stories in which common vocabularies and common hopes take seed. Consequently, perhaps education's greatest charge now is to vigorously imagine America's future community, one that includes the stories of all those who have been left behind, past and present.

———————

The Splintering of the American Mind argues that we are in danger of losing our civic culture. Instead of a forum for engaging in debate and achieving compromise, our public sphere has devolved into a blood sport in which scoring a point for the home team seems preferable to improving the state of the nation. A strong civic culture depends on having a society whose members are not only individuals set on improving their own lots, but also citizens who see their political interests as rooted in the commonwealth they share with their fellows. But since the 1970s, Americans have become increasingly isolated from the national community. As the right advanced an agenda of unfettered individualism and the left made crucial gains in defending minority rights, what was lost was the very idea of a commonwealth in which individuals and groups can adjudicate their differences.

There are myriad factors that have influenced this degeneration of the commonwealth, from loss of confidence in political processes and public figures; to consolidation of media ownership and proliferation of media outlets; to political tampering with the economy in the service of particular ideologies; to the depression of employment in some sectors due to technological advances, in contrast with spectacular growth in some sectors of the service and information economies. Behind these economic and political changes, however, a cultural, even philosophical, sea change has sifted up from our education system. That system, which was formed to cultivate the commonwealth, has devolved from a national, publicly funded project to an unequal pyramid of locally financed public schools, topped by an elite layer of private schools seen by the wealthiest parents as investments in their offspring's prospects. Colleges and universities, once envisioned as the capstones in a system meant to be, in Cardinal John Newman's words, "cultivating the public mind," have instead exacerbated the splintering of that mind by becoming exclusive clubs for social advancement and coddled self-exploration. For real cultivation, the public mind would need forums for unfettered debate, not syllabi that are extensions of V-chips and demands to use non-gender-specific pronouns.

The problem with such demands does not lie in the desire to protect people from gender bias or hate speech, which is and should be a goal of any civil society, but with their too-exclusive focus on the individual at the expense of community. This in turn leads to an unexpected political liability. As Vanderbilt University discovered when it instituted the kind of inclusivity campaign I saw near the beaches of UCSB, focusing on the policing of microaggressions feeds into the growing sense in the nonacademic world that universities and their students and faculty are hopelessly out of touch. The coverage of Vanderbilt's initiative in the popular press was merciless. One popular news site quoted a landscape foreman from the local community as saying, "I have found people here to be more on the traditional side—courteous, kind, and strong in their beliefs. This is a great example of lunacy attaching to one community—the collegiate community—and focusing not on education to get through life, but on ridiculous PC 'manners' just to get through the day."

While the impulse to protect traditionally and even currently victimized groups represents the brightest light of our tradition—what Rorty described as the conviction that cruelty is the worst thing we do—in the rarefied and decontextualized space that higher education is now preparing for its yearly wave of new clients, it turns into a sorry caricature of the intent that animates it, and only intensifies the balkanization that permits such caricaturing in the first place. When posters instruct students on exactly what to say if they have used an incorrect pronoun—"Thank you for reminding me. I apologize and will use the correct name/pronoun for you in the future"—can such anodyne public service announcements really substitute for robust debate about what individuals should expect from society and society from citizens, about the violence imposed on transgender people, and about how better to understand and empathize with those who don't easily fall within our expected categories? This book challenges us to rejoin that debate, to reengage with the history and contexts that have gone by the wayside, and to imagine our national community in new and more inclusive ways.

To that end, the book is divided into three parts. The first part, "Identity," tells how American colleges shifted their focus since the middle of the twentieth century from the study of a common core of "great books" to the exploration and celebration of marginalized racial and sexual identities. While this redirection was both necessary and beneficial for the women, gays, and minorities who suffered generations of discrimination and violence, it was hijacked by the cult of the consumer and the ever-increasing specialization of academic knowledge. The result of this convergence has been a withdrawal from dialogue in those very fields and arenas where future leaders should be learning to openly debate society's most pressing issues. The second part, "Inequality," shows how the shift in focus toward identity and the breakdown in civil discourse on campuses have been exacerbated by increased inequality in society at large, and how our education system has abetted this rise. The third part, "Community," recounts how the American democratic project emerged from the liberal tradition, and how a liberal arts education was conceived as key in the formation of a public capable of democratic self-governance. As early thinkers of the liberal tradition recognized, communities need to cultivate fellow feeling among their members, and the basis for such a social glue is the stories a people hold in common. Today the stories that dominate our culture are more often about individual excess and social destruction than about sacrifice and transcending differences for the sake of a common goal. The book thus ends by calling for a renewal of the liberal arts, both within our education system and beyond, as the basis for telling a neglected story—perhaps the only one capable of containing and nourishing the diverse array of identities that comprise today's America— about our community's shared commitment to the principle of equality.

PART ONE

IDENTITY

UNDOING HISTORY

In the fall of 2016 George Washington University's history department dropped the requirement of American history from its major. The dean of GWU's Columbian College of Arts and Sciences, Ben Vinson, is an expert on Mexican history as well as African American history. He told me that the department, which had made the decision before he came on board as dean, was conflicted about it, as he was, but felt that the change reflected the evolving role of the field of history in an increasingly globalized world. It was also about choice and accommodating student preferences, he added, as well as letting them go "deeper into the curriculum." Katrin Schultheiss, the chair of the history department, concurred: "The main gain for students is that they have a great deal more flexibility than they had before, and they can adapt it to whatever their plans are for the future. Whatever they want to do, there's a way to make the history department work for them."

While the irony of dropping American history as a requirement for the major in history is particularly trenchant in the school named after our first president, GWU is not alone. In fact, fewer than a third of the nation's top history programs currently require students majoring in history to study any American history. Obvious questions of intellectual responsibility aside, one of the problems with decisions like this one is how they play into a narrative spun by AM talk-radio personalities that pits professors and a global economic elite against a core set of American values. In a statement put out in 2016, ACTA, the American Council of Trustees and Alumni, a conservative watchdog group that describes itself as "committed to academic freedom, excellence, and accountability at America's colleges and universities," complained,

> many of the same institutions that do not require history majors to take a course on United States history do specify that they must complete coursework on areas outside the United States. And many allow some very strange, highly specialized topics to substitute for a course on the United States. History majors at Williams College could choose "Soccer and History in Latin America: Making the Beautiful Game." At Swarthmore, one choice could be "Modern Addiction: Cigarette Smoking in the 20th Century." At Bowdoin, it might be "Lawn Boy Meets Valley Girl."

As is often the case with politicized decisions in academia, the facts of the GWU decision have been exaggerated in the press and in reactions such as that of ACTA. The American history requirement at GWU was not a single course; it was a sequence of courses. Moreover, the strength and depth of the faculty in American history (the same faculty that came to the unanimous decision to remove the sequence as a requirement) make it highly improbable that a student can major in history without taking at least *a* course, if not more than one, in American history. But as is often the case, controversies like this one are less about the facts than about the underlying narrative.

Battles around curriculum in U.S. colleges and universities are expressing a deep cultural divide between two opposing ideas of community, based on two different understandings of human nature. One view holds that community's purpose is essentially paternalistic, that institutions exist to correct our selfish and rebellious impulses. The other view is that humans are essentially good, and that original goodness must be salvaged from the corruption brought about by communal institutions. In the former view, when universities change their curricula to meet student demands, they are betraying their purpose as representative institutions of the larger community. In the latter view, over time institutions like universities, churches, and governments become the sedimented repositories of society's worst prejudices and iniquities, and thus reforming a canon, like modernizing a religion, is necessary to shake free of tradition's limiting constraints on humanity's natural virtue.

What ACTA's statement and such popular ridicule of academic specialization overlooks is the profound progress in knowledge that has in fact accompanied the diversification of canons and the emergence of new fields of specialization. Just like the growth of the specter of political correctness, these caricatures stem at least in part from a failure to understand new methods and new interpretations in their proper context and history. Behind every enthusiastic but shallow graduate term paper about "queering the canon," there is the extraordinary scholarship of a professor like Stephen Orgel, whose research into the young men who played women's roles on the Elizabethan stage shed new light on our understanding of how gender roles and prejudices change over time.

Orgel, a legendary professor of English with whom I studied when I was a graduate student at Stanford, is the author of *Impersonations: The Performance of Gender in Shakespeare's England.* He was also openly gay well before it was widely accepted to be so. In his preface to that pathbreaking book he recounts a phone conversation with a teacher from his own schoolboy days, in which the teacher had objected to boys playing the female roles in school productions because it "was turning the boys into pansies." Orgel's research into the staging practices of theater companies in Elizabethan England provided him and his readers in the 1990s with powerful evidence that "everything we were taught in biology and sex education classes to the contrary notwithstanding, gender was obviously not a fixed category." Given our understanding of sexuality today and the broad support that gays and lesbians have won over the past twenty years and transgender people are winning today, this English professor's research was as prescient as it was historically accurate.

Until the 1960s most colleges, especially the elite ones, were overwhelmingly male and white. In the late 1960s and the 1970s, the number of black students attending such schools started slowly increasing, even as they remained significantly underrepresented. At the same time, some schools were opening their doors to women for the first time, allowing for an influx that eventually led to women outnumbering men in higher education. As they arrived on campuses where their race or sex put them in a distinct minority, blacks and women could often find strength and communal support in student groups, or with specific professors. Starting in the 1970s, they could also enroll in newly crafted majors intended to study the historical experiences of racial minorities and women in the United States. This same process was repeated about a decade later by gays and lesbians as they laid claim to their long-neglected civil rights, started coming out in larger numbers, and established departments and programs of queer studies on campuses around the country. In each case, exposure to others who had shared their experiences, in an environment that still resembled the white, male world of their parents' generation, gave these students a platform and an intellectual justification for insisting that their points of view be recognized and valued. At the same time, though, these students were being taught that their experience was incomprehensible to those who hadn't shared it with them, a position that implicitly justified excluding white, straight, or male students from their groups.

This engendered a paradox of sorts: by claiming the recognition and equality that was rightly theirs to claim and promoting the specificity of their perspectives—which had not been adequately accounted for either in the popular imagination or in college curricula—ethnic and gender studies programs and the professors and students who gravitated toward them were also perceived as undermining the very spirit of community that had made their emergence possible in the first place. As academic disciplines that focused on underrepresented groups achieved their goals of raising awareness about these groups' experiences and laying legitimate claim to equality, they also, rightly, drew attention to how the larger community has been and continues to be complicit in the oppression and disenfranchisement of these groups. The whites and men who had most benefited from strong federal investments in the national community felt personally attacked, and in some cases responded by belittling the new academic fields and thus intensifying those students' feelings of marginalization. What was lost in the mix was a philosophical commitment to the idea of community itself, and to the tradition of thinkers that had made it central to the American project.

Respect for minorities' and women's rights to equal representation and respect is the inevitable outcome of America's *idea* of community. But as groups have gained in confidence and risen to claim that recognition, the nation's real community, that emotional glue that holds it together, hasn't evolved at the same pace. It's as if we started down a road toward an important goal but got stuck in the mud halfway there. Now the challenge is to imagine that community anew, in a way that includes the multitude of new perspectives that have made their claim to be a part of the American project. The first step is to understand how we got to this point, where the necessary inclusion of a broader span of individual experiences has been won at the expense of a more expansive model of community.

As a result of the diversification of education brought on by the civil rights era, new fields of study and new approaches exploded into the academy in the 1970s and '80s, giving more people a place at the table and opening the doors to fresh insights and knowledge. This was positive not only for the humanities but also for the students who, seeing themselves in some of the new perspectives that were being explored, were inspired to become teachers and researchers themselves. This was a period of extraordinary democratization in higher education, and it should be recognized and celebrated for that. George Washington University's Ben Vinson and I were students together at Dartmouth College in the 1980s. Like I do, he remembers the foment of those times and believes that it was at least in part due to the intellectual revolution we lived through that a young black man like himself could go on to be a professor of history and eventually dean at GWU. When he and his colleagues decided to make the study of U.S. history optional for the major, they were doing so in this very spirit of expansiveness. They were recognizing that other parts of the world, the experiences of other nations, also deserve a place at the table.

At the same time, Ben admitted to me that he understood how this very revolution would feed a growing narrative in which the humanities professors of the academic left have abandoned a core set of values and stories that are essential to maintaining our broader sense of community. He conceded that while the new ways of reading texts and understanding our common past that opened our eyes when we were college students constituted a vital corrective to the naïve universalistic assumptions that preceded it, they also had the effect of undermining the idea that America shares a set of common stories and values. To the extent that those stories excluded huge portions of the population, it was necessary to undermine them. But it is also necessary to understand that those exclusions were themselves a violation of America's promise. Going forward it will be the task of the humanities not only to deconstruct, but also to rebuild; not only to undermine, but also to imagine anew. As Harvard president Drew Gilpin Faust would have it, this is the ultimate job of the humanities: to help "Americans explore and better understand how we came to be the nation, people and world we are . . . to reflect on our identities as citizens and human beings, to ask profound questions about origins, legacies and meaning, to contemplate where we are going as individuals and as a society and why."

———

A FIRST VOLLEY IN THE CULTURE WARS

In 1984, William J. Bennett, who was chair of the National Endowment for the Humanities and who would soon thereafter become Ronald Reagan's secretary of the recently created Department of Education, released a report authored by "a blue-ribbon study group of 31 nationally prominent authorities on higher education convened by the National Endowment for the Humanities." The report, entitled "To Reclaim a Legacy: A Report on the Humanities in Higher Education," excoriated the current state of humanities education, claiming that "over the past 20 years, the place of the humanities in the U.S. undergraduate curriculum has eroded and the overall coherence of the humanities curriculum has declined." Among a number of conclusions and recommendations, the report encouraged faculties to "put aside narrow departmentalism and work to shape a challenging common curriculum with a core of studies in history, philosophy, languages, and literature." Going further, it specified, "The humanities and the study of Western civilization should be placed at the core of the college curriculum, intended for all students and not just for humanities majors."

Bennett's report was followed by others, including one by his successor at the NEH, Lynne V. Cheney, four years later, in which she and her committee declared the principal ill affecting the life of the mind to be "viewing humanities texts as though they were primarily political documents," an approach she called "the most noticeable trend in academic study of the humanities today," adding that, under the sway of this trend, "Truth and beauty and excellence are regarded as irrelevant," and "questions of intellectual and aesthetic quality [are] dismissed."

Reagan's revolution had fundamentally altered the baseline for conservative politics in the United States. His philosophy favored a radical defunding of the federal government, which in the minds of those in his movement had draped the national spirit in cumbersome taxes and regulations in the service of cultivating a culture of dependency among the poor. By calling for the abolition of the Department of Education during his 1980 campaign, Reagan was signaling the importance that education would play in his revolution. At the same time, his consistent appeals for reforming education dissimulated the profound erosion that he would institute in the level of federal support for public higher education. In other words, his administration was simultaneously advocating for the restoration of a common legacy and culture at the heart of the U.S. academy, while setting in place the policy changes that would ensure that access to higher education would become increasingly unaffordable for the majority of Americans.

These twin impulses of the rise of movement conservatism in the United States were not arbitrarily linked. Reagan's fusing of the values of fundamentalist Christians, Nixon's "silent majority," and the economic theories of laissez-faire, small-government market fundamentalism was, in some ways, the key to his success. Reagan was part of a group of Republican politicians who, after the defeat of Barry Goldwater by Lyndon Johnson in 1964, retrenched and began to think carefully about how the right could regain its footing in American politics. In developing his ideas, he was guided by a relatively young journal, the *National Review*, spearheaded by the profoundly gifted writer and speaker William F. Buckley. Upon his graduation in 1950, Buckley had published a memoir of his time at Yale called *God and Man at Yale*. In the very first words of its foreword he lays out the foundations of the philosophy that would eventually guide Reagan's administration: "I had always been taught, and experience had fortified the teachings, that an active faith in God and a rigid adherence to Christian principles are the most powerful influences toward the good life. I also believed, with only a scanty knowledge of economics, that free enterprise and limited government had served this country well and would probably continue to do so in the future."

Buckley went on in his book to inveigh against his enemies, "secularism and collectivism," and "those who seek to subvert religion and individualism." These enemies he finds personified in the faculty at Yale, who, under the banner of "academic freedom," have "produced one of the most extraordinary incongruities of our time: the institution that derives its moral and financial support from Christian individualists and then addresses itself to the task of persuading the sons of these supporters to be atheistic socialists."

A great virtue of Buckley's book to today's reader is its honesty in presenting his own assumptions and positions. He states outright that the axiom that "all sides should be presented impartially" does not exist at Yale and that, more surprisingly, it "can never and ought never to be practiced." In other words, for Buckley, Yale's leftist professors were importing atheistic and collectivist thought under the guise of objectivity; and what was needed was an acknowledgment of their bias followed by open and honest battle against their ideas. Those to follow him, and eventually a more seasoned Buckley himself, would fall on a much more effective strategy, one we see put into action in the rise of the "culture wars," of which Bennett's 1984 report was the first open volley.

In this strategy, the academic left would be accused of injecting subjective and politically motivated standards into the academy and undermining the objective and pure quality of its conveyance of culture. The new avatars of Buckley's position would henceforth decry the decimation of the canon. As the literary biographer, editor, and eventual publisher James Atlas, one of many voices making this case in the 1980s, would write, "If we as a society can't agree that there is a body of knowledge to be mastered, much less what that body is, our very continuance as a literate culture will be in doubt. Saving our schools isn't just a matter of improving test scores or teaching children to read. There has to be a vision of what it is we wish them to know." But note how Atlas almost intentionally glosses inequality when making his case for the brutalization of our common culture as the cause of current decline. There is never any question that there should not be a divide between "elementary schools in the slums" and "graduate seminars in the Ivy League." If there is inequality today, rather, it is the kind produced by professors failing to teach both groups the same treasured tradition.

Of what texts exactly did that tradition consist? As the novelist and essayist Cynthia Ozick wrote in a widely read *New Yorker* article, those leaving the university today are deprived of the feeling of "exultation" felt toward poets and writers of the American tradition "by anyone who was an undergraduate in the forties or fifties." Today, in contrast, "high culture is dead. Tradition is equated with obscurantism. The wall that divided serious high art from the popular arts is breached; anything can count as text."

This erosion of standards famously took place, in Bennett's words, "over the last 20 years," counting back from 1984. This means that the golden age lauded by Ozick and others would have been in place prior to the 1960s, and that Buckley, with his keen feelers out, must have been sensing and anticipating in the late forties at Yale the oncoming attack decades in advance of its arrival. Be that as it may, if there was an academic consensus that lasted through the mid-twentieth century we will find it in the teachings of poets, writers, and professors like T. S. Eliot and Lionel Trilling, and their predecessor in criticism, Matthew Arnold. These and others like them defined the canon and the approaches to reading and teaching the liberal arts that would eventually give way to the onslaught of multiculturalism, relativism, and deconstruction, the movements that would do away with high culture and leave us in that perilous state wherein "anything can count as text."

MAKING THE PERSONAL POLITICAL

It was roughly thirty years ago, or three years after Bennett's report, that I stepped for the first time as a student onto Dartmouth College's hallowed Green, the quad crisscrossed with well-trodden paths connecting its academic halls, the historic Baker Library, and the tall glass windows of the Hopkins Center for the Arts, a miniature version of New York's Lincoln Center. Little did I know that I was arriving on a campus that would soon be at the heart of a culture war between two interpretations of the goals and purposes of the liberal arts education I had come to Dartmouth to pursue.

By 1987 Dartmouth had been admitting women for some fourteen years, since the moment its alumni became the last of the Ivy League to come to the collective realization, as others have wryly noted, that half their children were female. In 1970, three years before that watershed, Carol Hanisch, a member of the women's liberation movement in New York City, had published an essay in the journal *Notes from the Second Year: Women's Liberation*, in which she argued that "personal problems are political problems. There are no personal solutions at this time. There is only collective action for a collective solution." The article appeared under the title "The Personal Is Political," which went on to become a banner for a generation of feminists and political activists.

Women were well established on campus by the time I arrived, and the school was also on its way to challenging its reputation for ingrained sexism by becoming the first Ivy League school to have more women students than men and the highest representation of women on the faculty. It would be a long and painful journey. On my traditional "freshman trip" in New Hampshire's White Mountains the week before classes started, our trip leaders, upperclassmen involved with the Dartmouth Outing Club that maintained the local portions of the Appalachian Trail, schooled us well in the brewing controversy. "Feminists" were intent on destroying the school's traditions, they told us over the campfire at night, as we all, women included, nodded our heads in worried unison about the ominous threat. Traditions, after all, were fun. Feminism, clearly, wasn't. As the joke went at the time: "How many feminists does it take to screw in a lightbulb?" Answer (best yelled loudly and suddenly): "That's not funny!"

As it happened, I soon started to learn that tradition wasn't very funny, either. My first night on campus I was roped into a carousing group of fraternity brothers who soon started chanting decidedly vile songs about the women they still dismissively referred to as "coeds." The easy sense of victimized tradition that my summer trip had tried to bestow on me began to dissolve, and I started to see a different story at work. Dartmouth's image as a playground for privileged frat boys was well earned, but it was also given a national platform in the 1970s by alumnus Chris Miller. Miller had published a series of stories in *National Lampoon* magazine that were based on his experience as a brother at the Alpha Delta Phi fraternity—whose front yard, even in my day, filled as it often was with tattered couches holding the slumbering bodies of hungover partiers from the night before, regularly earned the house probation from the college administration. He later joined with Harold Ramis and Douglas Kenney to write the screenplay for the hit 1978 comedy *National Lampoon's Animal House*, starring the comedian John Belushi in his iconic role as the ultimate underachiever, sporting the now famous sweatshirt with the word COLLEGE stamped across the front.

In the 1980s many Dartmouth students secretly (or not so secretly) lionized their school's *Animal House* image. They took the film's goofy, laid-back brothers, more interested in beer and babes than in anything academic, as a good-natured, boys-will-be-boys look at college life. Conservative students and alumni liked the film's portrayal of the days prior to coeducation, when Dartmouth men would go on "panty raids" to nearby girls' schools to get dates for their wild toga parties. Many of Dartmouth's women had a very different response. For them, being in a minority meant being subjected to humiliating comments and innuendos on a constant basis. It meant being treated like a second-class student. And it meant being at risk of sexual assault any time you went to a party.

By 1987, women were pushing back, but so were the forces of reaction. There was a women's movement that was advocating for greater awareness of sexual assault and date rape, a new concept at the time, but stories also abounded of protests by "radical feminists" who threw supposedly used tampons on the Green in defiance of the school's old-boy ways. Freshmen like me were being exposed to both sides of a growing culture war: in one corner were the efforts at educating young men that "no means no"; in the other a countermovement led by an alliance between some fraternities and the conservative *Dartmouth Review* to ridicule "political correctness" and harken back to better, simpler times.

The *Review*—which received funding and guidance from William F. Buckley's *National Review*, the journal that had shaped the thinking of Ronald Reagan and helped pave the way for his rise to power—thought of itself as a sanctuary for freedom fighters who were busy speaking truth to the institutional power of the administration. They particularly reviled the school's official paper, the *Dartmouth*, which the *Review*'s editors dismissed as the "Parkhurst *Pravda*," eliding the building housing the school's administration with the Soviet paper well known to be the Kremlin's mouthpiece. The *Review*'s reporters often adopted intentionally confrontational stances and controversial tactics. They pilloried the new president, James O. Freedman, for his attempts to make Dartmouth's curriculum more academically rigorous, for his support for the hiring of more women and black faculty, and for establishing programs in women's studies and African American studies, even going as far as publishing caricatures depicting Freedman, an observant Jew, as a Nazi officer. In one incident that attracted national attention, they attacked a black professor of music, William Cole, mocking him with racist cartoons and confronting him physically in his classroom. When they published a transcript of him answering questions in class, Buckley himself weighed in in a column published in a New Hampshire daily, in which he opined that "Professor Cole, the tape recorder revealed, sounded as though he were strung out on dope, reciting a disjointed soliloquy on . . . poverty, racism, and the kitchen stove, peppered by the language of the streets, as one would most charitably call it."

The staff of the *Review* hated feminism and the changes in their traditions—such as the school song, whose line "men of Dartmouth" had been changed to "we of Dartmouth," a change that went largely ignored for a long time. Not all women were the enemy, though. Women who agreed with their conservative positions were welcomed with open arms. Laura Ingraham, who went on to become one of the most influential voices on conservative AM talk radio, was a staff writer and then editor during her four years at Dartmouth. They weren't necessarily against immigrants, either. Their most visible alumnus to date is the Indian-born conservative firebrand Dinesh D'Souza, whose book *Illiberal Education*, dedicated to Ingraham, was published in 1991, the year I left Dartmouth.

Illiberal Education accused universities like Dartmouth of buckling under pressure from leftist faculty and adopting policies that undercut the core democratic principles of free speech and equality. The two great sins that D'Souza cited were the institutionalization of political correctness, which, he claimed, prescribes what can and cannot be said on campus, and the adoption of affirmative action in admission, which strikes at the heart of a university's obligation to admit students based on merit alone (a standard that is as much a fiction today as it was then). D'Souza's larger claim was that campus policies were affecting national politics. Specifically, he tried to show how colleges and universities, with their doctrinaire adherence to identity politics, were actively changing U.S. culture and destroying the foundations of the U.S. political system. Affirmative action was an attack on equality, since it encouraged preference based on race. Political correctness was an attack on freedom of expression, since anything deemed offensive to women or racial minorities was summarily censored. And the faculty who were hired to teach subjects like literature and history were largely to blame, because they had sacrificed the transmission of enduring classics to the trendy politics of race and gender.

D'Souza was far from alone in his attack on recent tendencies in higher education. Allan Bloom's *The Closing of the American Mind*, published four years earlier, had already become a kind of bible for campus reactionaries. Bloom's target was less specifically campus policies and more the degeneration he claimed to see in his students' awareness of and engagement with the classic literature of the liberal tradition. In fact, these two questions—what texts are included in a student's education and what universities do to protect women and minorities and ensure a diverse student body—are separate issues, but by the middle of the 1990s Bloom's and D'Souza's books had managed to suture them into one.

In *The Closing of the American Mind* Bloom diagnosed a deep malaise on college campuses. Students in the 1980s were, Bloom reported, blissfully ignorant of the great books that constituted the Western tradition. With a generation of sixties radicals now comfortably tenured in English and history departments around the country, these students were no longer being exposed to Plato, Rousseau, Kant, and the other "dead white men" whose ideas formed the bedrock of the liberal tradition. The advocates of "women's studies" and "black studies" had discarded them, claiming that the greatness of these "great books" was an illusion born of the prejudices of white, male domination.

Bloom's evident social conservatism made him a darling of the right while also allowing reactionary politics to claim the intellectual high ground. While he could have complained about students' ignorance of Plato, Rousseau, and Kant without blaming feminism and the civil rights movement, not only did he do both, he also engaged in long, venomous screeds against the introduction of new programs like women's studies and black studies—both of which had been introduced into Dartmouth's curriculum under Freedman—and, of all things, the music and dancing of Mick Jagger. Looking back now, in an age in which intellectuals can venerate the Rolling Stones as cultural icons and Bob Dylan has won the Nobel Prize for literature, using Jagger's sexualized gyrations as evidence for the decline of intellectual standards only dates the author as a hopelessly out-of-touch curmudgeon and detracts from the value of his observation: namely, that students are not reading enough intellectual history and that we ought to be teaching some dead white men more, not less.

Likewise, by subtly associating those who do agree about the importance of intellectual history with the retrograde reaction against feminism and the civil rights movement, his work clouded the truth that these movements are the ultimate expression of the very tradition he claimed to be defending. In fact, what the editors of the *Dartmouth Review* and subsequent conservative torchbearers denigrated as PC was, at core, a symptom of how far

we have come as a nation in respecting those whose rights have been trampled on, just as the extent of their reaction is a sign of how far we still have
to go. At times the new efforts to rectify the historical underrepresenta-
tion of minorities undermined their own effectiveness by providing their
critics with examples of absurd abuses, such as with Yale University's
Stephen L. Carter, who as a student from Stanford was rejected by Harvard
Law School only to be called by a panicky admissions officer abjectly apologizing for having overlooked that he was black and offering him admission on the spot As Carter put it, "Stephen Carter, the white male, was not
good enough for the Harvard Law School. Stephen Carter, the black
male, not only was good enough, but rated agonized telephone calls urging
him to attend." But while individuals can always take a good impulse too
far, can anyone seriously think that we need to be less concerned with
racism and sexism now, when blacks are imprisoned at six times the rate of
whites and twice as likely to be arrested for the same crime, and one in five
women report being raped during their time at university?

THE BEST THAT HAS BEEN
THOUGHT AND SAID

As testified to by the popularity of Bloom's book, one of the main criticisms of the changes that swept through academia in the 1960s was the
damage wrought on the "canon," the ostensibly eternal list of great books of
the Western tradition that stands as an indelible monument to our culture's
impact on the world. In the 1989 piece in the *New Yorker* marking 101 years
of T. S. Eliot quoted previously, Cynthia Ozick reassessed her veneration for
the great modernist poet and critic in light of the biographical revelations of
the second half of the century that brought to light his bigotry, misogyny,
and anti-Semitism. She also reaffirmed her commitment to a core idea that
Eliot and his generation represented: "I admit to being arrested in the Age
of Eliot, a permanent member of it, unregenerate. The etiolation of high art
seems to me to be a major loss. I continue to suppose that some texts are

worthier than other texts . . . I would not wish to drop Homer or Jane Austen or Kafka to make room for an Aleutian Islander of lesser gifts, unrepresented though her group may be on the college reading list."

Ozick's drive to prioritize value, to refer to a contour map of culture on which the icons of literary greatness occupy the innermost circles and highest vantages from which they look down on an ever-encroaching army of pretenders to the throne, was bequeathed to her by Eliot and his literary generation. For Eliot art must be difficult, and its difficulty stems from the artist's location in a tradition. As he wrote in his famous essay "The Metaphysical Poets," "Our civilization comprehends great variety and complexity, and this variety and complexity, playing upon a refined sensibility, must produce various and complex results." This requirement in the artist of "complexity, playing upon a refined sensibility," created a standard that would allow Eliot to, implicitly or explicitly, rank artistic contributions in terms of objective quality, such that even a "poet of genius" like William Blake could pale in comparison to the kind of world-historical brilliance characterizing a "classic" like Dante: "The concentration resulting from a framework of mythology and theology and philosophy is one of the reasons why Dante is a classic, and Blake only a poet of genius."

A key assumption for professors prior to the 1960s under the influence of Eliot was that great works of literature needed to be understood as objects unto themselves. Reading them under the influence of biographical information about the author, the historical circumstances of their production, or, heaven forbid, the sociopolitical contexts that influenced how they had been received, was anathema, because reading literature with such external influences in mind seemed to undermine the very idea of literary greatness. But Ozick's frank admission and Eliot's criteria for excellence touch on a contradiction lying at the heart of the liberal arts education. On the one hand those of us who teach history and literature and philosophy tend to believe that there is intrinsic value in what we are studying and passing on to future generations. On the other hand, we study and pass on the tradition in part because we feel the need to protect it, as if its intrinsic value needed our study, our commentary, our clarification to ensure its survival.

Another way of putting this tension is that the value of the canon is, or must be, universal. Classic authors like Shakespeare, Dante, and Cervantes speak to all people regardless of their place in history, their race, class, or gender. At the same time, we must be constantly vigilant lest the universality of the canon be questioned, its authors shown to be mere products of their time, or class, or gender. When Ozick admits her prejudice favoring Homer, Austen, and Kafka over an Aleutian Islander of no name but of whom she can be sure was of lesser gifts, she reveals something of the logic of inclusion into the canon. At some point in the past, one could have, and probably did, resist dropping Homer for a nineteenth-century Englishwoman "of lesser gifts," just as at a slightly later point one could have, and probably did, resist dropping Jane Austen for an obscure German-speaking Jew from Prague, "of lesser gifts." The canon is and has always been one long history of admission into an exclusive club; it's just the nature of the club and its standards of admission that have been changing all along. Here I agree again with Richard Rorty when he writes, "We should cheerfully admit that canons are temporary, and touchstones replaceable. But this should not lead us to discard the idea of greatness. We should see great works of literature as great because they inspired many readers, not as having inspired many readers because they are great."

As I write these pages I have just finished the second week of teaching in Johns Hopkins's own Great Books course. Unlike our more famous sister programs at Columbia and Chicago, Great Books at Hopkins is decidedly modest in its approach to the canon. It is an elective, not a requirement, and, far from the two-year span of other "core curricula," our course lasts only the fall semester. We are also tentative, perhaps slightly embarrassed, by its title. As my colleague the Shakespearian scholar (and half of the well-known experimental music duo Matmos) Drew Daniel put it to our students on the first day of class:

> Please don't misunderstand the name of this course—one could teach many other courses called "Great Books" with entirely different syllabi. These are great books, and live up to Matthew Arnold's phrase in *Culture and Anarchy* that culture amounts to "the best that has been

thought and said"—but greatness, what the bestness of "best" consists in, is always something open to question and argument as cultures change and conflicts erupt . . . The greatness of these works lies not in the bare fact of survival over time or the sheer accumulation of intellectual prestige, but in the immanent intensity of what these works can generate in the present within your mind as you read.

Granted, our own little canon is modestly diversified. Virginia Woolf and the seventeenth-century British novelist Aphra Behn join nine men; Frederick Douglass makes an appearance in an otherwise white crowd; and Daniel's two picks, Shakespeare's *Othello* along with Behn's *Orinooko*, are works that, in his words, "pick at a sore that is still festering at present: racist violence." At the same time, the sheer absurdity of encapsulating a tradition in thirteen weeks makes a mockery of any claim to preserving the canon with such a course. On the day I met my section for the first time—ten freshmen nervously sitting around my seminar table wondering what they had gotten themselves into—I decided to grab that particular bull's horns and ask them—more women and people of color than white men—how they felt about a course that, at least implicitly, associated greatness with an exclusive, largely white and male tradition.

I needn't have been too concerned. This group of young people almost thought the question passé. Katy, whose sharp gaze and confidence belied her years, told me that for her, "there are two ways you can go about reading these books. One way is to gain a lot of knowledge, to have other people think of you as someone who knows a lot of classical references. The other way is to read them for all those moments that make you stop and circle a phrase, and just be amazed that someone could have put something in just those words, and in a way that means so much to you, here, today. If you're reading in that way, it's even more amazing when that someone is so different from you and has been dead so long." But does reading in this second way amount to misreading these texts, subjecting them to the concerns and pressures of the here and now instead of understanding them as they were intended in their own times? And would such an emphasis on personal interpretation decay all the more easily into an "anything goes" kind of relativism that forsakes the objective meaning of great literature in favor of the latest flavor of the month?

I think the choice is a false one. "As they were intended in their own time" is a red herring, an impossible standard that even the author and his immediate friends and family couldn't achieve. Every act of reading is necessarily a reconstruction of a different time and place in conjunction with the concerns, prejudices, and identity of the one doing the reading. What is important is not an "intention" lying in wait to be unearthed, but the rigorous practice of learning to understand, articulating interpretations, and then justifying them to others on the basis of evidence. As Daniel again put it on the first day, "Great Books is about the transmission of habits of mind more than it is about worshipping at the altar of potentially overfamiliar famous dead geniuses. Those habits of mind are going to emerge in each of you as you struggle with the grain of these texts, line by line, image by image, when you are alone in your rooms and when you are challenged in the classroom to light up their significance in discussion with each other . . . I'm not here because Shakespeare is great. I already know that. I'm here because I can't wait to read what you are going to write." This is how we teach Great Books.

***

THE RISE OF THEORY

The midcentury club for which cultural conservatives now feel the pangs of nostalgia shared much with the whites-only country clubs that would only slowly and reluctantly give way to social pressures of our time. These were tight-knit communities, but the tightness of their weave corresponded to the severity of their exclusions. As young scholars rose to become professors in the 1960s, not only did they challenge what and whom to teach, they began to question the methods and assumptions that guided both the formation of the canon and the understanding of literature. In 1966, a group of assistant professors at Johns Hopkins invited several philosophers, historians, and even a psychoanalyst to engage in some debates that had been raging for the last few years in France around a method of interpreting not only high art and canonical literature, but any and all sorts of cultural production. The method was called structuralism, and the intellectuals involved were so iconoclastic that by the time they gathered in Baltimore they were already starting to reject the term, and the vague moniker of poststructuralism arose in its place.

Soon thereafter the American academy was awash in "theory," as the radical ideas of these French intellectuals spread from Hopkins to Yale, SUNY Buffalo, UC Irvine, and eventually other universities around the country. As French-inflected theory spread, so did approaches that favored understanding literature and history from sociopolitical, racial, and sexual perspectives. The objective value of texts fell into suspicion, and "external" factors like race, class, and gender, once vilified as detracting from the essence of high art, became central concerns for all humanistic inquiry. These were the two decades preceding Bennett's report; these were the years when conservative culture warriors emerged to defend against the relativism of multiculturalism. But from the perspective of the newcomers, they were the years when the whites-only clubs were at long last being integrated, when assumptions of universality were being shown to be the congratulatory self-promotions of a privileged class, and when those Aleutian Islanders would finally have a place in the sun.

Culture wars construct straw men, and the one launched by Bennett and movement conservatism in the 1980s was no exception. In their case the enemy was relativism. According to their narrative, radical professors poured into the academy during the rowdy 1960s and swept aside centuries of established traditions, replacing them with a hodgepodge of multiculturalism and an "anything goes" attitude to evaluating works of art. Classics were disregarded because they had been written by "dead white men"; new authors of suspect quality were introduced because they represented previously marginalized groups; and the distinction between art and popular culture was trashed by an attitude that considered everything to be equally worthy of academic study. This was the meaning of Ozick's pithy line: anything could count as text.

That line had a specific reference. One of the French intellectuals who came to Baltimore in the spring of 1966 was an Algerian-born Jew, a so-called *pied-noir*, in France's colonially tinged taxonomy, named Jacques Derrida. Since rocketing to fame in the 1970s, Derrida's name has become synonymous with the excesses of academic trendiness. Upon his death in 2003 to pancreatic cancer—the same illness that took Richard Rorty several years later, causing him to wryly opine that he and Derrida must have shared the same vice, namely, reading too much Heidegger—the *New York Times* published an obituary that failed to refer to Derrida as a philosopher in its headline, calling him instead an "abstruse theorist." While he had not yet formulated it in 1966, the sentence that would be quoted and misquoted ad nauseam, leading eventually to Ozick's and others' dismissive characterization, was "*Il n'y a pas de hors-texte*," literally, there is no outside-the-text.

While the claim that "everything is text" is held up as the antithesis of midcentury critical practices that lionized the autonomy of the work of art and insisted on bracketing out external concerns like history or biography, in a strict sense, "there is no outside-the-text" is really a radical affirmation of that sensibility. Literary critics who learned in the newly created schools of "deconstruction" that were influenced by Derrida and his followers practiced an almost monastic level of "close reading" that in no way departed from the exigencies of Eliot and the critical schools he lorded over. In fact, there is more variation within the various new methods and approaches in the humanities that developed from the 1960s onward than between those methods and approaches and those of the period that preceded them.

Furthermore, Derrida's dictum was largely taken out of context. When philosophers, linguists, or anthropologists analyze how cultures create meaning, they tend to hierarchize that process into a series of gradations getting closer and closer to something like a "pure," unadulterated experience or intention. At the core of any such experience or intention would be the pure perception of what I am sensing right now. At a next step of remove would then be my using language to talk about it. Finally, at the furthest remove is written language, which freezes in time some idea about that original sensation. Derrida's point was that this hierarchy is an artificial construct that creates a kind of fetish of pure experience where there never in fact was one.

Just as any "pure," instantaneous moment of sensation is indelibly affected by our memory of it moments later and our expectations of it moments before, so the apparently purer oral transmission of culture is inflected by what he called a "general structure of writing," since even oral language works by constant reference to prior meanings circulating among the community of language users. As the comedian George Carlin once put it, "Tell us in your own words? . . . I'm using the ones everybody else has been using!" In this light, "There is no outside-the-text" encapsulates the very specific philosophical thesis that we're never going to be able to isolate pure, unadulterated experience because that experience depends on the same techniques of meaning creation that "higher" forms of communication like writing depend on: memory, expectation, referral, and holding meanings in time.

While such focus on ubiquitous textuality cannot be blamed for the flattening of distinctions and the dissipation of standards that cultural conservatives associate with the critical movements of the 1960s, one aspect of Derrida's theories did have a direct impact on those movements. Derrida thought the Western tradition was spellbound by hierarchies largely built around the sensation-writing opposition. His philosophical method turned around identifying implicitly biased pairs of terms to show how the more valued term often depended on the lesser-valued of the terms for its status. Just as what we take to be the essential operations of writing could be shown to have a general structure underlying all meaning creation, for instance, major or central cultures depended on the construction and exclusion of secondary and peripheral communities to establish their primacy. This technique or way of approaching a problem caught the attention of members of marginalized groups just as they started to assert themselves in academic circles, and in some cases a synergy developed between deconstruction and the new theorists of race, ethnicity, and gender.

One critical movement that took wind from deconstruction and that continues in full strength today is known as postcolonial studies, a blanket descriptor of approaches that have purchase in any number of humanistic and social science fields, from history to literature to anthropology. Post-colonial theorists such as Edward Said and Gayatri Chakravorty Spivak, both professors at Columbia University, were quick to see the power of Derrida's insights into the implicit hierarchies underlying apparently objective descriptions. Spivak, who translated Derrida's influential 1967 tome *Of Grammatology* into English, adding her own hundred-page preface to the mix, used the logic of deconstruction to shed light on the functioning of colonial and sexist ideologies that deprive colonized people, and colonized women doubly so, of a voice in which to articulate their own resistance.

For Spivak, women and colonized people are not only oppressed by the coercive power of imperialism and patrimony; they are "subalterns," meaning that the very language available to them to develop ideas of selfhood and agency is already loaded with implicit meanings that constitute them as secondary and lesser beings. There is no objective, unweighted playing field on which to position themselves and argue for equality, because the terms of the argument are already organized into one term that is central and one that is defined as different or opposed to the central term. In the case of colonized women, for Spivak, the othering is twofold: "If, in the context of colonial production, the subaltern has no history and cannot speak, the subaltern as female is even more deeply in shadow."

The double bind Spivak identifies in her essay was equally visible to artists and scholars of the African American experience. As the novelist Richard Wright wrote, "I'm black. I'm a man of the West . . . I also see and understand the non- or anti-Western point of view . . . Yet, I'm not non-Western . . . When I look out upon those vast stretches of this earth inhabited by brown, black, and yellow men . . . my reactions and attitudes are those of the West." Harvard professor of English and Africana Studies Henry Louis Gates quotes this passage as an example of Wright's "ambivalent relation to both the Western and non-Western cultures," adding, "So long as we retain a vocabulary of heritage and inheritance in defining our putative national cultures, it cannot be resolved."

Wright, in identifying his dilemma, drew a similar distinction to that noted by Spivak, but also to the one central to the conservative voices in the culture wars. There is the West, and then there are non-Western or anti-Western points of view, and the latter are defined as the inverse of the former. Indeed, as liberal arts curricula started to be diversified after the 1970s, one of the principal tools was the creation of "non-Western" distribution requirements. The great battle at Stanford University in the 1990s, when I was a graduate student there, was around the replacement of "Western Civ" with a more anodyne and less exclusive series of introductory humanities courses. Twenty-five years later the *Stanford Review*, the university's conservative newspaper, modeled on the *Dartmouth Review*, initiated a petition to reinstate Western Civ. In April 2016 the student body voted six to one to reject the initiative; ironically, fewer people voted in favor of it than had signed the original petition.

The standard argument for courses or tracks like Western Civ is that we have an obligation to "master our own culture" before learning about others. As Gates puts it, "To insist that we 'master our own culture' before learning others only defers the vexed question: What gets to count as 'our' culture? What makes knowledge worth knowing? Unfortunately, as history has taught us, an Anglo-American regional culture has too often masked itself as universal, passing itself off as our 'common culture,' and depicting different cultural traditions as 'tribal' or 'parochial.'" It is not the case, however, that the scholars I am glossing here were a unified block, by any means. Gates finds much to disagree with in the very deconstructive logic that Spivak found so compelling, according to which the structures of subjectivity are ineluctably male and colonial, and hence there can be no voice, even one of resistance, that doesn't in some way retrench and reinforce that power dynamic. As he points out, explicitly calling out Derrida as the origin of this logic, "to deny us the process of exploring and reclaiming our subjectivity before we critique it is the critical version of the grandfather clause, the double privileging of categories that happen to be *preconstituted*."

Nonetheless, whether more or less optimistic about the prospects of finding effective critical voices for the marginalized, scholars of African American studies, like Gates, or of postcolonial studies, like Spivak, as well as feminists and queer theorists, were energized by the task of unmaking the dominant, white, male, heterosexual assumptions that had passed for universal values and aesthetic standards until the eruption of new methods and points of view. The passion and electricity these new approaches brought to humanistic disciplines was transformative. As Gates could write at the beginning of the nineties, by which time multiculturalism had settled into a dominant position on most campuses even as the right was taking the fight to the streets, "For a scholar of African-American Studies, this new state of affairs is especially gratifying, given the link between the social and economic conditions of African-Americans and our field of inquiry. Debates about multiculturalism have given to literary studies a renewed urgency."

This renewed urgency was, and is, a remarkable achievement and a profound benefit to society. The intense critical gaze of theory, the upending of staid certainties of what counts as great literature, the incorporation of new voices and new perspectives, these innovations that revolutionized the American college curriculum from the seventies through the nineties were responsible for important contributions to students' understandings of themselves and the complex world they live in. At the same time, Gates expresses a certain ambivalence, which I share, when he notes that he agrees "with those conservatives who have raised the alarm about our students' ignorance of history," just as I share his rejoinder that "the history we need to teach has to be the history of the idea of the 'canon.'" In other words, we do need to teach history, we need to "master our own culture," and we need to know the classics, but more important, we need to understand the contexts, institutions, and exclusions that made them into classics, just as we need to understand the contexts, institutions, and exclusions that forged the identities we now strive to protect and cherish. Finally, rather than reject wholesale what came before, we should remain attentive to the ideas and methods that contributed to the strength of the whole community and not to the favoritism of one part and the diminishment of others. In this regard, there may still be much to salvage from the comfortable canon and critical consensus that reigned before the democratization of the academy.

THE LIBERAL IMAGINATION

While they were busily at work consolidating a canon of great works of literature and thought, midcentury critics like T. S. Eliot didn't think that their principal criterion in selecting authors was their gender or the color of their skin, even if de facto their canon was entirely white and almost entirely male. Rather, the critics who patrolled the canon's borders were enamored of an idea of what made a work great. That idea is worth paying attention to, because, as it turns out, it is the kind of idea that is both essential for a democratic community to function and instrumental in opening such communities to embrace new identities.

In an important essay called "The Function of Criticism," Eliot remarked that the reason a scholar had to read literature and discuss it with others, that is, the essence of what takes place in a humanities seminar, was to discover and explore "differences with as many of his fellows as possible, in the common pursuit of true judgment." The method of reading that he and others of his generation, like the critic I. A. Richards, developed was intended to cultivate in students an openness to "complex and unfamiliar" meanings, and to avoid "stock responses" and attitudes "already fully prepared in the reader's mind." This was important not only for the cultivation of students' intellectual capacities, but for the better functioning of society as a whole, which would benefit from its citizens honing the practice of standing back and dispassionately assessing "views that seem to conflict with our own prepossessions," in order better "to investigate them," instead of simply rejecting them.

In embracing this function of criticism, and in making judgments about which texts and authors had the intrinsic qualities conducive to promoting such reading and inquiry, the midcentury critics were appealing to an ideal of liberal education that they inherited from thinkers of the prior century. The great philosopher of liberalism John Stuart Mill wrote in his landmark essay "On Liberty" that liberty in a democratic society would depend on individuals learning the skills of discernment and judgment. As he wrote, "In the case of any person whose judgment is really deserving of confidence, how has it become so? Because he has kept his mind open

to criticism and his opinions and conduct. Because it has been his practice to listen to all that could be said against him . . . hearing what can be
said about it by persons of every variety of opinion, and studying all
modes in which it can be looked at by every character of mind." This
essential value, doubting one's own certainties and being open to the
possibility that others might have a better way, lies at the core of the liberal
tradition. It undergirded the powerful sense of community that built
U.S. society into the most stable and prosperous middle class the world
had ever seen. And it also inspired the moral imagination that would give
rise to and help legitimate the very multiculturalism that would come to
challenge it.

Mill's commitment to openness and tolerance was not just about
improving oneself, becoming smarter or more insightful; he understood
his position as a dialogue with opponents who, if they could be convinced
to share that sort of honest self-assessment, would become interlocutors
and partners in building a better community. In his critical essay on the
Romantic poet and cultural conservative Samuel Taylor Coleridge, Mill
urged his fellow liberals to acquaint themselves with this powerful thinker
and created a prayer that he wished his partisans would speak with him:
"Lord, enlighten thou our enemies . . . sharpen their wits, give acuteness
to their perceptions, and consecutiveness and clearness to their reasoning
powers: we are in danger from their folly, not from their wisdom; their
weakness is what fills us with apprehension, not their strength." While still
radiating condescension, it is a prayer for dialogue, understanding, and
community, not victory.

This passage from Mill is one of the first quotations in *The Liberal Imagination*, the influential book of another midcentury critic, Lionel Trilling.
Trilling begins with Mill because he exemplifies for him not only the right
critical stance but the essence of the politics he believes criticism should
embody. This liberalism is not so much a specific ideology or set of policy
recommendations; it is, rather, a philosophy about how democratic
communities—that is, communities not of like-minded but of other-
minded individuals—can survive and thrive. As he writes, "The job of
criticism would seem to be, then, to recall liberalism to its first essential

imagination of variousness and possibility, which implies the awareness of complexity and difficulty."

This conception of liberalism is wide and encompassing; it is generous, not exclusive. As Harvard professor of English Louis Menand describes Trilling's conception, it has a common core that makes room for much of the American political spectrum: "In Trilling's view, the assumption that all liberals share, whether they are Soviet apologists, Hayekian free marketers, or subscribers to *Partisan Review*, is that people are perfectible. A liberal is someone who thinks that the right economic system, the right political reforms . . . and the right moral posture will do away with unfairness, snobbery, resentment, prejudice, tragic conflict, and neurosis. A liberal is a person who thinks that there is a straight road to health and happiness." As Trilling goes on to argue and show, the job of criticism, and here we could add the job of teaching the liberal arts, is to help that hope by hindering it, by teaching us, in Menand's words, "that life is not so simple."

This liberal idea at the heart of the midcentury approach to liberal arts education was not opposed by the new movements that came into their own after the sixties. On the contrary, it animated them. A university, Cardinal Newman wrote, not long after Mill published his essay, should promote "the power of viewing many things at once as one whole, of referring them severally to their true place in the universal system, of understanding their respective values, and determining their mutual dependence." Sure enough, these are the exact words Gates quotes in the face of the crisis he sees in today's America, which he goes on to call a "world profoundly fissured by nationality, ethnicity, race, class, and gender. And the only way to transcend those divisions—to forge, for once, a civic culture that respects both differences and commonalities—is through education that seeks to comprehend the diversity of human culture." Importantly, he goes on to add: "Any human being sufficiently curious and motivated can fully possess another culture, no matter how 'alien' it may appear to be."

As we embrace the new knowledge that multiculturalism brings us and extend the promise inherent in the constitution of liberty for all, not just for some, it is vital that we heed that injunction. The divisiveness that has engulfed our society is predicated on incommunicability. Coastal elites can't possibly understand the "forgotten man"; whites can't possibly grasp what it means to be black in America, or honestly come to terms with white privilege; to try to analogize from one group's situation to another's risks engulfing the one making the analogy in a stream of vindictive accusations of intolerance. And yet the curiosity and motivation to understand others is the vital core of our democracy; without it we are lost.

Richard Rorty believed that the movement that we can refer to with the shorthand "multiculturalism" and that he cobbled together under the moniker "the academic Left" was responsible for a great deal of positive change in America. Shortly after the 2016 election a passage from his 1999 book *Achieving Our Country* went viral on Twitter because it seemed to predict the rise of a candidate like Donald Trump:

> At that point, something will crack. The nonsuburban electorate will decide that the system has failed and start looking around for a strongman to vote for—someone willing to assure them that, once he is elected, the smug bureaucrats, tricky lawyers, overpaid bond salesmen, and post-modernist professors will no longer be calling the shots . . . One thing that is very likely to happen is that the gains made in the past forty years by black and brown Americans, and by homosexuals, will be wiped out. Jocular contempt for women will come back into fashion . . . All the sadism which the academic Left has tried to make unacceptable to its students will come flooding back. All the resentment which badly educated Americans feel about having their manners dictated to them by college graduates will find an outlet.

I was a student of Rorty's at Stanford when he was working on this book and had the privilege of reading it in proofs before it was published. I recall feeling a vague presentiment of foreboding when I read it, but relegated it to the same compartment of "likely true, but what are you going to do about it" in which I filed the assessments of most of the theorists I was reading at the time. When I read it in November 2016, in contrast, it hit me like a proverbial ton of bricks.

Rorty's point in that book was that the academic left's divorce from issues of pragmatic, economic policy in favor of advocating for cultural awareness and changes in behavior toward socially marginalized groups was going to have unintended consequences. He began by insisting on how much real good that attentiveness to language and feelings on college campuses, especially in the form of the creation of academic programs focused on ethnic, racial, and gender identity, had accomplished:

> In addition to being centers of genuinely original scholarship, the new academic programs have done what they were, semiconsciously, designed to do: they have decreased the amount of sadism in our society. Especially among college graduates, the casual infliction of humiliation is much less socially acceptable than it was during the first two thirds of the century. The tone in which educated men talk about women, and educated whites talk about blacks, is very different from what it was before the Sixties. Life for homosexual Americans, beleaguered and dangerous as it still is, is better than it was before Stonewall. The adoption of attitudes that the Right sneers at as "politically correct" has made America a far more civilized place than it was thirty years ago.

The problem is not, as the right would have it, that colleges have become dens of intolerance ruled by liberal thought police legislating a conformist coddling of all things formerly marginal. For Rorty this accommodation and respect for difference was an unmitigated good for society. The problem, rather, was that the academic left made its powerful inroads in this fight just as economic inequality and insecurity for the majority of Americans regardless of race, gender, or sexual orientation were taking a drastic turn for the worse.

One shocking and sad fact about some of the numbers Rorty puts to his analysis in 1999 has barely changed in the almost two decades that have passed since then. As he wrote at the time, "If husband and wife each work 2,000 hours a year for the current average wage of production and nonsupervisory workers ($7.50 per hour) they will make that much [$30,000]. But $30,000 a year will not permit homeownership or buy decent daycare . . . Such a family, trying to get by on this income, will be constantly tormented by fears of wage rollbacks and downsizing, and of the disastrous consequences of even a brief illness." In 2017, as of this writing, the federal minimum wage is $7.25 and the median household income is just above fifty thousand dollars, even as the costs of day care and, more spectacularly, higher education have risen dramatically since Rorty wrote those words.

With the rise of multiculturalism in academia, was the baby of "community" thrown out with the bathwater of the midcentury consensus? In acknowledging difference and repression and exploitation were we also closing the door on uncertainty and the desire to form new communities? The multiculturalism that swept onto college campuses in the 1960s had great promise; but in some ways and in some cases it has lost its way. This is not because one side of the debate is incurably relativist and the other side of the debate is incurably racist and sexist. It's because both in society and in the educational setting that in its original mold was meant to combat balkanization, we have become so fragmented that we barely have occasions to disagree with one another, much less articulate those disagreements intelligently and risk changing our minds. As the critic Gerald Graff writes, "The habit of preaching to the already converted is not restricted to the academy. A dangerous inability to talk to one another is the price we pay for a culture that makes it easy for us to avoid having to respect and deal with people who strongly disagree with us."

––––––––––

A CONTAGION OF DISAPPROVAL

The June 2015 issue of *Vanity Fair* magazine featured Caitlyn Jenner on its cover, celebrating her courage for having embraced her identity as a trans woman. That same month, another woman, Rachel Dolezal, was forced to resign from her position as the head of the Spokane, Washington, chapter of the National Association for the Advancement of Colored People. Her disgrace was provoked by the revelation, to the surprise of many of her friends and coworkers, that she was not black. The daughter of white parents who had grown up with black adopted siblings, married a black man, and had children with him, Dolezal had long felt herself to be black and had gradually altered her appearance to better conform to that identity. In stark contrast to Jenner, who was lionized in the press for transitioning to a new identity, Dolezal was called, among other things, "a deceiver, a liar, and a cultural appropriator" for having allowed others to believe she was African American.

Two years later, another controversy erupted on social media, this time around an article published in a philosophy journal. Written by an assistant professor of philosophy named Rebecca Tuvel, the article argued that there were logical similarities between the transgender identity of Caitlyn Jenner and the transracial identity of Rachel Dolezal. Tuvel, despite being supportive of both women's choices, was mercilessly attacked on Facebook forums, her academic credentials ridiculed, and her chances of gaining tenure threatened. For comparing a person who identified with a different gender from the one with which she was born to a person who identified with a different race from the one with which she was born, she was pilloried as "transphobic" and "racist," as well as just plain "stupid."

Professor Tuvel, a young woman with long, straight hair and a kind, unassuming demeanor, politely declined my request to be interviewed. Because I was unable to talk to Professor Tuvel, I reached out to her former dissertation adviser at Vanderbilt, Kelly Oliver. She told me that Professor Tuvel had been deeply hurt by the personal attacks she had received and the media frenzy the affair had stirred up, and was taking some time off to recover. She then led me through the events in a calm, reasoned voice, weaving together complex arguments with the kind of effortless eloquence I would expect from the formidable philosopher I knew her to be. Shortly after the first reactions on social media, Oliver had intervened with the mild suggestion that the journal invite a series of critical responses to the article instead of retracting it entirely. Her proposal was immediately met with scorn, with colleagues asserting that the mere suggestion constituted an act of "epistemic violence" against marginalized scholars. Some of these scholars reported that Tuvel's original article had triggered symptoms of

PTSD in them and that Professor Oliver's suggestion had aggravated their suffering.

I should say right off that Professor Oliver, and I too, for that matter, have nothing but admiration and support for the real progress of scholars and activists who have made significant strides against the violence that has traditionally been perpetuated against people because of their race or gender orientation. We both find appalling the trolling culture that attracts some angry men to cases like Tuvel's, which they gleefully label as examples of "the lunacy of social justice warriors" who, when there is no one else to attack, turn on their own and "start cannibalizing their young," in the words of one YouTube troll. Today's increased tolerance for traditionally marginalized groups has led to very real improvements in people's lives and must be seen as an unmitigated social success.

I asked Professor Oliver what she thought was responsible for the seemingly disproportionate response to an academic article that was energetically supportive, not critical, of transgender people's rights. She allowed that she had been taken utterly by surprise by the firestorm, but that after some reflection, it occurred to her that "scholars who worked in transgender studies may have been concerned that by comparing Caitlyn Jenner to Rachel Dolezal, who had been so savagely denounced in the media, Professor Tuvel's article was opening Jenner and transgender people to a kind of contagion of disapproval."

In her article, Professor Tuvel had approached the issue with the dispassionate tone of academic philosophy. She had strictly limited herself to analyzing the logic and arguments that were at work in each case, suggesting only "that Dolezal offers an important opportunity for us to think seriously about how society should treat individuals who claim a strongly felt sense of identification with a certain race." Tuvel was not proposing to think seriously about restricting people's rights or treating them as lesser citizens. On the contrary, she was making an argument in favor of extending rights and protections from one group to another. Serious academic discussion could indeed follow from such proposals. One could imagine sociologists and scholars of race giving reasoned arguments as to why extending the rights of people born white to identify as black would indeed constitute harm to black populations, where the same extension of rights to people designated male at birth identifying as women would not. This was not what happened.

As Professor Oliver told me, one thing that struck her right away about the initial responses from other scholars was that they seemed to be not so much engaging with the content of the piece as exhibiting a kind of academic territorialism. Trans and queer scholars were reacting in outrage that Tuvel had not cited their work sufficiently when making her arguments. As the controversy ballooned and more and more people weighed in on social media, Oliver observed, "there still was practically no engagement with Tuvel's arguments; everything was couched in terms of her failure to adequately cite experts in the field."

Sure enough, about a month after the publication of Tuvel's piece a group of scholars published an open letter on Facebook, which garnered hundreds of signatures, that focused almost entirely on Tuvel's failure to respect academic norms. Specifically, the authors faulted her for "using vocabulary and frameworks not recognized, accepted, or adopted by the conventions of the relevant subfields," as well as for failing to "seek out and sufficiently engage with scholarly work by those who are most vulnerable to the intersection of racial and gender oppressions (women of color) in its discussion of 'transracialism.'" In other words, Tuvel's cardinal sin was not having sufficiently acquainted herself with the subfields she was writing about or scholarship produced by people most personally familiar with the kinds of oppression she was attempting to write about.

As Professor Oliver also noted, this academic turf protection quickly morphed into another, more general claim: namely, that as a white, cisgender woman (the prefix *cis-*, from the Latin for "on this side," denotes those whose identity matches their sex assigned at birth, and is used as an antonym to *trans-*, "across" or "beyond"), Professor Tuvel was by definition unqualified to make arguments about people of other races or genders. In an op-ed piece in the *New York Times* that appeared shortly after the blowup, Rogers Brubaker, a professor of sociology at UCLA (who is also white and cisgender), wrote that the most troubling aspect of this debate was "the belief that identity qualifies or disqualifies one from writing with legitimacy and authority about a particular topic." This "epistemological insiderism," he argued, not only limits outsiders who wish to enter and engage in specific fields of inquiry, it also "risks conveying the patronizing and offensive expectation that members of racial and ethnic minorities will focus their scholarship on race and ethnicity." Such patronizing expectations are real enough. I recall at one faculty event introducing a department chairman's wife to a newly hired assistant professor, a woman from Bangladesh. The older white woman politely inquired what the younger woman of color's field was. Upon learning she was an anthropologist who focused on South Asia, she smiled understandingly and said, "Well, of course you are, dear!"

AN AUTHORITARIAN UNDERBELLY

In 2014, a self-described contrarian feminist named Laura Kipnis published an article in the *Chronicle of Higher Education* detailing the "sexual paranoia" provoked by the expansion of the federal regulation called Title IX, originally established to ensure gender equity in higher education, to universities' investigations of accusations of sexual assault on campus. Indeed, this expansion and the policies universities have instituted in response have raised the hackles of not a few legal scholars. A letter signed by twenty-eight professors at Harvard Law School in response to policies enacted at Harvard in 2014 states, "As teachers responsible for educating our students about due process of law, the substantive law governing discrimination and violence, appropriate administrative decision-making, and the rule of law generally, we find the new sexual harassment policy inconsistent with many of the most basic principles we teach." Ironically, Kipnis's muckraking exposé of a professor's trial and eventual dismissal for allegations of sexual harassment at Northwestern University, where she also teaches, led to some students filing Title IX charges against her for creating a hostile environment with her article. Naturally, Kipnis wrote about that experience, too. Within twenty-four hours of her new article appearing on the *Chronicle*'s website, she was informed that she had been cleared of all charges.

One of the conclusions Kipnis draws from her ordeal is that "critical distance itself is out of fashion—not exactly a plus when it comes to intellectual life (or education itself)." As she continues, "Feelings are what's in fashion. I'm all for feelings: I'm a standard-issue female, after all. But this cult of feeling has an authoritarian underbelly: feelings can't be questioned or probed, even while furnishing the rationale for sweeping new policies, which can't be questioned or probed either." As it happened, the cult of feeling would soon strike with a vengeance. In March 2017, after Kipnis spoke at Wellesley University, a group of professors posted an open letter advocating for new policies limiting the kinds of speakers who should be invited to speak there, and cited Kipnis as the model of precisely the sort of speaker to avoid. The reason? The psychological damage her arguments could have on Wellesley's students, "who often feel the injury most acutely and invest time and energy in rebutting the speakers' arguments."

My first reaction to this letter was disbelief. Professors at a top university are actually arguing that students should not be asked to invest time and energy in rebutting arguments? As I thought more, though, I recalled a young woman who was a graduate student while I served as vice dean for graduate education, who reluctantly came to speak to me about a professor. The student—I'll call her Jean—was terrified that her complaints would make their way back to the professor, whose letter of recommendation would be essential for her chances of obtaining a job the following year. I immediately assured her that, although I was under an obligation to report claims of harassment, under no circumstances would her identity be revealed unless she permitted it. Jean seemed almost to melt with relief, as if the tension had been building up in her for months. She then described an incessant pattern of unwanted advances, touching, and proposals from the professor every time they were in private. She felt she couldn't avoid such situations because he was the only expert in her chosen field. She also felt that her refusals were clear enough, even if she was trying to issue them in friendly, nonconfrontational ways, to avoid the kind of conflict that might lead to her being dropped as his advisee. Today, the flood of revelations of powerful men in Hollywood, business, and politics who have used their influence to harass and assault women with impunity shows how widespread this dynamic has been.

Jean wanted nothing more than for the behavior to stop. Fortunately for her, the Office of Institutional Equity, which has responsibility for investigating harassment claims, was able to devise an approach that put an end to the behavior without drawing attention to Jean being the complainant. As it turns out, she was not the only student dealing with this kind of attention, and the compliance officer was able to call the professor into a meeting and present him with a pattern of behavior that was identifiable as unacceptable. He was told in no uncertain terms both that his meetings had to remain professional and that he was not to try to ascertain the identity of any complainants. He was also told that a determination that he had acted in any way that could be seen as retribution to students for having complained would be legally actionable. After that I never heard another complaint about that professor.

As unnerving as her experience had been, Jean was lucky. While frightening, the behavior she suffered through was not outright violent, and her complaint managed both to stop it and to safeguard her confidentiality. She finished her dissertation the next year and went on to get an excellent job. Other young women on campus are not nearly as lucky. While the statistic has been widely debated and there may in fact be no way of knowing the actual numbers, a 2015 American Association of Universities survey reported that almost one in four women are sexually assaulted during their undergraduate years. Since the assaults often occur behind closed doors at alcohol-fueled parties, it can be very hard to prove that sexual contact was not consensual. While each year there are high-profile cases where young men are disciplined and even expelled for sexual assault, many more cases end with much lighter punishments, or none at all—with the result that a woman may spend some part of her college career brushing shoulders with her attacker. These are the students the Wellesley professors had in mind when they wrote their letter.

One of the problems is that awareness of and discussion about sexual assault today are taking place in the midst of a cultural change, as the now prevalent term "rape culture" would seem to indicate. As Saida Agostini, a representative of an organization called FORCE: Upsetting Rape Culture, put it at a recent roundtable on immigration and race at Hopkins, today, women and people of color can feel assaulted merely by virtue of being in a space that sorts them as "black," "women," or "queer." But if that is the case, then it would appear that "identity" can be a truly be a double-edged sword, a much-needed anchor for forming communities that safeguard and heal, even while running the risk of provoking and reinforcing some of the same attitudes that caused so much damage in the first place.

For this very reason it is all the more crucial that these debates take place and that these feelings and attitudes be aired. While understanding that individual students may have had deeply painful experiences that cause them to react in anguish to discussions of, for example, sexual assault on campus, it seems to me that when groups speak up to ask that debate be stifled, we need to ask whose interests are being served. The professors at Wellesley went on in their letter to recommend that "those who invite speakers to campus should consider whether, in their zeal for promoting debate, they might, in fact, stifle productive debate by enabling the bullying of disempowered groups," and I agree that this is a legitimate question to ask. They also added that "standards of respect and rigor must remain paramount when considering whether a speaker is actually qualified for the platform granted by an invitation to Wellesley." As far as how to determine whether said speakers are "actually qualified," they added this: "In the case of an academic speaker, we ask that the Wellesley host not only consider whether the speaker holds credentials, but whether the presenter has standing in his/her/their discipline." It seems that, yet again, legitimacy of opinion rests on contested academic turf.

Was Henry Louis Gates right when he insisted that "any human being sufficiently curious and motivated can fully possess another culture, no matter how 'alien' it may appear to be"? In 2017 a controversy erupted when the Whitney Museum selected for its Biennial a painting by the artist Dana Schutz depicting the body of Emmett Till, a black boy who was murdered by white supremacists in 1955. Among a number of vocal critics, a British artist and woman of color named Hannah Black started a petition demanding the painting be destroyed. As the critic Kenan Malik has written about this case and others like it, "Campaigns against cultural appropriation reveal the changing meaning of what it is to challenge racism. Once, it was a demand for equal treatment for all. Now, it calls for cultures to be walled off and the boundaries to be policed." As Malik recalls, when Emmett Till was killed his mother called for photographs of his body to be published and for him to be laid out in an open casket, the better to tell the world the horrific story of his death. In this way, his murder helped inspire the movement that resulted in the Civil Rights Act of 1964.

Hannah Black's letter invokes the pleas of Till's mother, too, however, even as she contests that they had the effect that is often claimed for them. As she puts it, "That even the disfigured corpse of a child was not sufficient to move the white gaze from its habitual cold calculation is evident daily and in a myriad of ways, not least the fact that this painting exists at all. In brief: the painting should not be acceptable to anyone who cares or pretends to care about Black people because it is not acceptable for a white person to transmute Black suffering into profit and fun, though the practice has been normalized for a long time."

The conflict would seem to be irresolvable: on the one hand the heartfelt cry of those who are of a race or culture that has been slaughtered, enslaved, and systematically oppressed for centuries, that their suffering not be appropriated by those who have never felt the stigma of that oppression; on the other, the desire on the part of those not afflicted to engage in what another critic, Adam Shatz, calls "acts of radical sympathy, and imaginative identification." Can it be that such desire has no place in a community trying to heal? Conversely, can a community built on a foundation of oppression and violence ever heal itself without such acts?

I think the answer can only be that we not only allow but demand such acts—with the caveat that they always be subject to critique and debate, and that their emotional reverberations be openly felt and discussed. I think that an artwork that is clearly not an expression of hate but an attempt at understanding, however flawed, should not be destroyed; but it need not be silently accepted or admired either. Likewise, arguments or comparisons that trigger trauma, despite the best of intentions, should be held account-able for that, not by retraction, but by engagement.

The ideal place to learn the tools for such engagement is in classrooms where art, literature, philosophy, or history is the subject matter at hand. These are precisely the spaces where one could hope that students are learning how to engage in "acts of radical sympathy, and imaginative identification." Yet, as "epistemological insiderism" becomes the default position on socially high-tension topics like race and gender, we should perhaps wonder along with Rogers Brubaker if teachers will "avoid assigning controversial materials or discussing controversial views in class" or if professors will "stop exploring controversial topics in their research."

It seems to me that in some cases this is already happening, and has been for some time. Recently one of my graduate students, a young man from Italy, posted a flyer for his course on contemporary Mexican culture, a topic he can rightly be considered an expert on, given that he has been studying Mexican culture and literature for years and is writing a dissertation in that area. Within days one of his flyers was covered in writing that warned students that this course was an example of "whites-plaining." The instructor's name was circled and next to it was written, "not Mexican."

As universities have increasingly become places where one's race, gender, or sexual orientation is assumed to be the source of an ineffable and ulti-mately incommunicable knowledge, the very classrooms that used to be forums for wide-ranging discussion with professors who prided themselves for the reach of their inquiry are becoming increasingly constrained and limited in scope. For institutional reasons that we will see in what follows, professors are less likely to offer students an open space for boundless inquiry and debate precisely because they themselves are gravitating toward the narrowest definition of their fields, and are more and more fearful of being caught venturing out from their confines.

BOUTIQUE MULTICULTURALISM

By the 1990s multiculturalism was firmly entrenched as the reigning ideal in colleges and universities. The term was also well established in common parlance, with mentions in the press having increased fiftyfold in the prior decade. Despite something close to a consensus among college professors that multiculturalism was a good thing and a goal to aspire to, there was no explicit agreement on what that would mean, since the term was used to designate everything from expanded curricula to "African motifs in the fashion business, called 'multiculturally-aware wear.'" When I was a graduate student at Stanford, a group of fellow students and I invited the famed literary critic and academic gadfly Stanley Fish to come speak, and he chose as his topic what he called "boutique multiculturalism." As was (and still is) his way, he did his best to puncture the faculty's sanctimoniousness, insisting that no one present could in fact hold true to the ideal of multiculturalism, which at some point would demand a self-negating tolerance of intolerance itself. Hence all we could ever hope for was a boutique multiculturalism of colorful fashion and ethnic cuisine.

Fish was a multiculturalist at heart. Nevertheless, his deeper point about the inherent limits of the ideal of cultural openness was shared by critics participating in a cultural backlash against multiculturalism that started in the 1980s. As one of these, Richard Bernstein, would argue, "The power of culture is utterly contrary to the most fervently held beliefs and values of the advocates of multiculturalism. Multiculturalism is a movement of the left, emerging from . . . the 1960s. But culture is powerfully conservative. Culture is what enforces obedience to authority, the authority of parents, of history, of custom, of superstition. Deep attachment to culture is one of the things that prevents different people from understanding each other." While there can be no doubt that the multicultural movement from the 1960s to the 1980s did much to, in Richard Rorty's words, decrease "the amount of sadism in our society," the unquestioning embrace of culture has at times gone too far. Respecting the culture of another is a vital element of civil society, but equally important is sharing a basic vocabulary and standards for reasoned disagreement, as well as an understanding of the histories that led different cultures to share the same space in the first place.

The multicultural movement had a profound impact on what was being taught, not only on college campuses, but in schools. In 1987 both New York and California revamped their primary and secondary school curricula to make more room for non-European cultures. In New York this meant that the time devoted to the history and culture of western Europe was reduced from a full year to half of one semester, and U.S. history was cut down to "a section on the Constitution; then a leap across Jefferson, Jackson, the Civil War, and Reconstruction to 1877." Despite these changes, the 1987 revisions didn't go far enough for some. In 1989, New York convened a new Task Force on Minorities, which issued a report condemning current curricular standards for perpetuating "a terribly damaging effect on the psyche of young people of African, Asian, Latino, and Native American descent." While the 1987 revisions had made more room for materials focused on historically excluded cultures, it was not enough to counteract "deeply rooted racist traditions" and still left students with a "Eurocentric multiculturalism," the new report said.

As it turns out, one of the authors of the new report and the member of the task force representing African American culture was a professor of black studies at City College in New York named Leonard Jeffries. Professor Jeffries, a leader of the Afrocentric movement, has been disavowed by many scholars of African American studies, but his theories, including one dividing the world's cultures into "ice people" and "sun people," still manage to find an audience. Professor Jeffries is reported to have attributed the slave trade to "rich Jews," and derides the Constitution, saying it is "vulgar and revolting" to glorify "a process that heaped undeserved rewards on a segment of the population while oppressing the majority."

The Afrocentrism that Jeffries preaches is intended to overturn the implicit valuation that raises some cultures above other ones. But instead of focusing on the role of history in creating arbitrary hierarchies and then naturalizing them, it creates and naturalizes its own hierarchies. European "ice people" are "cold, individualistic, materialistic, and aggressive"; African "sun people" are "warm, humanistic, and communitarian." More than simply overturning hierarchies, thinking of culture in such deterministic ways presumes that our cultures set an absolute limit to what we can think and communicate. If this were the case, though, a truly pluralistic society would be impossible, because there would be no way for differences in value to be adjudicated between cultural groups. Unfortunately, this presumption appears to be on the rise today, and its vanguard is on college campuses.

In the spring of 2014 Brandeis University announced it had canceled its plans to give an honorary degree to the Somali-born Ayaan Hirsi Ali, author of the book *Infidel* and a vocal advocate of women's rights. In defense of its decision the administration claimed it was unable to "overlook certain of her past statements that are inconsistent with Brandeis University's core values." The statements that Brandeis found too shocking to permit Hirsi Ali to speak at commencement were criticisms of Islam, including calling the religion a "destructive, nihilistic cult of death," and her 2004 film *Submission*, which criticized the treatment of women in Islam, after which she received death threats in her adopted Netherlands, where she also served in Parliament. Hirsi Ali's criticisms of Islam stem from her own life experience growing up in Somalia, where she was subjected to genital mutilation and resisted her family's attempts to force her to marry against her will. They are political opinions, which she supports with clear and forceful arguments, even if many would disagree with them or find them offensive.

Indeed, Brandeis's official position on recipients of its honorary degrees makes explicit that political positions are not part of their decision process, as its president observed in 2006: "Just as Brandeis does not inquire into the political opinions and beliefs of faculty or staff before appointing them, or students before offering admission, so too the University does not select honorary degree recipients on the basis of their political beliefs or opinions." But the decision to rescind the invitation was not political in any normal sense of the word. The administration had come under pressure from student groups and outside advocacy groups like the Council on American-Islamic Relations, which characterized Hirsi Ali's positions not as political criticism but as religious bigotry. In other words, her arguments about a religion's beliefs were interpreted as feelings about a people's identity. As the chair of the Department of Islamic Studies put it, she "makes Muslim students feel very uneasy." Doing and saying things that make people uneasy is not popular these days. There is even a word for it: microaggression. The idea of a microaggression is that something someone says or does can offend a member of a minority group with or without it being the intention of the speaker or doer to offend. This much seems obvious and uncontroversial. The culture of policing microaggressions, however, has led to some extremes that beg the question of whether communication is even possible without groups engaging in microaggressions against one another. It can also be just plain silly.

A few years ago, also at Brandeis University, a group representing Asian American students put on an exhibition about the microaggressions that might be particularly offensive to their constituents, which included asking questions like "Aren't you supposed to be good at math?" or assertions like "I'm color-blind! I don't see race." (The latter seems little hard to believe in today's media environment, given how thoroughly Stephen Colbert lampooned that very sentence by having the persona of his archconservative talk-show host consistently claim not to be able to discern whether his interviewees were black or white.) Unfortunately, as Greg Lukianoff and Jonathan Haidt reported in a widely read piece in the *Atlantic*, at Brandeis "a backlash arose among other Asian American students, who felt that the display itself was a microaggression. The association removed the installation, and its president wrote an e-mail to the entire student body apologizing to anyone who was 'triggered or hurt by the content of the microaggressions.'"

As Lukianoff and Haidt go on to argue, today's movement differs from the political correctness of the 1980s in that it "is largely about emotional well-being. More than the last, it presumes an extraordinary fragility of the collegiate psyche, and therefore elevates the goal of protecting students from psychological harm. The ultimate aim, it seems, is to turn campuses into 'safe spaces' where young adults are shielded from words and ideas that make some uncomfortable." Could it be that such safe spaces are a bit like that marvelous "cone of silence" from the TV series *Get Smart*? Ostensibly there to protect us from those who would hurt us, they really prevent us from being able to hear ourselves, much less each other.

Conservative news outlets are having a field day with universities over what they are now terming "disinvitation season," the period just around spring break when administrations get hit by a wave of protests and angry letters over the most recent commencement speaker to rile up liberal ire on their campus. The pundits then blame the pressures that lead to such regular and embarrassing backtracking on political correctness, which they understand as the illiberal policing of language to pursue ostensible liberal ends.

Liberal policing of speech is real enough; any given day's morning paper can carry an example of the latest example of student outrage silencing a (usually conservative) speaker. As I write these words this morning the news was about Middlebury College, where students protesting a speech by Charles Murray, an author known for peddling discredited theories linking intelligence to race, shouted down the speaker as well as his left-leaning faculty interlocutor as they tried to conduct their dialogue, even assaulting them as they tried to leave the venue. But this popular image—hordes of intolerant liberal students shouting down speakers whose views they disagree with—fails to grasp the complexity of the move-ments and emotions that underlie the occasional excessive outbursts that are so eagerly spread by the media consumed by the public.

A PRESUPPOSITION OF INCOMMUNICABILITY

As both a university administrator and chair of a large department I've had many occasions to witness firsthand how attempts to communicate and adjudicate differences run afoul of the politics of race and gender. One spring semester around midterms (and here I'll change names and some details of the case to respect the students' privacy), Giselle, a second-year African American student, came to my office to talk about her experience in a section led by a graduate student, Beth, who is white. According to Giselle, Beth was ignoring or belittling the positions she would take in class, especially ones stemming from her experiences as a black woman. In one incident, Giselle and another student who, as Giselle told me, "identifies as black" tried to bring their perspectives as "black women attending a predominantly white institution like Hopkins" to the analysis of a story the class was reading, thinking their perspective could offer insights, since the character they were discussing "often feels like an outcast."

According to Giselle, while Beth's "intention was only to relate, she interrupted this student to say that when she was in Korea as an exchange student before starting her PhD, she felt the same sense of being an outcast." As she continued, "I found this frustrating because Beth is a white woman, and benefits from white privilege, so I pointed out to her that her experience in Korea does not compare to our experience here as black women. Beth appeared to be embarrassed, and said, 'I am not sure if I benefit from white privilege.'" For her part, Giselle found this reluctance on Beth's part to accept that she had benefited from white privilege "incredibly frustrating," and pointed to other moments in class where she, "as a brown-skinned woman, was the one to point out the necessity of addressing race or gender in our discussions, and feel that this should not be [her] job because [Beth] is the instructor and should be cognizant of her presence as a white woman who directly benefits from white supremacist and patriarchal structures in academia and elsewhere."

When I talked to Beth about the incident and the complaints she was getting in class, she was visibly shaken. As Giselle had surmised, bringing up her own experience was nothing other than an "attempt to relate" and support what the women had said. She didn't go out of her way to bring up race precisely because of her fear of being called out for making points that weren't hers to make. When I asked her about how she had reacted to Giselle's claim that she benefited from white privilege, she confessed that it had taken her aback, and that she had reacted with skepticism. She told me that Giselle didn't know her and shouldn't make assumptions about the privilege she may or may not have benefited from, especially now, when she was finishing her PhD without any job prospects in sight and little but accumulated debt to her name. I told her that I understood how she felt, but that as the instructor in the class she was responsible for being as inclusive as possible of different positions and perspectives.

I also told her that to my mind she and Giselle were facing off across the kind of fault line that has been spreading across the American social landscape for the last generation. As underrepresented minorities have slowly increased their representation on college campuses since the 1960s, they have often done so at a high emotional cost. Students of color are more likely than whites to be the first in their families to go to college and hence not have immediate family members who can relate to the culture shock that higher education can bring with it. For those who do enroll in college, their feelings of alienation are often exacerbated by finding themselves isolated on campus and having far fewer peers than they had in high school who look like them or have had similar upbringings to theirs; and their graduation rates lag far behind the average. "White privilege" is one of the terms that students like Giselle have found to put a name to the continued feelings of exclusion they feel.

The same term, however, often strikes whites like Beth as a slap in the face. They find implicit in the term the accusation that they have been dealt a better hand and have not gotten to where they are on the strengths of their merit and hard work alone. They bristle at the term because it is telling them the same thing that blacks have been made to feel for so long: "You don't really deserve to be here." When Beth made an honest attempt to "relate" to Giselle's perspective, she was trying to tell her, "I know what you're feeling." For Giselle, her attempt undermined the specificity of her situation and failed to recognize how whites continue to enjoy higher socioeconomic status because they have benefited from policies that have excluded African Americans from the spaces, institutions, and wealth that provide and reproduce that status. From Beth's perspective, her attempt was to relate and understand; from Giselle's perspective, it was an attempt to equate conditions and histories that are de facto different. As the administrator trying to adjudicate this dispute, my quandary was that both perspectives were justified, but that acquiescing to either one necessitated finding fault with the other.

Emphasizing the real differences of a group's conditions and history is what underlies the continued support for separate institutions for women and minorities, as well as a new trend in mixed institutions: separate graduation ceremonies. In 2017 Harvard held its first separate ceremony for

African American graduates. The ceremony didn't replace general graduation; not all graduating students of color attended; and whites were not
explicitly excluded from attending. But for the first time, some eighty graduates of color at Harvard marched in their own ceremony. The mood was
festive as the graduates and their families celebrated their achievement. One
of the student speakers, Duwain Pinder of Columbus, Ohio, focused on
the need for a feeling of community with other students of color in a society
that seems not to value blacks as much as whites. He recalled how in his
first year as a student in a joint degree program between the Kennedy
School of Government and the business school, "while reviewing notes on
the ethics of public office, I watched replays of the senseless execution of
Walter Scott, and the overwhelming question during this first year at
Harvard was: How can I survive in a world that seems not to value my
life?" Then he continued, "We have survived. Just look at us."

Separate celebrations like Harvard's are seen by the participants as a way
of recognizing and appreciating the communities that gave them a sense of
belonging when they left the safety and protection of their families and
homes. At a similar celebration at Columbia University, this one for students
who are the first in their families to go to college, graduate Lizzette Delgadillo spoke of "impostor syndrome—feeling alone when it feels like everybody else on campus just knows what to do and you don't." Critics of such
ceremonies see something else entirely. For the anti-affirmative-action
crusader Ward Connerly, for instance, there's a certain hypocrisy to students
graduating from the most elite institution in the country focusing on their
disadvantages. "Think about it," he said. "These kids went to Harvard, and
they less than anyone in our society should worry about feeling welcome and
finding comfort zones. They don't need that." Michael Huggins, one of the
Harvard event's organizers, disputed that students at Harvard don't need
such protections: "Our journeys at Harvard have not been easy," he said.
"Our families have had to overcome everything from Jim Crow segregation
to poverty to an oppressive criminal justice system, yet we still persist."

The controversy around separate graduations and the run-in between
Giselle and Beth share a common thread. In both cases, individual members
of a disadvantaged group are pointing to the shared experience of that group

as something that needs to be recognized. From their perspective, those who have not shared in this experience cannot possibly relate. Worse, trying to relate by drawing comparisons can seem like an attempt to delegitimize the claim to a different status. Over the past generation, the painful integration of minorities into the upper echelons of the education system has left a residue of resentment on both sides. Most troubling, perhaps, has been the emergence of a presupposition of incommunicability that has become most intense precisely where issues of identity and history should be talked about: in college classrooms. One reason for this may be a parallel development among the professors teaching these classes. As Upton Sinclair famously said, "It is difficult to get a man to understand something, when his salary depends on his not understanding it!" In the modern university, professors' salaries seem to depend on narrowing the range of what they believe they can legitimately talk about, which in turn is undermining their students' confidence that they can empathize with people who are different from them.

HYPERSPECIALIZATION

Hardly a viral grenade is launched on AM talk radio, or a venomous screed let loose by a populist politician, that doesn't have the "pointy-headed professor" somewhere at its core. Like faceless Bond villains ensconced in their secret headquarters, chortling over their plans to take over the world while stroking white felines, the "socialistic eggheads of the professoriate," in Yale history professor Beverly Gage's ironic phrasing, have consistently embodied Ronald Reagan's negative fantasy of "a little intellectual elite in a far-distant capitol" who can "plan our lives for us better than we can plan them ourselves."

This nefarious image of a conspiring, intellectual liberal elite—an obvious correlate of stories used by generations of anti-Semites to stir up popular rage against Jews—finds its lighthearted counterpart in the ridicule heaped upon some academics, especially humanists, when politicians periodically report on the ostensibly frivolous topics of their research, normally to justify further reducing the paltry public resources dedicated to the National Endowment for the Humanities. As a Texas congressman once reportedly said about a funded research project focusing on sex and sexuality in the Middle Ages, "Sex in the Middle Ages? Hell! Even I can tell you what we know about sex in the Middle Ages. There were men. There were women. Some of them had sex, which is why we are here today."

Academics, especially literature professors like me, at times seem to revel in feeding that cartoonish image. Take the annual conference in my field, the meeting of the Modern Language Association of America (MLA). Each year thousands of English, literature, and language professors and graduate students converge on a major U.S. city for three days of lectures, meetings, and job interviews. The novelist and literature professor David Lodge memorably lampooned the MLA in his globe-trotting bar brawl of a novel *Small World*, in which self-indulgent English professors engage in debates about deconstruction and trysts between the sheets while jet-setting from one boondoggle to the next. It all ends at the MLA conference in New York, where, Lodge writes, "you can attend the cocktail party organized by the Gay Caucus for the Modern Languages, or the Reception Sponsored by the American Association of Professors of Yiddish, or the Cash Bar arranged in Conjunction with the Special Session on Methodological Problems in Monolingual and Bilingual Lexicography, or the Annual Dinner of the American Milton Society, or the Executive Council of the American Boccaccio Association, or the meetings of the Marxist Literary Group."

I came of age as a scholar during the time that Lodge depicts in scenes like this one. Along with the history of European and Latin American literature, I studied philosophy and intellectual history, but also quite a lot of literary theory. Already as an undergraduate I sat in a classroom with other budding literary scholars and learned about strange and exciting approaches like Marxism, feminism, psychoanalysis, and deconstruction from a generously tattooed and pierced young professor. This was also the age of the canon wars, when young professors like mine challenged generations of syllabi that had included more or less the same authors, goading other professors like Allan Bloom to respond with books like *The Closing of the American Mind* in which they equated diversifying the canon with dumbing down the curriculum. At the same time, the grimace-inducing lecture titles and subgroups that are so common at the MLA were becoming symptoms of the hyperspecialization required by the research university, a trend that was risking undermining its educational mission.

The truth is, while much of the scholarship produced by the turn to multiculturalism and theory in the seventies was both groundbreaking and liberating, many of the academic trends that conservatives like Bloom were reacting to were just that, trends; and some enthusiasts of psychoanalysis or deconstruction were taking an intellectually easy road, springing impressive-sounding concepts on unsuspecting texts without really understanding the former or in any way enlightening the latter. That such approaches to literature made it out to the general public was bad for literary studies. It made well-educated nonacademics snort derisively about modern criticism having lost all standards and any interest in getting to the truth. This, I believe, is utter nonsense. What is true, however, is that the drive to hyperspecialization induced by today's university culture is undermining the broad, boundary-breaking kind of thinking that is one of the real benefits—both for individuals and for society—of a liberal arts education.

Specialization is one of the great motors of civilization. It was only when communities of humans began to have individuals focus on one task or trade and exchange the products of their labor for the other necessities of life that those communities advanced beyond the basic technologies of subsistence farming. This logic holds through to the miraculous discoveries and inventions of modern science. Without individuals putting aside the knowledge and practices that are essential for survival in more traditional societies so that they can dive deep into a field—molecular biology, material engineering, atomic physics—the innovations that allow modern humans to live longer, shelter more people, and know more about the physical world we live in would never have gotten off the ground. The modern university that produces much of this knowledge and practical know-how also thrives on and fosters specialization. If it didn't, the innovation we have come to depend on would grind to a halt.

Sometimes, though, when a system's incentives push its elements exclusively in one direction, it can end up producing too much of a good thing.

It may be that in the case of some fields, too much specialization can work against the university's mission and society's best interests. Let's take an analogy from health care. There is no question that, like so much else the modern, industrialized world has produced, modern medicine is a product of specialization. The American medical system, with its elite medical schools, continues to produce both some of the top medical specialists in the world along with some of the best research, leading to ever-greater innovation in diagnosing and treating illness. As a result of the obvious benefits of specialization and the premium placed on specialists, there is an enormous incentive built into the American medical educational system for a student to become a specialist—including average salaries that are double what primary-care physicians earn. Given how much talent, time, and money it costs to become a physician in our highly competitive education system, it stands to reason that many talented people will be drawn to make good on their investment by becoming specialists.

This state of affairs has led to a significant shortage of primary-care physicians, even as it has continued to make the American medical system the most expensive in the world, with spending on health care as of this writing well over three trillion dollars per year. At the same time, this lavish spending on health care has done little to improve the actual health of average Americans, with the United States still ranked last among developed nations on many of the key measures for health outcomes. As Jamie Koufman, a clinical professor of otolaryngology and the director of Voice Institute of New York, puts it in explaining this trend, the counterintuitive combination of ever-greater cost and declining or stagnating quality is due to the influence the specialists have on the medical system: "There are so many specialty organizations because each develops authority over a niche market and vigorously guards its turf." While there are limits to the analogy, since the first half of the twentieth century colleges have functioned increasingly in a similar fashion, often at the expense of the quality of the education they offer to their students.

In the last years of his life, the philosopher Richard Rorty was hired by the comparative literature department where I was working on my doctorate. He had great love and respect for literature, but worried that the field of literary studies was likely to suffer from the same trend he had witnessed in his own field. As he once put it, "The main reason I am prey to such suspicions is that I have watched, in the course of my lifetime, similarly gloomy predictions come true in my own discipline. Philosophers of my generation learned that an academic discipline can become almost unrecognizably different in a half-century—different, above all, in the sort of talents that can get you tenure." The trend that Rorty saw in philosophy and feared for in literature was the shift from wisdom to what he called knowingness. Where the former is characterized by a wide-ranging knowledge and a passionate attachment to deep questions, the latter is highly focused and dry but technically accurate: "As philosophy became analytic, the reading habits of aspiring graduate students changed in a way that parallels recent changes in the habits of graduate students of literature. Fewer old books were read, and more recent articles." Rorty's fear was that under such circumstances, "the study of the humanities may continue to produce knowledge, but may no longer produce hope."

While this is a classic fear that older scholars have about generational change in their fields, I am convinced that the trends Rorty saw in philosophy have influenced the development of other disciplines as well. And although I do see much value in specialization (after all, where's the fun in all of us knowing exactly the same things?), I also believe that the institutional pressures created by the modern university have led to a hyper-specialization that is inimical to the very idea of a liberal arts education. These trends are structurally similar to those that have led to our medical system having some of the best specialists in the world while being too costly and not providing very good health care: namely, a tenure system that incentivizes ever more minutely focused research; the organization of the university into departments that ultimately seek to protect their "turf" and maintain near total control over who is hired and promoted; and pressures from the government and university administrations to uniformly quantify the value of teaching and research as measurable outputs.

THE TRAP OF RELEVANCE

Shriver Hall sits at the far end of the lower quad of Johns Hopkins University's Homewood campus. When you climb the marble stairs and enter one of the three sets of massive white-painted doors overlooking the quad, the first sight to greet you is a set of murals from the previous century, depicting some of the school's founding faculty in medicine and the arts and sciences. The tableau on the right wall is particularly striking. There the visitor is treated to a scene taking place in an operating theater. An audience of eager students gazes down at a table surrounded by the greatest physicians of their day—luminaries like William Osler, who is credited with creating the first residency training program for medical students, and William Stewart Halsted, who introduced procedures for maintaining sterility in the operating room and invented the radical mastectomy as a treatment for breast cancer. The only woman in the painting is an unnamed patient lying prone on the operating table, her breasts exposed.

The mural separates the building foyer from an ornate room known simply as the boardroom, which is where the Johns Hopkins Board of Trustees traditionally met. Now it is the meeting place of a body with a far greater impact on the day-to-today workings of the schools of Arts and Sciences and Engineering that occupy the Homewood campus. That body is called the Homewood Academic Council. The academic council has a host of responsibilities, including oversight over curricula and regularly reviewing the departments of the two schools. But its most significant and, for the faculty, fearsome charge is that of granting and denying tenure.

Tenure is a loaded word nowadays. In the United States, academia is the only field of employment where something like tenure, which protects those who hold it from termination, exists. The existence of tenure stokes the ire of pundits and politicians like the Missouri Republican state representative Rick Brattin, who in January 2017 introduced a bill to eliminate tenure at Missouri State and nullify it for already tenured professors, in the belief that "in the academic world, you can get away with literally anything and taxpayers are paying their salaries—not to mention students being burdened with millions and millions and millions of dollars of debt." Such broadsides notwithstanding, the idea behind tenure is noble. Freed from concerns about how their work will be received by their employers, professors may pursue the truth, regardless of political pressures. A tenured professor of political science may investigate how her university is involved with the development of advanced weaponry; a tenured professor of humanities like myself can write lines critical of his institution, with a reasonable expectation that his words will not lead to his losing his job.

Because each general field of knowledge has only a few representatives on the council, a single unscrupulous busybody can exert enormous sway on its decisions regarding tenure and promotion. I have seen cases where a council is persuaded by a professor with a single, short and unimpressive book to his name and very little standing in the field to deny tenure to clearly superior colleagues who are world-renowned scholars. The justifications are easy to come by. Since the council ostensibly makes its decisions based on a slew of letters from other scholars in the candidate's field, one humanities professor on the council need only start focusing on the one or two inevitable critical sentences in this or that letter to trigger a cascade of doubt. Because the administration has been putting pressure on the council to tighten its tenure standards, it has become easier for professors to game the system and ensure that an up-and-coming colleague they don't like is denied tenure. And the most surefire way to ensure denial of tenure is if a candidate has erred into a field that is not her own and earned some critical comments from an expert in that field. Consequently, the safest bet for young faculty as they prepare for tenure is to hew closely to a very narrowly defined field in which they can develop a justified claim to be the best—because they are in practical terms the only—scholar working today. If your dissertation analyzes the critical reception of translations of, say, a single Latin American novelist in China since the 1980s, you can be pretty sure you'll know more about your field than anyone else.

It only takes a few cases to cast a pall over young humanists' desire to think big. A recent case at Hopkins involved a junior professor whose second book had just been published by one of the most prestigious university presses and had received a top prize from the academic association closest to his research interests. Given his outstanding credentials, his chair proposed he be put up for tenure early, and the dean agreed. What neither the chair nor the dean counted on was the resistance of a senior colleague in the department who resented the encroachment of younger scholars on his field, in which he considered himself to be one of the reigning experts. By the end of the process, the junior scholar, whose work had seemed so promising that he was put up for early promotion, was denied tenure and his employment was terminated. A university in Europe happily took advantage of Hopkins's mistake and offered him a professorship, and he has since moved with his family to continue his career there.

Academia is a small world. Word got around very quickly that Hopkins had denied tenure to a rising star who had been making a name for himself in a cutting-edge, interdisciplinary field. Young scholars and those advising their PhD students learn a simple lesson from these cases: Universities like to talk about interdisciplinary work and emerging fields. But faculties grant tenure, and among faculties, field protectionism is the law of the land. The safest path to a tenured position is to dig deep and straight down, be as narrow as possible, and don't rock the boat. In other words, never try to know too much outside of your own field.

This caution is handed down to future professors in the most concrete possible way: directly from faculty to the graduate students they are mentoring. One of the most curious trends I have witnessed as someone who trains graduate students is how the idea of "relevance" has come to be treated. A first, my naïve assumption was that relevance is a good thing, something everyone should strive for in his or her work. But more often than not relevance is used in a cautionary way these days, as in directives to students and colleagues to "avoid the trap of relevance." The idea of the trap of relevance is that humanistic inquiry, especially into historical periods at a distance from our own, should be driven by interest in and concern for the events and works being studied and their cultural contexts, not the relevance of these to our own times and concerns. The latter is disparaged as "presentism," and contrasted with a healthy attitude of "historicism." But a salutary respect for historical context does not preclude explaining why an interest in the past, in literature, or in a philosophical problem has relevance for our lives today. Yet it is precisely this kind of interest that is being driven out of graduate students, out of a concern that they not appear to be straying too far from the narrow field they are specializing in.

I should immediately interject that the faculty giving this advice have only the best interests of their students in mind. Often the adviser admits that personally, she appreciates the broader context being brought to the analysis, but then she adds that she is concerned about how the student's claim will be received when he is on the job market. Beyond the individual relationship between the faculty adviser and the graduate student, at Hopkins the moment for these admonitions is the dissertation defense, when the PhD candidate responds to questions from a committee of at least five professors including his or her adviser and at least two faculty from outside his or her department.

I participate in a half dozen or more dissertation defenses per year, and have often witnessed this dynamic taking shape, even among my most brilliant and respected colleagues. At Hopkins "disciplinarity" is almost a sacred word, and professors guard the borders of their disciplines, which apparently align perfectly with their departments, as if they were the last sentinels of a besieged nation. Historians sitting on a literature committee will, almost as if programmed, ask "the historical question," and make a huge show of how the candidate's claims fail to grasp the subtleties of the political and social movements of that moment in history. Likewise, literature professors like myself who are called to sit on a philosophy defense will jump on readings of literary texts that the candidate might call on as evidence in, say, a thesis about moral reasoning. In one recent defense that I attended as an external reader, a dissertation focused on public morality in Victorian literature concluded with a chapter on the degeneration of political discourse in the present day. The connections were, to my mind, both real and elegantly made. The committee advised that the dissertation should be accepted . . . without the concluding chapter. The trap of relevance was decisively avoided.

THE TIME TO THINK

Specialization is part of the DNA of the modern American university, an institution that Johns Hopkins played a key role in establishing. One of our founding documents states, "The Johns Hopkins University provides advanced instruction, not professional, to properly qualified students, in various departments of literature and science." The mention of departments in this context is vital. Hopkins was founded in the late nineteenth century on a new model of the university imported from Germany, in which, instead of studying the classical curriculum that had previously been uniform for all, students would now focus their studies in elective areas. These areas were defined and controlled by the faculty, who organized themselves into departments.

While Hopkins was the first research university expressly organized according to the model, the man most responsible for bringing the new spirit of higher education to the States was Charles William Eliot, a chemist who was denied promotion at Harvard, taught in Europe and at MIT for some time, and then returned to Harvard as its youngest-ever president. Architects of the university prior to Eliot, like the English cardinal John Henry Newman, were skeptical of combining a research faculty with a teaching mission. For Newman, the object of the university was "the diffusion and extension of knowledge," not "scientific and philosophical discovery." If that were not the case, he reasoned, "I do not see why a University should have students." In contrast, it was Eliot's firm belief that the modern university could advance knowledge and educate its students at the same time. As he wrote in an article in the *Atlantic* in 1869, "To make a good engineer, chemist, or architect, the only sure way is to make first, or at least simultaneously, an observant, sensible, and reflecting man, whose mind is not only well stored, but well trained also to see, compare, reason, and decide."

This elective system allowed students to choose from a wider array of more specialized subjects, which in turn incentivized the universities to invest in faculties with a more diverse set of specialized expertise. New graduate programs were founded to produce PhDs to fill the demand for new faculty positions. Johns Hopkins was a key player in this development; in the early years of the twentieth century fully a quarter of the PhDs teaching at America's top universities had their degrees from Hopkins.

As the historian Hal Lawson has described it, "Specialized faculty required equally specialized academic homes and supervision, leading to the formation of an increasing number of academic departments and resulting in a new balance of power between the faculty and the administration." Along with the addition of new professional schools to the major universities and the development of new majors for undergraduates, "the American university played a central role in advancing specialization in society. At the same time, the university's internal specialization was responsible for its bureaucratization." This occurred as the faculty, newly organized into departments and increasingly responsible for deciding on the standards of excellence in their field, organized themselves to increase their political capital within the university. The historian Laurence Veysey noted already in the 1960s that the tendency to increased specialization under the sway of departments was undermining the educational goals of the American university. "The most pronounced effect of the increasing emphasis upon specialized research," he wrote, "was a tendency among scientifically minded professors to ignore the undergraduate college and to place a low value on their function as teachers."

As the costs of attending university have risen alongside the economic pressures to attend, colleges have doubled down on the specialization model by investing in a managerial class that emphasizes metrics like efficiency and productivity. This has resulted in a further decline in precisely that resource that is most valuable in a liberal arts education: the time needed to read, think, and discuss. As Cambridge professor of English Stefan Collini puts it,

life in contemporary universities has become so hurried and harried that the processes that generate this frenzy of ostentatious busyness now threaten to frustrate the purposes for which such institutions exist. Spending time applying for grants to do research rather than actually doing research; spending time reporting that the outcomes of a course conformed to the guidelines rather than thinking about how to teach the course next year; spending time sitting on committees that report on how many grant applications were successful and how many course outcomes satisfactory rather than exchanging ideas with colleagues— these are all symptoms of a system in which managerialist imperatives displace the activities they are meant to be supporting.

While colorful, Collini's complaints are not hyperbole. Less than a year after I became chair of my department, a new dean swept in and, as is expected of a good academic leader these days, mandated a strategic planning process that required every department to produce a white paper and undergo an external review. The process took two years, and the white paper I produced (with input from and countless meetings with my faculty) was 150 pages long. Other than the creation of what was essentially a small book about the department, in hindsight it's not at all clear to me that anything concrete arose from all that work.

About a year after completing the strategic plan, Hopkins was up for review by our local accrediting agency, the Maryland Higher Education Commission (MHEC). This process, which also takes several years and thousands of collective hours of meeting and preparing documentation, is a necessary hurdle for a university to qualify for federal funding. Since Hopkins, like all major research universities, relies for an enormous portion of its operating budget on the indirect costs recovered from its federal grants, there is no question that the administration must comply with the accreditation agency's requirements, the number of which is continually growing.

When I served as vice dean for graduate education, I was assigned to the task force working on accreditation. I recall making my way to the downtown Baltimore campus of the Bloomberg School of Public Health, where I sat down at an enormous table with a gaggle of vice deans and vice provosts from the university's ten schools. There we were treated to a detailed presentation drawn from the websites of other, "peer" universities, showing how their various schools and departments had risen to the challenges of their respective accreditations. At some point a colleague from the medical school raised her hand and asked the question that was on everyone's mind: Please tell us again why we are doing this? As the representative from MHEC informed us, in a gloriously circular response to my colleague's question, we were there to make sure Hopkins success-fully passed MHEC's accreditation requirements.

Among the latest requirements is demonstrating that all departments have published "learning outcomes" for their majors and classes. More important, departments must establish procedures for assessing that these outcomes have been achieved. This is done by faculty committees who select a sampling of the work done each year by majors and judge it according to the standards published on syllabi and department websites. The jaw-dropping conclusion of these assessments, performed by faculty reviewing their department's own outcomes, tends to be that, indeed, the published standards have been achieved.

Even in a best-case scenario in which going through such exercises in fact induces professors to become more conscientious teachers, Collini's complaints prove true: instead of spending time on our students and research, we are spending time preparing reports. And this loss of time is translating directly into a diminution of faculty's capacity to gain knowl-edge outside their fields. As shown by one survey taken within the last ten years, "regardless of discipline, career stage, or gender, the overwhelming majority of respondents indicated that they had less time than in earlier stages of their career for reflective and creative thinking and that their reading and knowledge of scholarly literature was narrower and more specialized than it used to be or than they liked it to be."

What has been widely described as the "corporatization" of the univer-sity is now an established phenomenon. Given the high rate of return on certain areas of research—biomedical, for instance—some fields quickly rise above others in funding priority. Northwestern University's ten-billion-dollar endowment makes it the tenth-best-endowed university in the country, and almost a fifth of that endowment comes from its patent on one pharmaceutical product: Lyrica, a drug used for treating seizures. But beyond simply influencing how universities select fields in which to invest, the corporate model has, as English professors Maggie Berg and Barbara Seeber argue, "infiltrated the ways in which all of us, across the disciplines, conduct our research and the way we think about research. The push towards the easily quantifiable and marketable rushes us into 'findings,' and is at odds with the spirit of open inquiry and social critique."

If that's the case, though, it strikes me that it is even more at odds with the spirit of education. Universities like Hopkins are referred to as research universities, but we also admit students, and continue to do so despite literature professor Terry Eagleton's impression from some universities in the United Kingdom, where "security staff move students on if they are found hanging around," that "the ideal would be a university without these disheveled, unpredictable creatures." Many of these students are undergraduates, which means that they can on occasion be as young as sixteen or seventeen when they first come to study with us. Can it really escape us that at least as important a charge as the creation of new knowledge is the cultivation of a new generation of young intellects? And can we further ignore that who these young people are, including their histories and, yes, identities, is not incidental to how we can best help educate them?

Around the time I was working on the university's accreditation committee, I was teaching a course on Latin American literature, a course that tends to attract a good number of "heritage speakers," often Latino students whose spoken Spanish is quite solid but who have never read or written in that language. One of my students, Alvaro, a tall, charming young man whose parents immigrated from the Dominican Republic, began the semester thoroughly engaged with the class, excelling in the discussions, and improving rapidly in the quality of his writing. Around midterms, though, I noticed him slacking off, missing classes, and handing in assignments late, if at all. I asked him to come to my office hours, and there I asked him what was happening. When he realized one of his professors was taking a personal interest in his progress, he broke down and started crying. He told me he was the first person in his entire family ever to attend college. He told me that his parents, while proud of him, were not even sure what he was doing here or why it was important. No one from his circle of friends back in Miami had gone to college, and he felt completely adrift.

The decline in investment in public universities in the United States and the shifting priorities of what are now euphemistically called enrollment-sensitive colleges almost perfectly reflect the values of the market economy. Schools now think of students as clients and attach a dollar value to them in their quest to meet revenue-driven demands. Hunter Rawlings, a former president of both Cornell University and the American Association of Universities, put it this way in an op-ed article in the *Washington Post*:

> Most everyone now evaluates college in purely economic terms, thus reducing it to a commodity like a car or a house. How much does the average English major at college X earn 18 months after graduation? What is the average debt of college Y's alumni? How much does it cost to attend college Z, and is it worth it? How much more does the "average" college grad earn over a lifetime than someone with only a high school degree? (The current number appears to be about $1 million.) There is now a cottage industry built around such data.

As Rawlings goes on to point out, though, unlike a car, a college education depends as much on what the "consumer" brings and puts into it as it does on the "product itself." Yet despite this essential difference, "most public discussion of higher ed today pretends that students simply receive their education from colleges the way a person walks out of Best Buy with a television." For Rawlings, this consequence of the corporatization of education encourages the scenarios that are rampant on campuses today: "If colleges are responsible for outcomes, then students can feel entitled to classes that do not push them too hard, to high grades and to material that does not challenge their assumptions or make them uncomfortable. Hence colleges too often cater to student demands for trigger warnings, 'safe rooms,' and canceled commencement speakers." For me, an even more important consequence is that we may forget the awesome nature of our responsibility to students like Alvaro.

The overall effect is this: faculty today are under almost constant surveillance focusing on the "impact" of their research and teaching, a standard that is hard for any humanist to measure but that is interpreted by most administrations and by our academic council at Hopkins in terms of numbers of publications and citations, rather than the far more impactful yet amorphous influence that professors may be having on the intellectual development of the young people whose lives they touch. While teaching is ostensibly a part of the current vogue for measuring outcomes, the time we now spend listing "learning goals" in a college syllabus and then creating committees to collect and read samples of students' work in order to assess what percentage of those goals have been achieved by what percentage of students . . . this is time that, to my mind, could have been better used reading more widely, acquainting ourselves with the fields and experiences of others, advising and getting to know our students on an individual basis, and perhaps even occasionally falling into the trap of relevance.

But who am I kidding? Later in the day after Alvaro had broken down in my office, I went down to get my afternoon espresso, and I happened to pass a colleague in the hall. We exchanged a few niceties and went on our way, and I was relieved, happy even, not to be "exchanging ideas with colleagues," at least in this case. At Hopkins, and here you can insert the name of any top research university, professors are hired and retained in an atmosphere of almost cutthroat competitiveness. The humanities at top American universities, even more than the sciences, where research is often collaborative and funding can require teams of experts, is the purest example of market capitalism at work. Salaries, research budgets, and even frequency of sabbatical depend on proving one's value, which is demonstrated by "going on the market" and obtaining external offers. Since there is no straightforward way to assess the effectiveness of a professor of, say, art history to the university's core mission, the value of a humanities professor is ultimately determined by how much another university is willing to offer to take her away from you. And unlike, say, an international soccer star like Cristiano Ronaldo—who depends on the magical synergies of a team of stars to rack up the spectacular scoring records that put him among the most expensive players in history—humanists tend to work in sublime isolation, because there is no incentive to do otherwise.

A NEOLIBERAL ETHIC

The current wave of "disinvitations" and gender pronoun activism that has reinvigorated the forces of reaction is related to the story I've been telling, but not necessarily in the way one might expect. The sad fact is that the restriction of free speech on campus that the right ridicules as political correctness has some demographic truth to it. According to a 2010 survey, only 35 percent of university students strongly agreed with the statement that "it is safe to hold unpopular views" on their campus. Even more dismaying, the number of faculty who agreed with the statement was less than 19 percent. Perhaps most scandalously, there is a demonstrable inverse relation between the level of education achieved and exposure to a diversity of opinions. In other words, education appears to be doing precisely the opposite of what advocates believe it does: broaden our intellectual horizons.

Conservatives have scored terrific victories by framing campus politics since the 1980s as an assault by the forces of PC on the fundamentally American commitment to freedom of speech. In the early nineties Dinesh D'Souza held a series of debates with Stanley Fish, then already a famous professor of English from Duke University's Literature Program. Fish's position in those debates eventually became part of a book he published in 1994 with the provocative title *There's No Such Thing As Free Speech (And It's a Good Thing, Too)*. Fish's aim, both in the debates and the book, was to undercut both D'Souza's and the right's claim to be defenders of timeless American values, as well as the academic left's own pieties, especially their belief in the achievability of a society in which no one is marginalized or feels slighted. In attacking the right's embrace of free speech, Fish argued that designating one group of advocates as politically motivated and the other as "free" was simply a politically savvy way of veiling the actual political motivations underlying any set of positions. "There's no such thing as free speech" because at any given time and in any given culture, some groups and individuals are always freer than others.

Using a standard like free speech and its ostensible undermining by the forces of political correctness has become a model for effective political strategies today. Internet trolls like Milo Yiannopoulos can spark predictable outrage by spewing hate-filled rhetoric and then pointing to rioting protesters—like those who forced Berkeley to disinvite him in February 2017—as examples of the left's war on free speech. In a similar way, when a politician like Martin O'Malley naïvely embraced the phrase "all lives matter," he walked into a political quagmire. The benign tautology that all lives do in fact matter had already shattered against the raised political consciousness of a generation of young people who have come to learn the dismal truth that being black in America is a statistical disadvantage in any number of ways. But once uttered, his gaffe could not be withdrawn without conservatives basking once again in the hilarity of a liberal apologizing for defending an apparently universal value.

The perception of liberal outrage on college campuses is a powerful political weapon for the right. However, as much as such outrage is the expression of a specific politics, it is also the result of a powerful historical conflation between the increased sensitivities to racial and sexual bias inculcated in humanities courses since the 1970s and a society-wide resistance among students to having their sensibilities challenged by opposing viewpoints. When literature and history seminars started drawing attention to marginalized works and perspectives, this privileging of the categories of race and gender was a much-needed corrective to an assumed universalism that was in fact far from impartial. As these perspectives were encouraged and cultivated, however, they were accompanied by a growing unwillingness to challenge and debate the interpretations that emerged from those underrepresented points of view.

At the same time, the very socioeconomic trends that have led to ever-greater income inequality and demographic sorting in the population at large were contributing to a new way of understanding college education, namely, as a desirable consumer product. As Frank Fear, a professor emeritus from Michigan State University, has put it, "a neoliberal ethic has infected America's institutions. Many organizations have become self-absorbed—hyper-focused on internal matters, lathered with self-promotion . . . And while I don't think it happened overnight, I also believe—that over time—neoliberalism has become a prevailing ethic in

American higher education. Higher education today, I believe, is a largely neoliberal institution."

"Neoliberalism" normally refers to the reemergence of economic theories advocating limited government intervention in markets that have become dominant since the latter half of the twentieth century. But what Fear means here is that our universities have become like department stores: instead of being driven primarily by a desire to pursue truth and educate a new generation in that pursuit, they have become more and more fixated on branding, competition, and marketing themselves to a well-researched brew of the wealthiest and most academically stellar students. Rather than ask these students to challenge their own assumptions and engage a true diversity of perspectives, universities often encourage them to pursue a path of self-realization and fulfillment unencumbered by classes that don't fit either their chosen path to success or a vision of the world tailored to their identity. And despite the protestations of conservatives, this tendency cuts both ways.

One visible result of this infection of higher education by the ideology of extreme individualism is the increased incidence of students' complaints about the contents of their humanities courses. Even as cultural conservatives interpret recent incidents on college campuses as a renewal of the liberal excesses of political correctness, it has become increasingly clear that much of such excessive progressivism masks a very different set of core values, ironically those stemming from the very individualistic philosophy that those same conservative voices do everything possible to champion in the public sphere. On the one hand, these values are at work in the increases in specialization among the faculty as universities compete with one another for the grants that subsidize huge portions of their budgets. On the other hand, these values can be seen in the general increase of intolerance among students to perspectives that make them uncomfortable.

This explains how Duke University student David Grasso's refusal to read Alison Bechdel's graphic novel in preparation for his freshman year is in some ways identical to the protests by supposedly left-leaning students at colleges around the country that have resulted in prominent intellectuals being disinvited because their view might be offensive to, say, Muslims on campus; or, more recently, the demand of the student union at London's School of Oriental and African Studies (SOAS) that philosophers like Kant and Plato be dropped from their curriculum because they were white. As one of the founding documents for the union stresses, "decolonising" the university and "confronting the white institution" are some of its priorities for the academic year.

The first thing to point out in the SOAS case is that the students' demands had a legitimate basis. SOAS itself has a complicated history, evolving as it has from the British Empire's primary school for training its colonial administrators to its reality today as an academic institution focused on studying the history and culture of African and Asian societies. The 2017 protests were in some ways a natural outgrowth of this gradual transformation, with its current students reacting to what they perceive as vestiges of the institution's colonial past.

Typically, however, the mainstream press saw the protest by the SOAS students as another example of leftist hysteria. The *Telegraph*, a popular London paper, reported that "students at a prestigious London university are demanding that figures such as Plato, Descartes and Immanuel Kant should be largely dropped from the curriculum because they are white," and quoted the students as insisting that when studying philosophy, "the majority of philosophers on our courses" should be from Africa and Asia. As someone who regularly teaches all three of the above-mentioned "white" philosophers, I decided to take a deeper look at the case, so on a recent trip to London I looked up my good friend Kevin Jon Heller, who is a professor of international criminal law at SOAS.

Here's a snippet of our conversation as we strolled under the dense canopy of trees outside one of the campus's modern concrete and glass buildings:

> ME: So, Kevin, did your students really demand that you all drop the teaching of Kant from the philosophy program?
>
> KEVIN: Oh, for fuck's sake! No, they didn't. There isn't a philosophy program at SOAS; they were talking about the general survey course. And they didn't demand dropping anyone—they simply

wanted the selection of philosophers to reflect the Global South orientation of the school, even if that meant trimming the number of canonical philosophers. I think the students are misguided, but they weren't attacking Kant or Voltaire or Aristotle. The right-wing press in the UK is remarkably dishonest, like another country I know.

Sure enough, when I consulted the left-wing UK press, in this case the *Guardian*, I got a very different story. In those pages Tom Whyman wrote,

> it must be noted that despite the headlines no one, at any point, has actually called for white philosophers to be dropped from the curriculum at Soas—aka the School of Oriental and African Studies. Even at its most extreme, all the Soas students' union demands (and note that their demand has no binding force whatsoever) is that European philosophers only be taught in preference to African and Asian ones when necessary. Adopting this principle, if it turns out that say, Kant, has expressed some insight that is vital for understanding some aspect of reality, then he should be allowed to remain in the curriculum.

Then he goes on to provide something that was entirely missing from the *Telegraph*'s coverage but supported by Kevin's glib remarks:

> You wouldn't know it from reading any of the other news articles on this topic, but Soas doesn't actually have a philosophy department—and nor does it offer a BA degree in philosophy. Rather, Soas offers a BA in world philosophies, which is run by the department of religions and philosophies. Given the nature of this course and the nature of Soas as an institution, it makes complete sense for the students to want to study more African and Asian thought at the expense of European. Of course if nearby Birkbeck [part of the University of London] decided to purge its curriculum of European thought, that would be an entirely different issue. But these matters are context-sensitive, and diversity across curricula should be welcomed.

Context-sensitive—there it is in a nutshell. Virtually all our position taking, our principles, our admonitions, our rage, are based on stripping the context away from the statements we are invested in. If the student union's demands are misguided, as Kevin agrees, it's only because the belief that reading less Kant and more, say, Valentin Mudimbe (the African philosopher whom Kevin and I both studied under, at Duke and Stanford respectively) would be tantamount to "decolonizing" the university fails to adequately grasp the extent to which Mudimbe's anticolonial thought emerged from a careful generational dialogue with the very tradition that Kant exemplifies. Likewise, the rush to find another poster child of PC extremism always fails to see the context of student demands, demands that, when seen in that context, are often far less unreasonable and indeed extreme than they are made out to appear.

What can be seen in a case like that of the SOAS student union, however, is how idealistic demands on the part of students overlap with the transformation of universities under political influences that are, paradoxically, coming from the right rather than the left. In the United Kingdom the majority of universities are public institutions that have been forced over the last decades increasingly to compete with one another for diminishing resources. The factors taken into account have been focused on "measurable impact," mainly through the counting of publications and citations in annual research assessment exercises; but a recent proposal in Parliament aims at placing student satisfaction squarely at the heart of decisions regarding resource allocation, a decision that has led many in the United Kingdom to warn that universities "will be forced to pander to the demands of 'snowflake' students if controversial changes to the ranking system are approved."

It goes further than that. Just as most students now think that an education is something to be purchased and shown off, like a car, citizens in today's economy treat reality itself like a commodity. Like any other entertainment, my news should deliver customer satisfaction, and so my information, like my education or my politics, becomes an expression of an identity that is unhinged from its community. We become uprooted from a common civic space with long-established norms for adjudicating differences. We lose sight of the common principles of toleration that permit the expression of our identities in the first place. We continue to burn fossil fuels despite an almost universal acceptance that doing so is incompatible with the future of civilization as we know it. And in a similar way, we have given up on the idea that the very existence of our diverse perspectives is guaranteed by a common intellectual tradition now being destroyed by fragmentation. It is for this very reason that the task of a liberal arts education is more vital today than ever before.

SOUNDING THE ALARM

Colleges aren't the cause of our current crisis in civility; but they sure aren't helping, either. At a time when, as a recent Pew survey has established, Americans are more divided politically than they ever have been before, the last thing our colleges should be promoting is a myopic culture wherein professors jealously guard the borders of their ever-shrinking fields of expertise. Nonetheless, some of the same economic and institutional pressures that have led to the almost unprecedented levels of inequality and divisiveness that are buffeting our society have had a hand in pushing the culture of higher education in this very direction. If we want a society in which more young black women like Giselle graduate from places like Johns Hopkins and go on to successful and rewarding careers; if we want a society in which two thirds of the country, regardless of race, isn't left behind with stagnating wages and no sense of a viable future; if we want a society in which people aren't valued less and exposed to sexual violence because of their gender, how we educate our citizens is going to play an essential role in getting us there.

I'm not pretending for a second that changing our culture of higher education would magically fix all of society's problems. Our present levels of social and economic inequality, which we will look at more carefully in the next part, have their own complex origins and ramifications and need to be understood in their own light. But trends in our education system are deeply intertwined with inequality, and if how we currently conceive of college and the liberal arts is a symptom of where we are today, it also has a role to play in getting us somewhere else.

To put it simply, when a college degree is the clearest dividing line between those who are making it and those who are slipping behind, it doesn't help heal a wounded body politic for university students to be seen by those outside academia's ivory gates as "special snowflakes," throwing a fit any time someone uses a wrong phrase, or bringing professors like Laura Kipnis up on Title IX charges for "creating a hostile environment" with an article she wrote about Title IX. Nor does it help for professors to promote that image by shying away from the kinds of teaching and thinking that cultivate the spaces and tools for civil confrontation, because like Rebecca Tuvel they have learned to fear the firestorm it might provoke if they make a controversial claim not legitimated by their sexual or racial status. If we want a world where our politicians can learn to work together for the common good, and where citizens can make decisions about complex issues based on solid evidence and the merits of the arguments, it stands to reason that our colleges should be teaching those practices as well.

What I was witnessing in the late 1980s at Dartmouth was the result of a cultural change in the way people thought about their relation to politics; and it wasn't just feminists and graduates of the civil rights movement. An entire generation of students had learned to make their ideas an outgrowth of their identities, instead of regarding their identities as conditioned by history. On the right as well as the left, students were basing their political positions on an ideal of authenticity that they felt they could find by identifying with a specific group. Like the legions of AM radio listeners who would flock to her programs a decade later, Laura Ingraham found authenticity in the traditional version of America—white, rural, with well-established gender roles—that she and others at the *Dartmouth Review* felt was being trashed and denigrated by feminists and leftist intellectuals on the faculty and among their peers. Women and minority groups and the liberals who supported them were just as strongly repulsed by a version of America that they saw as rejecting their claims to an equal degree of freedom. In all cases, these groups doubled down on those feelings of authenticity, to the detriment of better understanding the context of their claims.

Perhaps most perniciously, the resistance to context in these and so many other cases contaminated the real, historically grounded inequities suffered by those students who, regardless of race, gender, or sexual orientation, *do* so often arrive on campus without the invisible blankets of some of their peers' unquestioned privileges, who *do* have to overcome unacknowledged but real prejudices, who *should* have the benefit of policies that take into account the inequities of race and class. That minority, transgender, and first-generation students are left without adequate support and assault victims forced to relive their traumas while other students demand safe spaces because they voted for Trump or call for their departments to stop teaching "traditional" philosophers because they were white European men—this is perhaps the worst irony. For it was precisely thinkers like Kant who developed the fullest elaboration of the very notion of universal rights that the defense of underrepresented peoples depends on today. So it is undeniable that the connection between the thinkers of the liberal tradition and the actual history of racial and religious oppression is something that can and should be taught *along with* their thought; as many of the great anticolonial and feminist thinkers of the twentieth century knew well, some of the most powerful intellectual tools for human liberation are to be found in that very tradition.

Bloom was right to sound the alarm, but wrong in both his diagnosis and his proposed cure. While some students and faculty have indeed agitated for a diminution of the liberal tradition in college curricula, falling standards in liberal arts training are as much a result of increased pressures toward specialization in research, the increasingly instrumental understanding of the purpose of education, and the tendency to view education as a consumer product like any other, destined to be tailored by its producers to fit consumers' desires and expectations, as of political pressures to diversify the canon.

What is lost in all this is the very idea and purpose of the liberal arts, which regards and elevates those aspects of being human that are not reducible to today's dominant model of the individual. The individual at the heart of the liberal tradition, far from a desire-fulfillment machine, is a delicate balance of self-legislation and respect for community. In fact, as we will see in the third part of this book, the very Immanuel Kant whose influence in their curriculum some students now want to diminish made it the centerpiece of his teaching on moral philosophy that an individual's autonomy was inconceivable without taking into account the universal community of humanity. For Kant, in order to be truly autonomous an individual had to act according to reason, not simply follow his or her inclinations. In practical terms this meant that the individual should opt for only that course of action about which he or she could say, "Anyone else in my position should also be doing this." Any apparent freedom of choice that didn't ask itself this question was nothing other than slavery to one's own appetites.

In losing sight of the balance between individual identity and the larger community, while at the same time devolving into a product we purchase to better ourselves, education has ceased to be the means by which our community transforms a child into a citizen. This change has been a while in coming. Its story is intellectual, economic, demographic, and political, as we will see in the sections that follow. But the outcome and the prescription are clear. Thirty years ago a conservative college professor found traction by accusing tenured radicals of closing the American mind. But the American mind wasn't closing, it was splintering into a thousand different individual selves, sorting itself into ever more specialized explorations of identity and into gated communities that could only see value in what would give those selves a competitive edge. By treating liberal arts education as an optional elective, an ornament to be enjoyed by those privileged enough to be able to afford it, but unnecessary for really getting ahead, we are running the risk of losing the most precious and vital tool a democracy has: the citizen whose role it is to ensure its survival.

PART TWO

INEQUALITY

THE GREAT EQUALIZER

For people in my world, with book-lined offices overlooking the red bricks, white towers, and immaculate lawns of a private East Coast university, the morning of November 9, 2016, was like the morning after the apocalypse. Having dragged myself to campus after a short and fitful night, I found myself looking across my desk at an ashen-faced colleague suffering from a combination of politics-induced sleep deprivation and almost clinical despondency, as he recounted trying to teach his introduction to moral philosophy earlier that morning. "How can I mention it? How can I not?" he agonized, recalling the solitary young man in the front row with TRUMP emblazoned across his sweatshirt.

A few hours later, I made my way down to the espresso bar in my building's main atrium. In this pleasant space faculty and students can purchase lattes and panini and sit on an Italian marble patio hovering two stories below the spectacular glass ceiling built by a German architectural firm as part of an eighty-five-million-dollar renovation to Gilman Hall, Johns Hopkins University's fabled home for the humanities. The line to order drinks was strangely subdued, the normal buzz of small talk stamped out by an oppressive silence. A hastily scribbled sign was taped to the cash register: "Don't be an asshole. Listen to each other."

"Are people being assholes today?" I asked Calvin, the appropriately hip and scruffy barista who passed his colleague the handmade Mexican coffee cup that relieves me of any need for me to ask for my daily cortado. "Oh yeah," he replied curtly, "total assholes."

Tensions ran high during the weeks and months after Donald Trump's surprising (for the left) electoral win. On some campuses, conservative students called out faculty, administration, and fellow students alike for treating their candidate's victory as if it were a cataclysm, even adopting the stereotypically progressive tactic of calling for "safe spaces" in which to hold and protect their minority views. Even on that first day, back in my fourth-floor corner office with its alcove window looking out over Baltimore, the collective reaction I had seen below started to gnaw at me. Here, in the literal pinnacle of the humanities, those disciplines dedicated to debating the core issues of human culture, ideas, and values, where professors like me are supposed to train students to support arguments with evidence and communicate their ideas with elegance and persuasion—here, instead of debate, I was registering a kind of shocked and sullen unanimity.

The problem is not simply that the great majority of faculty and students around me share my political ideology—expecting half a building full of literary intellectuals to have voted for a man like Donald Trump would be as realistic as going to dinner with a large Italian family hoping to tuck in for some shepherd's pie in contemplative silence. The problem is far deeper. Where political debate used to be something one could take for granted in all sorts of forums, from backyard barbecues to workplace water coolers, today the opinions and positions one might have argued about in the past have morphed into something else. They have become attributes of our deepest selves, aspects that are not up for evaluation but are treated as vital parts of a personal identity better to be cherished and protected than exposed.

This shift has, in part, taken place on college campuses. Aaron Hanlon, now an assistant professor of English at Colby College in Maine, who was an outspoken campus conservative in his student days, recalls the moment this transformation occurred for him: "I was a reasonably good-natured kid from a modest Catholic household when I showed up to my liberal arts campus. Then suddenly I wasn't me, the individual. I was just white. It seemed that everyone was celebrating diversity and multiculturalism, and

I didn't see a role for myself in that. It occurred to me, as it has to count-less other conservative students, that I might also be a kind of minority—an 'ideological minority'—because of my conservative political views."

As he further explains, "The left talked about women and students of color as victims of historical and institutional inequality because of things like patriarchy, slavery, and Jim Crow. Most of us conservatives didn't suffer from similar injustices, but we saw ourselves nevertheless as victims of ideological oppression." But if the purpose of Hanlon's reminiscence is to admonish conservative students today not to assume the mantle of victimhood, I draw a different lesson. At some point in the recent past, as America was sorting itself demographically into a nationwide family feud, college, which should have been both an equalizer and a place for vital conversations to take place, stopped being both.

While educational attainment level has long been known to correlate strongly with income and has become among the most important drivers of inequality in the United States, it was only with the 2016 presidential election that level of education attained became an equally potent indicator of political persuasion. In some ways, it was even this shift that accounts for why the major media outlets were all surprised by the outcome of the election, since pollsters were not adequately weighting education when adjusting their raw data. As the *New York Times*'s Nate Cohn writes, "The tendency of better-educated voters to respond to surveys in greater numbers has been true for a long time. What's new is the importance of education to presidential vote choice. Hillary Clinton led Trump by 25 points among college-educated voters in pre-election national polls, up from President Obama's four-point edge in 2012." Pollsters hadn't weighted by education in the past because the effect wasn't statistically significant enough to do so. By 2016 it became so significant that it likely threw off their models and made them miss how popular Trump actually was.

On a call-in radio show in the spring of 2017, Michelle Goldberg, then a *Slate* columnist, got into an altercation with a caller named Scott from Tennessee, who berated her and fellow members of the coastal elite for a tone that "dripped with condescension" when talking about Middle America. She responded angrily that she was "repulsed" by the sentiment the caller expressed, that the heartland was somehow more authentic than America's urban centers. The irony is that there were no obvious policy differences or arguments separating Scott and Goldberg. Rather, they were separated by their emotional commitments, by their rage.

Goldberg's rage against real and persistent racism and sexism is entirely legitimate in a country where black men are imprisoned at six times the rate of whites and where the same proportion of women are sexually assaulted while in college as currently serve in the U.S. legislature (one in five). Scott's rage is legitimate, too, in a country where the suffering of blue-collar workers from Michigan gets dismissed, or where the rural poor of Kentucky are summarily tossed into a "basket of deplorables" for expressing their anger. But that rage is also self-fulfilling, because it cuts off the very conversations that could lead to a world in which all these identities were better able to achieve their goals. In other words, a white man working in a meat processing plant in "Middle America" would benefit from supporting racial and gender equality, and a Latina woman cleaning houses in an East Coast city would benefit from policies supporting economic equality for all, but neither will make gains without understanding that the recognition they are demanding entails invoking a common story and recognizing how their interests overlap.

In the words of Larry Laughlin, a small-business owner from the outskirts of Minneapolis, politics today is "like a hockey game. Everyone's got their goons. Their goons are pushing our guys around, and it's great to see our goons push back." Laughlin's vote, like his choice of fringe, right-wing news sources, reflects an emotional attachment to an identity and the story underlying it. Laughlin put himself through community college after escaping from a broken family at sixteen and went on to create a metal company with more than a dozen employees. Yet despite his humble upbringing, personal struggles, and even his decision to adopt three mixed-raced children, Laughlin feels attacked and dismissed by liberals. " 'You have a nice house and got it made because you are a white guy,' " he recounts being lectured by a friend of his children. "There are all of these preconceived notions that I'm a racist, idiot, a bigot, and oh, uneducated."

Laughlin's experience, like the radio run-in between Goldberg and Scott, is part of a much larger story in America today. As we know all too well by now, Barack Obama's famous speech notwithstanding, there are indeed two Americas: a red America and a blue America, a rural America and an urban America; a white America and a multihued America. And these two Americas are increasingly also a high-school-educated America and a college-educated America. These two giant populations are continuing to draw apart, geographically, economically, and politically, and as long as both sides fail to see that they share a common country, a common history, and a common future, our country will continue to flail about in political dysfunction, with countless lives and resources going to waste. But what is crucial to grasp is that what we understand and rightly decry as divisiveness is really another word for inequality, and our education system, which was conceived of as a bulwark against inequality, has become a veritable machine for building and entrenching rigid class hierarchies.

As the saying goes, state universities used to be state funded, then they were state supported, now they are located in a state. Today all too many students are arriving at college from disadvantaged backgrounds, only to drop out years later, saddled with debt and worse off than when they began. One daughter of a working-class family, who made it into a moderately selective state university in the Midwest, described the experience of being a student surrounded by people of means in this way: "Coming from where I come from, and not really being able to relate to some of the girls that were there, really kinda made it hard. I'm from a small town, have to make do with what I have . . . I feel it came a lot easier for them than it did for me. It took a lot of studying and sacrifices for me to pull off my grades and to do well, and I just wasn't the same as them. They could go and do whatever they wanted, and I was kinda limited on money." Because she had worked to support her parents all through high school, and was now working to stay in college, she felt like she was in a different world from her roommate, who came from a family that could easily have afforded the twenty-three thousand dollars her school charged for out-of-state students, not to mention the twelve thousand dollars for in-state students.

As decisive as a college degree is for success in today's economy, though, the problem doesn't start at college. The quality and availability of education from the earliest years has been repeatedly shown to have a significant impact on later earning power and quality of life. Throughout the twentieth century, local school districts carried the lion's share of the responsibility for funding public education, with states and the federal government increasingly sharing those costs in the second half of the century. The percentage of the federal budget going to education peaked in 1949 due to the GI Bill, declined until the 1960s, then began to rise again. The period between the 1950s and 1970s saw increases in the percentage of local and state budgets going to public education, but these increases tapered off in the 1980s, only to rise again until the great recession of 2008, when funding for education was slashed by states to plug growing budget holes.

That said, the problem with public education in the United States has never really been about overall spending, which, at around eleven thousand dollars annually per child as of this writing, ranks fourth in the world. The problem has instead been that inequality is baked into our system, and has only intensified as America has sorted itself into more and more socioeconomically distinct communities. In 1973, the Supreme Court ruled 5–4 that the Fourteenth Amendment's guarantee of equal protection did not extend to education, and that therefore unequal funding by school districts was not unconstitutional. Justice Lewis F. Powell, who authored the majority opinion, based the decision largely on the reasoning that education did not constitute a "fundamental right" and hence was not subject to the protections provided by the Fourteenth Amendment. In his words, "Though education is one of the most important services performed by the State, it is not within the limited category of rights recognized by this Court as guaranteed by the Constitution." In a powerful dissent, Justice Thurgood Marshall wrote, "I cannot accept such an emasculation of the Equal Protection Clause in the context of this case."

Contrary to the court's reasoning in 1973, most state constitutions do include education as a fundamental right, and funding disparities have led to lawsuits in almost all fifty states. Nevertheless, if you were a student in

New Trier, Illinois, in 2009, you would enjoy the resources, teachers, and class size afforded by three times more money than was available to the Farmington Central Community district, only a few miles away. It seems to me that the failure to recognize education as a fundamental right, along with our reliance on local property taxes as the basis for the funding of public education, is in many ways the policy root of our inability to maintain a baseline equality in our education system. And the situation is only getting worse. Since the financial crisis of 2008, state and local funding for schools has plummeted, in some cases by nearly 40 percent, and has shown no sign of returning to prerecession levels.

Because of its dependence on local tax bases, the biggest factor in public education inequality has been the geographic divergence in economic development in the United States since around 1980, leading to ever-greater differences in local property values. For the four decades leading up to that year, the poorer sectors of the American economy were slowly catching up to the richest. But that all started to change with the rise of free-market fundamentalism and the information economy of the Reagan and post-Reagan years. Since 1980, economic success has more and more accrued to those with higher degrees living in urban centers, while the economic situation of those with only a secondary education or less, and those living in rural areas, has stagnated or declined. This regional disparity is mirrored by the higher-education gap. Prior to 1980, the poverty rate among those with only a high school diploma was relatively low, around 7 percent. Today only those with a college degree enjoy such low poverty rates, and the percentage of impoverished high school graduates has more than tripled, to 22 percent. But while college graduates in general are more upwardly mobile than people who are not college graduates, there are also increasing degrees of inequality within the college-educated populace at large, including vast numbers of students who have borrowed excessively to join that world, only to drop out with no degree and encumbered by debt. Instead of leveling the playing field, education seems to be making it more uneven.

It is this unevenness more than any other factor that is directly contributing to the patent failure of democratic dialogue in the United States today. While the thought leaders of the Republican Party are all college educated, the base that they depend on is a mixture of white conservatives who felt alienated when they were at college and working-class whites who never went to college and are now deeply suspicious of what they think of as the coastal elite. In fact, as a recent Pew Research Center poll showed, for the first time, a majority of Republicans and right-leaning independent voters now believes that universities "have a negative effect on the way things are going in the country," a number that rose sharply in the year leading up to the 2016 election. To put it plainly, in the middle of a growing culture war, our education system, created to cultivate a national civic culture, is only making things worse.

WHAT HAPPENED TO THE AMERICAN DREAM?

As a child I used to visit my grandfather out at his house in Mattituck, on the North Fork of Long Island. He was already retired and had plenty of time to take walks on the shore with me and to give me painting lessons. By the end of his life he was as known in the local art scene for his stunning watercolors depicting the tranquil wetlands of the Long Island Sound as he was for leading the local church choir. While I may have been too young to understand what owning a house on the North Fork meant in financial terms—even if in those days it was certainly far less than what it would mean today—what stuck with me was the image of a successful man with many grandchildren, living at ease in an idyllic setting and reaping the rewards of a successful life.

Most people today might assume that my grandfather had retired from Wall Street. But Grandpa Stack wasn't a stockbroker or a hedge fund manager. He was a teacher. My grandfather flew bombers over Germany in World War II. Returning home to Long Island, he did what so many of his generation did with the help of the GI Bill: he went to college and graduated; he looked for a job that would allow him to support his wife and six daughters, the oldest of whom was my mother; and he bought a house in a Long Island suburb. Flying was no longer an option, because he had an ailing wife, so he got a master of education degree by attending night school while working in a cement factory, then landed a job as a chemistry teacher in a public school. Education, in other words, played an essential role not only in determining my grandfather's standard of living, but also that of his six daughters, their children, and now their children's children.

When we talk about "the American Dream," we have in mind an image like this, or like Norman Rockwell's iconic paintings of idyllic suburban Americana. And for about thirty years after the war this story would have been recognizable to many Americans. The historian James Truslow Adams, who is credited with first using the phrase in 1931, defined it as "a dream of being able to grow to the fullest development as man and woman, unhampered by the barriers which had slowly been erected in older civilizations . . . for the benefit of classes rather than for the simple human being."

The idea was simple: you sacrifice for something greater than yourself, for your country and your community, and that community gives back. It supports you, educates you, allows you to succeed. And, in fact, for American society in general, but especially for white men coming back from the war and those coming of age in the fifties, this would be a golden age. As a reporter from *Time* magazine wrote in 1953, "Even in the smallest towns and most isolated areas . . . the U.S. is wearing a very prosperous, middle-class suit of clothes." This same period of time saw the greatest level of bipartisanship that the U.S. Congress had ever seen, a degree of cooperation bolstered by equally high levels of what the economist and Nobel laureate Paul Krugman has called "minority-party overlap," namely, the number of members of one party whose political views are further from their own party's core than those of the closest opposing party's member. As would surprise no one, this index has dropped to zero in contemporary politics, whereas in 1958 there were more than a hundred members of Congress who fit this description.

This golden age was in part produced by an almost exponential spread of educational opportunity. Since 1940 the percentage of people with a college degree has increased eightfold. Wages also increased across the board as opportunities grew for both white-collar and blue-collar workers. The middle class exploded, and the portion of families owning their own home rose from under 50 percent in the early 1940s to almost 70 percent by 1980. While there was still a divide between the college-educated and those with little or no education, working-class whites didn't have to feel disadvantaged. They too could earn a good living and support their families. The wealthiest Americans were doing plenty well, but the growth of their fortunes was held in check by the estate tax, which Teddy Roosevelt had helped bring about, and top marginal tax rates that peaked at more than 90 percent and remained above 70 percent until well into the 1960s.

The thirty-year period of relative economic equality began to unravel in the 1970s. While the average income of Americans has indeed increased since 1973, median income—the index that measures the take-home salary of the family who does better than one half of the country and not as well as the other half—hasn't changed at all. What this means is that the increase of the average is entirely due to the rich getting richer, while the poor and middle class either stay where they are or become worse off. According to Krugman's analysis, "only the top 1 percent has done better since the 1970s than it did in the generation after World War II. Once you get way up the scale, however, the gains have been spectacular—the top tenth of a percent saw its income rise fivefold, and the top .01 percent of Americans is seven times richer than they were in 1973."

There are some quibbles among economists and sociologists who study such income trends, of course. As the economist Richard V. Reeves has argued, "too often the rhetoric of inequality points to a 'top 1 percent' problem, as if the 'bottom' 99 percent is in a similarly dire situation. This obsession with the upper class allows the upper middle class to convince ourselves that we are in the same boat as the rest of America; but it is not true." As Reeves goes on to document, the top quintile of earners in the United States saw an overall gain in income of over four trillion dollars between the end of the 1970s and 2013, compared with something closer to three trillion dollars for the other 80 percent of the population. There was no comparable divergence anywhere below the top quintile.

There is no doubt truth to both these analyses. While there are enormous inequalities between the 1 percent and everyone else, it is also the case that the upper middle class have been successful in pulling out ahead of the rest of the country, as well as at putting up barriers to ensure that they stay there. And education has been one of the most successful barriers. As Reeves puts it, "Education has therefore become the main mechanism for the reproduction of upper middle-class status across generations," what Anthony Carnevale, director of the Georgetown University Center on Education and the Workforce, coined "an inequality machine." While Carnevale is referring specifically to postsecondary education, our entire system is at fault, sorting children by zip code and means into neighborhoods and classrooms with vastly different resources, intellectual as well as material, and making the upper echelons more necessary for success even as they become ever more difficult to attain.

Part of this sifting seems almost nefariously deliberate. Just as parents swoop into municipal hearings to voice their opposition to the construction of affordable housing in their covetously protected school districts, constituents in affluent and often ostensibly liberal districts rose in unison when Barack Obama proposed eliminating the tax-free college savings plans known as 529 plans. The plans should have been a clear-cut target for progressives hoping to make tax policy more equitable, given that 90 percent of their benefits go to "families with incomes in the top quarter of the distribution." But when word got out, then congressman (and now one of my senators) Chris Van Hollen roped together the Democratic leadership and squelched the plan.

While they may disagree about where to draw the line, both Krugman and Reeves agree that inequality isn't necessarily the natural outcome of market economies, but is rather a result of specific policies and practices. Reeves focuses on policies and practices that the upper middle class have adopted with the express purpose of safeguarding their wealth and privilege, which have the ancillary effect of making it far harder for those trying to climb the socioeconomic ladder to break in. Krugman, for his part, traces the machinations of a very specific political organization. In his view, since the 1970s one of the United States' two major political parties has been taken over by a radical wing intent on rolling back all the social advances put in place by the New Deal and that took hold after World War II. Their aim is to dismantle the very institutions that helped create the postwar period of prosperity and relative equality. As he puts it, "The empowerment of the hard right emboldened business to launch an all-out attack on the union movement, drastically reducing workers' bargaining power; freed business executives from the political and social constraints that had previously placed limits on runaway executive paychecks; sharply reduced tax rates on high incomes; and in a variety of other ways promoted rising inequality."

The stories are not incompatible; they simply have a different focus. But wherever the focus lies, the correlation between inequality and political divisiveness is hardwired, and the influence runs both ways. On the one hand, the divisiveness of our system drives inequality insofar as it has allowed populist discontent to be packaged with and subsumed by a political platform that pushes deregulation and tax cuts for the wealthy. This is the situation that Thomas Frank famously describes in his book *What's the Matter with Kansas?*:

> The trick never ages; the illusion never wears off. *Vote* to stop abortion; *receive* a rollback in capital gains taxes. *Vote* to make our country strong again; *receive* deindustrialization. *Vote* to screw those politically correct college professors; *receive* electricity deregulation. *Vote* to get government off our backs; *receive* conglomeration and monopoly everywhere from media to meatpacking. *Vote* to stand tall against terrorists; *receive* Social Security privatization. *Vote* to strike a blow against elitism; *receive* a social order in which wealth is more concentrated than ever before in our lifetimes, in which workers have been stripped of power and CEOs rewarded in a manner beyond imagining.

On the other hand, it is equally true that rising and entrenched inequality leads inexorably to greater polarization and divisiveness. If the economic and political playing fields of the three decades after World War II had grown remarkably flat, by 1980 things started moving in a decidedly different direction. In 1970 only around a tenth of the U.S. population had a college degree, and those degree holders were relatively evenly spread throughout its different communities. That rate has leapt up each decade, as the journalist Bill Bishop has shown, "to 16.4 percent in 1980, nearly 19 percent in 1990, and 27 percent in 2004." Now, more than ten years after he accumulated that data, we know the number to be almost a third of the population.

More education, of course, is a great thing. The problem is that this growth in the educated populace took place unevenly. Very unevenly. Entire swaths of rural America, along with certain cities, saw no or relatively minor increases in the educated population. Other urban areas saw astronomical growth: "The percentage of adults with a college education increased in Austin from 17 percent in 1970 to 45 percent in 2004. In Cleveland, the change was only from 4 percent to 14 percent. Not only was Cleveland behind, but it was falling further behind."

This sorting of the population by education levels is a primary mover in what Bishop has called "the big sort," the name he gives to the increased tendency of Americans to cluster into communities of people with similar tastes and economic resources. As Americans have become more educated and more mobile, those with educations are increasingly moving to communities where there are others who have similar levels of education. At face value, this seems both obvious and innocuous enough. Why wouldn't we expect a recent college graduate to head to a city with other recent grads and a lively economy where she can more easily find gainful and interesting employment? A young man I know named Tray (I'm changing his name and story slightly to protect his identity) grew up in a small town in rural North Carolina. He was the first person in his family to go to college. After completing his bachelor's degree at UNC, where he majored in French and studied abroad in Paris, he came to Hopkins and completed a PhD in literature. Now he is moving to New York and has no intention of ever moving back to his hometown. As he understands it, education has fundamentally changed who he is. His horizons and interests can no longer be satisfied by a small town in rural America.

While this is an understandable choice at the individual level, the darker side of this trend begins to become clear when hundreds of thousands of new graduates each year start to leave communities they are from and cluster in a small group of urban centers. While there was always some level of difference between the levels of educational attainment in rural and urban America, by the year 2000, "the percentage of young adults with a college degree in rural areas was only half that of the average city." Inevitably, perhaps, the sorting of people and places by educational level correlated closely with growing differences in how much people earned. The turn of the century saw rural Nebraskans earning on average less than twenty thousand dollars a year, compared with over fifty thousand in San Francisco. And wages were increasing at starkly different rates as well, going up by "7.1 percent a year in Austin, but only 1.8 percent a year in Wheeling, West Virginia," as Bishop has shown.

Inequality has tracked with race as well as geography. Postwar America was characterized by a broad consensus of support for the democratic project and its expansion, a consensus that helped pave the way for the signature successes of the civil rights movement in the 1960s. But the health of that commonwealth belied its many exclusions: women had gone back to the household after a period of independence during World War II; and African Americans were largely blocked from the economic progress enjoyed by whites by means of legally sanctioned discriminatory practices. The government-backed housing loans provided for by the GI Bill, for example, were largely unavailable to blacks, since they were kept out of the growing suburbs and banks refused to issue mortgages for properties in black neighborhoods. As the historian Nathan Connolly has shown in great detail, the communities that black families have been left with have often become targets for predatory commerce, from payday loan sharks to overpriced convenience stores to a disproportionate number of liquor and tobacco merchants spreading addiction for profit. The consequences of such "economies of extraction" stemming from systemic and legally sanctioned discrimination have been devastating to black communities, with the result of these exclusions—combined with generations of systematic oppression under slavery and Jim Crow laws—that the average wealth of black families today is less than a tenth of that of white families.

The successes of the civil rights movement in achieving the dismantling of legal segregation depended on the extraordinary efforts and suffering of the movement's leaders and adherents. They collectively showed Americans that segregation was an abomination precisely because it violated the social contract that the American spirit of community was built on. But as new social movements reverberated on college campuses from the 1960s on, redefining notions of what counts as literature and whose history gets told, similar movements were also disrupting the idea of community under-lying the policies that had moved so many white families like Grandpa Stack's into the middle class. As the ideal and the reality of community expanded for whites in postwar America, a series of developments pushed back on those gains. In the South, the civil rights movement provoked backlash among those committed to segregation; deception by govern-ment leaders during the Vietnam War led to unprecedented public distrust in government; and the euphoric promises of globalization gave way to an exposure to world labor markets that undercut the livelihoods of working-class whites.

At the same time, just as success in an increasingly competitive global market was requiring more higher education, the federal and state govern-ments were reducing their investments in public higher education, leaving state colleges and universities no alternative but to start raising their tuitions. As a result, college was becoming less and less available to the very sectors of the society that would have needed it most. Meanwhile, the faculty and students at those colleges, embracing the expansion promoted by the new social movements, began to shift their focus away from the ideals and philosophies of community toward a decontextualized individualism that was being pushed equally by both left and right, for very different reasons. As Mark Lilla describes it, for the past four decades "our politics have been dominated by two ideologies that encourage and even celebrate the *unmaking* of citizens. On the right, an ideology that questions the exis-tence of a common good and denies our obligation to help fellow citizens, through government action if necessary. On the left, an ideology institu-tionalized in colleges and universities that fetishizes our individual and group attachments, applauds self-absorption, and casts a shadow of suspicion over any invocation of a universal democratic *we*." While the left rebelled against the constraints of a community it saw as inherently oppressive, the right chafed at a form of community it saw as supporting the worst in humanity instead of cultivating the best, a betrayal through permissiveness of what they saw as community's ultimate purpose—to correct individuals' natural rebelliousness and enforce conformity with traditional morals.

This is where we are right now. Our democracy is not functioning because we have lost sight of the community that grounds it. We are unable to repair community because of the persistent toxicity of economic inequality. And our education system, which was intended to thwart inequality by generating opportunity and disseminating the tools for democratic participation and empowerment, has instead turned into an inequality-generating machine. To understand how that works, we can't just start with college; we need to jump on at the ground floor.

TODDLER TRENCHES

Guido and Marion are a young couple from Paris with a toddler, an adorable brown-eyed girl named Clara. They recently moved to Baltimore so that Guido could take up a position as a postdoctoral scholar at Hopkins. In Paris, where they taught French and Italian at a school for languages, they sent Clara to their neighborhood day care near the Place Gambetta. Behind the Place Gambetta are two parks where you can see children playing after school every afternoon. In France, day care is considered an essential social benefit and is universally available as soon as the state-mandated period of paid leave for parents has run out, usually when the child is around eight months old. Parents can choose to send their child to a public or to a private facility. There is little difference in the quality (very high) or the ratio of children to caregivers (very low). Moreover, cost is barely a factor. All families receive a monthly check from the government to cover costs, and how much one pays is calculated on the basis of salaries, the highest price being around four hundred euros ($450) a month. In Guido and Marion's case, they were paying less than three hundred euros for full-time day care, including warm meals (this was France, after all) as well as medicines and even diapers, at a beautiful, light-filled facility only blocks away from their house. And even that price was largely covered by their monthly child-support check from the government.

France has wonderful family support programs, but this kind of commitment to early childhood care is not exclusive to France. Most European governments offer some form of subsidized childcare. Julia and Adi are an Austrian couple who live in Vienna, where my wife is from and where we spend a portion of each year. Their daughter, Vita, attends a private school—in fact, it's the school run by the world-renowned Vienna Boys' Choir—where she has been since preschool. I went with Julia one day to pick Vita up from school and marveled at the beauty of the school's architecture, including the luxuriant green park in its courtyard, where it seemed the children never wanted to stop playing. When I mused aloud at how expensive such a private school must be, though, Julia almost choked with laughter. As she went on to explain, the 250 or so euros it cost to send Vita there is entirely covered by their monthly child-support check, just like in France.

Since I was the one who had enticed Guido and Marion to Baltimore, I felt a little chagrined to find out how much trouble they were having finding the kind of quality childcare for Clara that would allow them both to work. At first I naïvely suggested they could look into Hopkins's own childcare facility. The Hopkins Homewood Early Learning Center is nothing short of state-of-the-art. It opened a couple of years ago to much fanfare, after almost a decade of faculty and student advocacy, protests, and meetings, all intended to draw attention to the lack of quality affordable day care facilities for Hopkins employees. I had been aware of and very much supported that movement, and was delighted when it led to the creation of the Early Learning Center, although my own children were well past the age when it could have been useful to me. When Guido and Marion arrived, I had just referred the Hopkins day care to a couple of junior faculty members who had also moved to Hopkins, and they were very happy with it.

And what's not to be happy about! The brand-new modular buildings are bright and sunny examples of modern architecture, surrounded by beautifully landscaped playgrounds. For the youngest age group, there were three highly trained early-childhood specialists for the four infants I saw in the room. The downside? The basic monthly rate for an infant at the Homewood Early Learning Center is around nineteen hundred dollars. And that's without meals. It's also without access to the playground, which requires the purchase of a second insurance option. The grand total for an eight-month-old child thus ends up running a young family around twenty-five hundred dollars. That is ten times the cost of equivalent care in France or Austria, before we have even taken into account that, there, the state is in fact paying for most of that cost.

My junior colleagues who did decide to send their child to the Hopkins day care on my recommendation, it turns out, were paying over 40 percent of their monthly net salary so that their child could be taken care of for the time they needed to be working to make that money. They decided to bite the bullet and pay those rates after having tried to leave their son at another facility, farther away, and realizing that they just weren't happy with the quality of the care—despite also paying around a thousand dollars a month there. Happily, Guido and Marion, for whom the Hopkins day care would have cost well more than half their monthly salaries, found a workable option.

A few blocks away from Hopkins's Homewood campus is an economically struggling neighborhood called Waverly, which many students and faculty try to avoid. There, in a quiet row house, a woman named Angela runs a private day care that caters to some of the Hopkins professors and foreign visitors who can't afford or simply can't bring themselves to pay what they see as the Early Learning Center's extortionate rates. The rooms are small, but warm, bright, and colorful. The four children I saw there, who all greeted Clara by name, were babbling and happy, and being lovingly cared for by the caretaker in charge that day, a woman named Francisca.

As far as I could tell, Francisca, who is from Honduras, didn't speak much English, but she clearly had a great deal of love for and experience with babies. Guido and Marion pay around a thousand dollars a month to send Clara here. It's still much, much more than they are used to. But they can live with it. As Marion told me, they had reached a point where they were almost ready to pay for the Hopkins day care, but then something one of the administrators told them stopped her cold. "She told me that, best of all, I would be certain that my child was only around other Hopkins children," Marion said. "Is that what they want you to pay all that money for? So that your child doesn't have to be around children whose parents can't?"

It turns out that not only is quality childcare important for families' economic well-being, it can be decisive in the success of their children's later education, and consequently has a multiplier effect on the next generation's socioeconomic status. A study released in 2014 intended to measure the efficacy of an early Obama-era policy initiative called the School Improvement Grant (SIG) program, showed that the program was not turning around failing schools, as was intended. The primary reason for its failure was that, even while SIG funds were being spent in elementary schools in disadvantaged areas, the gap in how prepared kids are to begin elementary school had persisted. While the administration proposed adjustments to the program, including allowing districts to use SIG funds to support pre-K initiatives, there were few incentives for districts to apply funds in this way, since testing was only instituted as of third grade.

Even more troublingly, the research revealed that almost insurmountable cognitive and emotional differences between relatively advantaged and disadvantaged groups of children were emerging long before third grade, and indeed by children's third year of life. In 1995, the education researchers Todd R. Risley and Betty Hart had shown, for instance, that three-year-olds from better-off families had been exposed on average to ten million more words than their peers from less advantaged families. What is now known as the "word gap" directly predicts a future achievement gap, which only grows in kindergarten and grade school as those who start life with the word deficit fall further and further behind.

Such studies seem to suggest that education is limited in what it can accomplish, since the word gap is produced in the home environment before kids arrive in classrooms. Indeed, a good number of states already have some degree of universal pre-K, and the data is decidedly mixed. One reason for this is that, by definition, universal pre-K allots money to early education independently of a family's ability to pay. This means that cash-strapped states are in fact diluting resources that could be used to benefit poorer families and more effectively close the achievement gap to subsidize childcare for families for whom that subsidy will make far less difference. As some researchers have argued, though, maximizing the cost-effectiveness of such programs may become secondary for political reasons. In the view of Stanford professor of education emeritus Larry Cuban, even if universal pre-K dilutes states' attempts to close the achievement gap, it may be the only alternative politically, since "it's politically impossible to get it passed if it's only aimed at poor kids of color, so what you do is you spread it to everyone so that white, middle-class families have access."

The fact remains that simply putting kids in pre-K programs is not a panacea. The quality and training of teachers is essential. As the journalist Alia Wong has reported, "many of the country's existing private preschools are little more than glorified daycare centers. Their staffs often consist of unskilled, low-paid employees who work under the guise of classroom teachers. They don't use prepared lesson plans; they don't focus on developing the cognitive, physical, and social skills expected of today's kindergartners; they don't have the kinds of facilities a quality classroom needs." Moreover, even long-established programs like Head Start, which does focus on lower-income children, often fail to close the achievement gap in the long run. The reason for this is straightforward enough: even quality pre-K won't be enough if children are then thrown into subpar primary schools. If we are going to try to use our education system to ensure and maintain equality, intervening at just one level won't be enough.

SCHOOL HAZE

There are few things that Americans agree upon these days. But one of them is that our schools are a mess. Under Ronald Reagan in the 1980s, the title of the watershed report on that state of public education was called "A Nation at Risk." Under President Clinton the rhetoric continued, with his administration signing the rather unimaginatively named Improving America's Schools Act of 1994. The preamble to that bill stated unambiguously that "a high-quality education for all individuals and a fair and equal opportunity to obtain that education are a societal good, are a moral imperative, and improve the life of every individual, because the quality of our individual lives ultimately depends on the quality of the lives of others."

In the early 2000s, President George W. Bush signed "No Child Left Behind," which instituted an age of increased accountability on a national scale, or at least of more frequent and widespread standardized testing. Under President Obama, school districts were invited to submit more individualized proposals under his signature "Race to the Top" initiative, which was intended to rectify the fact that, as he put it, "despite resources that are unmatched anywhere in the world, we've let our grades slip, our schools crumble, our teacher quality fall short, and other nations outpace us." Even President Trump, who normally would make a point of saying the opposite of anything his predecessor said, toed the line, lamenting that "our beautiful students are being deprived of all knowledge."

This consensus on the abysmal state of public education is belied, however, by the data. One of the key talking points for politicians as they support their favorite education platforms is to point to declining test scores, implying how much higher they were in the past. But as the early childhood educator Erika Christakis has reported, "not only is the idea that American test scores were once higher a fiction, but in some cases they have actually improved over time, especially among African American students. Since the 1970s, when the Department of Education began collecting long term data, average reading and math scores for 9- and 13-year-olds have risen significantly."

These improvements are all the more impressive when certain demographic factors are taken into account, such as the fact that for the first time a majority of U.S. public school students are from families classified as low income, or the increasing number of students who are newly included in public schools. For instance, since the passage of the 1975 Individuals with Disabilities Education Act, public schools have been required to admit disabled students. Today's student body also includes a far greater number of children for whom English is not their native language. What this data points to is that, on average, public schools are doing an admirable job; it is society as a whole that is letting our children and families down.

The foundation of this failure is America's inability to stem the tide of both racial and socioeconomic segregation. As the U.S. population continues to sort itself into racial and socioeconomic enclaves, the inherent inequalities that define and separate these enclaves profoundly affect the quality of education that students living in specific environments receive. Just as increases in average income over a population are biased by outsize increases at the top, the average improvements in some metrics for public education outcomes mask staggering inequalities between school districts. And it is almost always the case that the most underresourced, crowded, and unsafe schools are the ones that serve poor, crime-ridden urban neighborhoods.

Victor is an illustrator who has transitioned into a second career as an art teacher. He currently holds two jobs, teaching art in the morning at Windsor Hills, a public school in West Baltimore, before driving out to the country in the afternoon to teach in an after-school program at an elite private school. When I asked him about his daily commute he broke into laughter. "It's like moving from Iraq in the morning to Tahiti in the afternoon," he said. From a war zone to paradise in one day. Victor tells this story of his first day teaching eighth-grade art. He looked out at a classroom packed with almost forty kids. In the front row sat a boy, let's call him Terence, who is around six foot five and plays offensive tackle for the middle school football team. He glared at Victor, crossed his arms, and growled, "I don't like art."

Luckily, Victor is an empathetic and compelling teacher, and soon Terence, who towers over Victor's five-foot-seven frame, took an interest in drawing. It's still hard to keep the classroom focused, though. Even with an excellent teacher's aide working at his side, Victor feels that every time he gives his full attention to someone like Terence, two or three disturbances erupt behind his back.

Victor's experience of shuttling back and forth between Iraq and Tahiti on any given day reflects the real chasm between the quality of education and livelihood that exists in two very different neighborhoods in Baltimore. It happens to be the case that one of his schools is public and the other private; but he could have just as jarring an experience in two public schools in different parts of the city. Unfortunately, though, the contrast supports the stereotype that public schools in general are quagmires of failure, for which private schools are the only possible solution. This is the kind of thinking that animates the school choice movement and the push, largely from the Republican Party, to replace public education with vouchers.

Vouchers are grants, paid for with taxpayer money, given to families so that they can pay for private education. The idea behind them is that the more effective schools will attract the most students and thrive; the least effective schools, in contrast, will fail to attract students and over time will lose funding and close. According to an ideal market-based model, entrepreneurs would see the successful schools and the demand they are fomenting, and would open new schools that model themselves on the successful schools to replace the failing and closing schools. Before long, the entire district will be brimming with successful schools pushing well-educated students out into the workforce.

Unfortunately, there is a gaping chasm separating this sunny image from how vouchers work when they are actually implemented. One issue is that the theory depends on assumptions about families making decisions in ways that fail to reflect how actual families often make decisions. As David Osborne, director of the Progressive Policy Institute's project on Reinventing America's Schools, puts it, "Experience teaches that some parents will stick with a school if it is safe and nurturing, even if test scores are abysmal, so we cannot rely on parents to abandon all failing schools." In fact, rather than equalize opportunity, the evidence suggests that a universal voucher system that aims to convert all public funding of education into what are often called "educational savings accounts" would radically exacerbate inequality. "Those who can afford it will add their own money to the voucher and buy more expensive educations for their kids, and the education market will stratify by income, like every other market."

Indeed, this is exactly what is already happening with public education, as we see the largest differences in resources and quality not between private and public schools, but between public schools in different zip codes. The irony is that having schools be publicly funded doesn't do any more to diversify our education system in fundamental ways; rather, the quality of public education available to families is strongly biased toward the preservation of upper-middle-class privilege, with nearly "40 percent of top-quintile families" living in areas "with public schools in the top fifth of their state" and 25 percent being zoned for schools in the top 10 percent. These schools, while ostensibly public and hence dependent on taxpayer money, can, depending on the community they serve, often afford the kind of opportunities that only the most elite and expensive private schools can offer.

Take the admittedly extreme example of PS3 in lower Manhattan. The school's district serves one of the most expensive real estate markets in the country, whose residents include not only families of Wall Street bankers, but also entertainers who like to live in and around Greenwich Village and the professors at NYU who live in university-subsidized housing. Faculty are delighted to be able to send their children to a top public school and avoid paying a large chunk of their salaries for private education; and the other parents are equally delighted that their children will be attending school with professors' kids, who have grown up surrounded by books and ideas, and often come from different cultures.

PS3 has effectively turned itself into a private school subsidized by state money. The school's parent-teacher organization actively fund-raises in the heart of one of the world's most affluent communities, and has an operating budget of more than $680,000. Plaques adorn the walls of PS3 celebrating the highest donors; and 100 percent participation is the goal of their giving campaigns. This is apparently not unusual, since "some Manhattan schools raise over a million dollars annually." If money were only window dressing and incidental to the quality of the education being offered, then perhaps these kinds of differences wouldn't have too profound an effect on overall levels of inequality. But as Reeves has shown, "every researcher that looks at the question finds that teacher quality is higher in schools in more affluent areas." And teacher quality, more than any other single factor, even including class size, is instrumental in providing students with effective education.

The take-home, then, is that each family's decisions about how to educate their own children contribute to overall educational inequality. The journalist and now MacArthur Fellow Nikole Hannah-Jones has drawn a line in the sand around the decision between public and private schools, making a public point of her own decision to send her daughter to her local public school. As she puts it, "I think that we can't say 'This school is not good enough for my child' and then sustain that system. I think that that's just morally wrong. If it's not good enough for my child, then why are we putting any children in those schools?" She has also been publicly dismissive of the hypocrisy of liberals who decry inequality and then, as she puts it, contribute to it by sending their children to elite private schools. But as noble as that sentiment is, many families are not willing to make a political point with their own children's education. As the liberal commentator and Brookings Institution scholar E. J. Dionne has put it, "I spend my weekdays decrying the problem of inequality, but then I spend my nights and weekends contributing to it."

Dionne's conundrum and Hannah-Jones's *j'accuse* feel personal to me. As educators ourselves, my wife and I feel it is important to invest in our children's education. And invest we do, dedicating almost a third of our net income to private-school tuition for our three children. Consciously and explicitly, what our choice says is that we place a premium on our kids' future and their development as human beings, and are willing to make sacrifices for that future. Implicitly, though, our choice is contributing to inequality in America.

So, what does making that choice get us? The name of the Park School of Baltimore is a bit of a misnomer, since it is located outside the city limits, and many of its several hundred students drive in from the surrounding counties rather than from the city. In stark contrast to the faux stone facades and asphalt streets lining so many of Baltimore's neighborhoods, the Park School sits astride a luxuriant green campus, its brown-brick modernist buildings nestled around a tree-lined pond.

Recently I sat on a bench in the school's lobby and watched the jubilant parade of students tumbling out of their classrooms. Despite the chatter and laughter of kids of all different ages and colors, the halls seemed strangely silent—until I realized that what was missing was the bell. In the schools that I attended growing up or have visited since, the times when students were due in or released from class had always been strictly marked by a bell that sounds for all the world like a fire or burglar alarm. Here at Park, the end of the school day was marked merely by kids leaving class.

A tall white boy with spiked hair wearing a heavy-metal T-shirt walked by a black girl in shorts and sandals in an animated conversation with a teacher. No one seemed to notice as a middle-schooler dressed in what looked like gray camouflage pajamas slid backward down the stairway's central banister . . . while reading a book. A flock of girls dressed for lacrosse moving toward my left passed through a small orchestra moving toward my right on its way to the music rooms; like colliding galaxies they momentarily merged and then parted with no observable mishaps.

Outside on the spacious campus, kids are playing sports, of course. But they are also building lean-tos in the woods, taking water samples from the creek, and building trebuchets with which to launch pumpkins across an open field. That may sound like a lot of fun; but the kids I saw were also busily calculating launch angles and x-displacement in a frantic quest to come up with the most accurate predictions of where, exactly, those pumpkins were going to go splat.

At Park School I spoke with two teachers, Kirk Wulf, who teaches English, and Peter Warren, who teaches history. A lanky, blond, bearded man, Kirk could just as easily be a surf instructor in Venice, California, as an English teacher in Baltimore; indeed, he brings something of the former vibe to his job. Peter, his counterpart in the history department, has intense and empathetic eyes framed by short-cropped white hair and a neatly trimmed beard. Peter's classroom is wallpapered with film posters, prominently among them the famous orange spiral from Alfred Hitchcock's *Vertigo*. When I commented that I have the same poster up in my house, Peter became effusive as he described bringing a class to see a showing of an original print of the film at a historic Baltimore cinema.

When I asked the two men about their choice to teach at an exclusive private school, they both allowed that they were conflicted. "The way I see it," Kirk opened, "I think that we do really good work with kids, but it's certainly true that that's largely because we get to teach kids who can already think and feel—who have been treated like reasonable people from early childhood—because they come from households in which the dinner table conversation is already a very good education in being human." Peter followed suit, also admitting some discomfort at having chosen to spend his career teaching "the most selective kids from families who can afford to send them to study with other kids who were similarly selected."

I asked Kirk if this meant that he and Peter were, in some ways, training a generation of mandarins, increasingly sophisticated in ways of thinking about both diversity and inequality, but without the means to create substantive change. He clarified that while "no one intends to become a mandarin, it's easy to end up that way: really sophisticated in the ways that you understand personal identity and in the ways you avoid giving offense, but substantially powerless to change the underlying causes that make all this identity stuff so important and full of pain." So, the teachers at Park were drawing a distinction between the rules of behavior that govern offense and the actual conditions linking identity to power and pain? Yes, Kirk answered. For him, "sophistication about identity is one passport into the culture of power, and even if that sophistication is in the service of sincere purposes, ways of thinking and feeling don't, on their own, change the structures of power."

I know where they are coming from. I spent the first part of my career teaching at a major state university, SUNY Buffalo, before accepting an offer to come to Johns Hopkins. For most professors who got their PhDs because they like doing research as well as teaching, such a move would be understandable. While both are research universities with similar teaching loads, the allure of better pay and resources, a more prestigious institution, and smaller classes with some of the nation's top students is hard to resist. As Kirk, Peter, and I sat in Peter's classroom—three highly educated white men with beards talking about diversity in education—I couldn't help being reflective as well: To what extent do all our individual decisions—where to work, where to send our children to school—end up contributing to the inequality and divisiveness that our much-vaunted commitment to diversity is intended to roll back?

I left Park with mixed feelings that day. On the one hand was my conviction, if anything strengthened, that the school my wife and I had chosen for our kids had some of the best, most thoughtful and articulate teachers I could ever hope for. I continue to believe that "a Park education for all" would be transformational beyond any social program one could imagine, if only our society had the means and will to bring it about. I also believe that what would be transformational in such a generalization would have less to do with the curriculum than with the people teaching it—people like Peter and Kirk, or like the dozens of other teachers at Park whom I have come to know over the years my children have attended the school. Dedicated, reflective, creative, and passionate teachers.

But my other hand was starting to itch a little. What if "a Park education for all" was not just a pipe dream because of the expense (at around twenty-five thousand dollars a student, Park costs more than twice the average annual per-child expenditure in the United States)? What if, instead, an essential ingredient in what makes a Park education so magical is the selectivity that produces that student body, and in turn helps attract teachers like Kirk and Peter, just as the students at Hopkins helped attract me? What if, in other words, an inherent roadblock preventing excellent liberal arts education from combating inequality is that the excellence of that education feeds on inequality in the first place?

This is the dilemma so many families face. On the one hand, we believe that education should be a public good, equally available for all; on the other hand, we undermine that public good by sending our own children to cloistered private schools, at considerable cost to ourselves. We know this choice is largely dependent on the quality of public schools available. In wealthy suburbs with high-performing schools, middle-class families tend not to send their children to private schools. However, black families have often been systematically excluded from precisely those neighborhoods whose tax bases would allow them to send their children to such high-performing schools. In other words, the principled stance that it is up to families to make responsible choices to invest in education is predicated on an utterly false assumption of equal opportunity. The high-quality public option is really only available to the very same demographic who have the option to send their kids to private schools if they should so choose.

From the early twentieth century until the passage of the Fair Housing Act in 1968, federal statutes actively ensured that loans for housing developments in the suburbs would only be granted under guarantee that black families would not be permitted to buy those houses. Concomitantly, zoning in the parts of cities where blacks were living ensured precisely the kinds of developments, from factories to waste facilities, that would guarantee that those who could move out to the affluent suburbs would do so. Hence, racial segregation that was also economic segregation was legally encouraged. While the Fair Housing Act officially outlawed such practices, the damage was already done, and the inequities were almost impossible to eradicate. Indeed, while blacks today earn on average only 60 percent of what whites earn, the wealth accumulated by black families equates to only 6 percent of white wealth.

Truly equal opportunity based on truly equal access to the same educational opportunities would seem to be what's needed for escaping from this vicious circle. But how do we get there from where we are now? We can imagine a truly public education system, one in which the 25 percent of affluent families' take-home income that in some cases is going to private schools would be transferred to public schools, and for that to be the case across the board. But now we're describing the system that exists in Austria, Finland, France, and all those other countries that regularly outperform the United States in educational standards and don't suffer from either the same levels of inequality or the lack of political engagement that we do—and where affluent families pay more than half of their income in taxes. But even if that were feasible in this country, would it be enough?

EDUCATIONAL ECOLOGIES

As we've seen, where one chooses to send a child for day care in the United States can turn out to be the first in a long series of decisions that often end up being about how much a family or parent is able or willing to spend to keep a child in a better, safer, or more enriching school. This is true whether the parents choose public or private schools, since having a child attend an excellent public school usually depends on living in the right school district, which means paying more for your housing. Some cities, as a result of entrenched urban poverty and white flight to the suburbs, have developed a particularly strong culture of private schools, which, in a kind of vicious circle, exacerbates the problems with the public schools, as wealthier families increasingly remove their kids from the public school system. Baltimore is just such a city.

The migration of white families out of urban school districts from the 1960s on has left a significant racial gap within city schools, one that mirrors the economic discrepancies between urban and suburban school districts. After decades of black migration into the city, followed by further decades of "white flight," Baltimore is one of many urban centers that are majority black, with African Americans accounting for 65 percent of its population. Baltimore City public schools, however, are closer to 85 percent black, a race gap in urban public education that we see repeated in other majority-black urban centers. Ultimately, the segregation of students by race and socioeconomic status into a pyramid of private schools, public suburban schools, and public urban schools correlates to a downward curve in average test scores. In Maryland, where all students, regardless of their school, take a standardized test called the ERB every few years from third grade on, the discrepancies among these three categories are such that a student's percentile needs to be measured in each category. A student who scores in the eighty-ninth percentile when measured against all schools may well fall into the eighty-fifth percentile of suburban school test takers, and only the eightieth of private school students.

The clustering of families into neighborhoods according to economic means, reinforced by the desirability of the local school, has been a major factor in creating the current levels of racial, economic, and performance segregation we see in a city like Baltimore. But while inequality of spending on students in different districts is part of the problem, it is not at all clear that just redistributing tax dollars, even if that were politically possible, would be enough to solve the problem; and there is plenty of evidence that it would not be. Rather, reversing the stratification of schools by reintegrating schools on all levels would yield better results. Public charters are one way of encouraging districts to reintegrate, since they have the potential to be attractive to families who might have otherwise made the choice to send their children to private schools or to move out of district. Emerging data from charter schools have demonstrated as much, with some school districts seeing marked improvement in new charters despite their being underfunded in comparison with traditional schools in the same city.

Ten years ago, Baltimore began an experiment it called Baltimore School Choice. Unlike the voucher programs that currently go under the euphemism "school choice," Baltimore's program is a public-school initiative, in which rising ninth graders throughout the city are permitted to choose their top five high schools anywhere in the city during the fall of their eighth grade year. Sometime in the following May they learn which of those five they will attend. Some of these schools are magnets whose admissions depend on high performance in middle school, while others are open-admission public schools.

In 2016 and 2017, Baltimore's program was reviewed by an independent commission, which concluded that the program had not met its goal of shaking up the pattern whereby family income largely determines whether children go on to college. As Nikole Hannah-Jones pointed out in a discussion of the commission's findings, the high schools that are capable of preparing kids for college themselves have high academic expectations. You can't have a system where kids are confined to under-performing schools through eighth grade and expect them magically to be prepared for an academically rigorous program when "choice" is introduced. The fact remains that most families will continue to send their children to the closest school, and in cities like Baltimore, which remains effectively segregated by wealth as well as by race, "choice" is likely to continue to benefit a population that is statistically both wealthier and whiter than the average Baltimore family.

Recognizing that the positive effects of a school choice program are limited when the program is limited to high school, Baltimore has been working to expand the program to all levels of the school system, essentially adopting for its public-school system one of the key attributes of charter schools. Charter schools are, as David Osborne defines them, "public schools operated by independent, mostly nonprofit organizations, free of most state and district rules but held accountable for performance by written charters, which function like performance contracts." Advocates of traditional public schools are often critical of charter schools, claiming that they direct funds away from "public schools." This charge is misleading, since charters are, by definition, public. It is true, however, that successful charters can deprive traditional public schools of funding if parents who are given the choice to send their children to a new charter school do so and remove their children from the traditional school. Since teachers in traditional schools are, by and large, unionized and benefit from tenure, whereas those in charter schools may not be, teachers' unions such as the American Federation of Teachers have actively lobbied against the adoption of charter schools, which they see, not incorrectly, as watering down their leverage.

Where charter schools have been widely implemented, and where they have been implemented according to the fundamental ideas animating the charter movement, the evidence of their efficacy has been overwhelmingly positive. Key to successful implementation of charters are two principles: first, that failure to live up to the standards in their charter leads to closing, so that other charters may take their place; and second, that attendance not be "cherry-picked" by the application of selective standards, such as are used by public "magnet schools." Once such basic principles have been applied, the evidence is clear. Even the studies cited by most critics of charter schools show significant educational gains for students in charters over the students who attend traditional schools in the same district.

As Osborne shows, a "natural experiment" resulting from a natural disaster has provided significant evidence that if school districts were to replace traditional schools with charter systems they would see tremendous improvement in educational outcomes. After Hurricane Katrina hit New Orleans in 2005, the city began a process of turning virtually all its public schools into charter schools. The results have been stellar: the city's schools, Osborne says, have "tripled their effectiveness. The district has improved faster than any other in the state—no doubt in the nation. On several important metrics, New Orleans is the first big city with a majority of low-income minorities to outperform its state."

Of course, it is difficult to generalize about charter schools because, by definition, each one is different. That is why it is so essential for a district to be able to shut down those that prove not to be working. I wanted to see in person how a successful charter school might function, so I spent several days as a guest at the Afya Public Charter School in East Baltimore. Afya, which is Swahili for "health," was founded by a small group of Baltimore public-school teachers some ten years ago to offer kids in an economically disadvantaged area of Baltimore an alternative to a public-school experience that can be drab, uninspiring, and even dangerous. On my first day at Afya I met Pat Njenga, one of the teachers who founded Afya along with Will McKenna, who had been the principal of the school in the Waverly neighborhood of Baltimore where she taught fourth grade.

Njenga is a spry Kenyan woman with a quiet, calming manner and an infectious smile. She spends most of her time running the school's programs these days and is no longer teaching, and as we walked through the busy hallways and poked our heads into several rooms, she confessed that talking with me about Afya's educational philosophy was making her miss being in the classroom. Njenga came to Baltimore to study at Coppin State University, where she majored in English before going on to get a master's degree in education. Afya began as a forum for bringing kids together to read books. I asked Njenga what it was about that simple act of gathering together around a book that she found so transformative. She answered, "When you sit in a circle and you've just read a chapter of a book like *Roll of Thunder, Hear My Cry*, the point is not to be telling the kids what it's about. You ask them questions. You ask, 'What was this character thinking?' or 'What would you do if that had happened to you?' You listen to each other, and the kids start to feel that their ideas matter, that what they are thinking is important to you. In some cases, they've never been given that sense before."

Afya takes the guiding notion of health seriously. The school uniforms are quick-dry tracksuits and T-shirts in bright colors like orange, blue, and purple. Students do at least an hour of sustained movement a day, and teachers often interrupt class if they see that students are lagging and exhort them to a quick game of wall ball or a set of calisthenics. Sodas are taboo, and students are taught about diet and nutrition from their first year in the school. In the decade since the school opened, Pat and the other teachers have seen a noticeable drop in obesity, which is endemic among children in many of Baltimore's poorer neighborhoods due to lack of education about nutrition and a dearth of healthy options.

The Afya school is a middle school, and enrolls about 340 kids from sixth to eighth grade. As a charter school, it is open to children from anywhere in Baltimore; but like many successful schools, there are always more applicants than there are spots, so each year the entering class is chosen by lottery. Currently about a third of Afya's students make it into one of Baltimore's four elite magnet high schools—far above the citywide public-school average—an extraordinary achievement given that many of these students were testing two or more years below grade levels when they matriculated at Afya.

Key to Afya's success is that students are made to feel like active members of a community. The school has identified six "core values" that were articulated by Afya students: compassion, self-control, honesty, teamwork, curiosity, and perseverance. On the first Wednesday of each month the entire school gathers in the cafeteria in the basement for a discussion of one of those core values. The teachers and coordinators I met, people like Scott Johnson, the school's student support coordinator, who runs community outreach for the school and coaches its boys' soccer team and its girls' basketball team, seemed to embody those principles. One morning shortly after the start of school, Elijah, a small, normally sunny sixth grader, showed up in his office, his eyes puffy from crying and his clothes soaked from having been caught in a rainstorm on his way to school. While his clothes were bothering him, he was particularly anxious about his copy of a *Percy Jackson* book that he was reading for his language arts class, which was so soaked as to be unusable. Johnson quickly reassured him, gave him a dry shirt to change into, hung his dripping shirt and jacket in his office, and took him to see Molly Grant, his English teacher.

Grant was also quick to comfort Elijah and gave him a new copy of the book. Before long Elijah was back to normal. When I saw him later, at lunch that day, he had a big smile on his face and happily fist-bumped me and Scott when we entered the cafeteria. I asked Grant during her free period whether she felt that kids at her school had extra challenges to deal with that might interfere with their ability to learn She told me that many of her kids, probably the majority, come from households with serious pressures that take an enormous toll on their ability to concentrate at school. By being aware of this, she and the team at Afya have been able to turn their school into a kind of sanctuary. She recalled how one of her students, Greta (I've changed her name to protect her privacy), had become extremely agitated and refused to put her purse in her locker one morning, as school policy requires. Instead of elevating passions by threatening her with punishment for her "willful disobedience," as can happen at many schools, Grant sat down with her and asked if there was anything going on. She learned from Greta that her mother, who had been in prison for several years, was now at home and didn't know or understand the rule about not having phones or purses during the day. Her agitation was due to her not knowing how she could both remain available to her mother and follow the school's rules. Knowing her situation, Grant was able to tell her that she would keep her phone for her and would call her right away if her mother called and needed her for anything.

Even the discipline at Afya is different from traditional schools. We now know that suspension is a form of punishment that unequally affects minority populations, and is often applied in response to teachers' perception of students being "willfully disobedient." What the research shows is that most cases of such resistance on the part of students stem from problems or distractions they are facing at home, and that simply asking students about what's bothering them can both increase trust between teachers and students and reduce suspensions, which are harmful to kids' academic and personal development. At Afya, when students are disruptive and need to be disciplined, they are told that they have earned a "workout" session and must stay after school for a period of time, during which they do supervised homework. On another occasion, when Greta was told she would have to serve a workout session, she again became agitated and refused. This time her teachers, again by talking to her and asking why she was so upset, learned that her older sister, who could drive, was taking her to see her father that day after school, and that if she was late she would leave without her. The Afya teachers told her that if she agreed to come serve her workout the next afternoon, she could leave as planned that day.

Sometimes it takes students time to transition into the culture of a school that allows for more autonomy and at the same time asks for more responsibility. When Gary, a very slight boy who had been systematically bullied at his previous school, first arrived, he was suspicious of all the other kids and would immediately jump to the conclusion that they were also going to bully him. When an older boy, Harold, saw that Gary was afraid of him, he took things into his own hands and confronted him on the playground—not to put him down, but to do the opposite. In front of the other kids he told him, "Look, we like you! Just give us a chance and play with us."

The Afya school is in a tough neighborhood. Some of the streets around the school are home to the sorts of stretches of boarded-up houses that Baltimore became famous for in shows like *Homicide* and *The Wire*. While overall graduation rates have increased since 2010, there is still a significant gender and race gap, with black boys being the demographic group in Baltimore's public schools who are most at risk of failing to graduate. For many, school is a place of danger and fear, not learning and support. What charters like Afya show is that a public school can become a sanctuary and a family, creating real possibilities for learning even for kids whose families are fractured and whose prospects seem the most at risk. A few schools here and there that are like Afya, however, aren't enough to do the trick; and school choice is only a solution to the fundamental inequality of our education system if it leads to real systemwide change, with parents opting for better-performing schools, leading to other schools following suit or being replaced by better schools. If that doesn't happen, then "choice" is just another word for continuing inequality.

It turns out that how a school performs is difficult, if not impossible, to separate from environmental factors. These include the level of funding available to the school, but other factors, such as what kind of neighborhood it is located in, what stresses are affecting kids at home, and the intellectual and cultural resources other families and kids bring to the school, are just as or even more important. Shakeer, who attends Franklin Square Elementary / Middle School in West Baltimore, is ambitious and brilliant. In 2016 he won an award as outstanding scholar of the year from a local charity organization. But Shakeer's eagerness to excel in school requires him to endure taunting and even threats of violence. His family is his support network, as are his teachers; but getting to school each day means walking through streets where, as one of his schoolmates put it, pointing across from their front door, a body was found right there just the other day. Kids who are frightened, undernourished, or hopeless are less capable of learning, but are also less able to contribute to an environment that helps others to learn.

Because of this complex network of environmental factors, increasing a school's funding levels alone has little chance of improving its effectiveness. While more money can translate into more books and computers, and even smaller class sizes, the single most important factor in a school's success is how good the teachers are. As Reeves has pointed out, "Every researcher that looks into the question finds that teacher quality is higher in schools in more affluent areas. In Louisiana, for example, 38 percent of the teachers in affluent neighborhoods are rated as 'highly effective,' compared to 22 percent in the poorest schools." Teacher quality is notoriously difficult to measure. In fact, there is almost something tautological to the statement that what makes the most difference is the quality of the teacher, since sometimes the only way we decide who the good teachers are, well, is that their presence has made a noticeable improvement in their classes' outcomes. Be that as it may, a brilliant teacher can do with a class of thirty as much as or more than a mediocre teacher can do with half that number. And it can be a wonder to see it happening in person.

At Afya, I spent several days in Molly Grant's sixth grade humanities class marveling at how her warm, firm, encouraging demeanor helped unlock and channel her young students' exuberance and vitality. The thirty-some desks in Grant's class seem to change configuration each day, a trick that I quickly learned helped to keep students alert and interested by subtly changing their perspective from day to day. The pacing of her classes—which can be long, up to eighty minutes—was also variable. At times, she held their attention by leading a group discussion, eliciting excited responses and even peals of laughter. Before the productive enthusiasm can boil over, though, she redirects the class into small discussion groups to work out a problem she's just given them. Marquez, a boy with sandy colored hair, doesn't have a partner. Grant looks meaningfully at Kylee, a girl with long, tight, multihued braids who sits in front of Marquez and is animatedly working through the question with her partner. Without missing a beat, Kylee turns her chair and the pair has become a threesome. No one is excluded.

As a charter school Afya cannot be selective. As noted earlier, the kids who arrive here in sixth grade are sometimes reading two or three years below grade. What I witnessed, only a few months into their first year there, seemed miraculous. Grant was teaching them to produce warranted inter-pretations of a literary text based on the application of secondary literature supported by close reading. She was teaching them to construct an exposi-tory paragraph making a concise argument grounded in textual evidence. And she was making all of this relevant to the kids' lives in a way that had them emotionally invested in the work they were doing. After rapidly elic-iting what a "theme" is from examples the whole class could identify with, Grant asked them, "Is it enough for me just to say, this is a theme?" "No!" a chorus of voices erupted. "What do I need to do, Madison?" Grant asked, turning to a quiet girl who had been studiously writing in her notebook.

She looked up and grinned. "I need to offer evidence," she said. I caught myself smiling as well as I thought to myself, this is a lesson we could all stand to learn.

———

THE COLLEGE BOTTLENECK

Let's say it again. The single most important indicator for whether a person is likely to get ahead or to stagnate in today's America is whether she has a college degree. For those in the top quintile of income, 60 percent have them, twice the rate of those in the middle 40 percent and six times the rate of the bottom 40 percent. And it is not just any old college degree that the children of the affluent are getting. As the economist Richard Reeves has shown, "The majority of children from top-quintile families attend a selective or elite college." Elite college education then becomes a virtuous (for those who benefit from it) or vicious (for those excluded) feedback loop. The economist David Autor writes that "children of better-educated parents are doubly advantaged—by their parents' higher education and higher earnings—in attaining greater education while young and greater earnings in adulthood." It's important to add that this correlation does not imply a necessary causality. It is undeniably the case that having a college degree corresponds to where one is on the socioeconomic spectrum; but this does not imply that simply having that degree exclusively determines one's upward mobility. College in this regard is one of a web of factors that benefit those who come from wealthier backgrounds.

Reeves refers to the way college admissions affect the nation's opportunity structure as "the tightest bottleneck" preventing movement into (and out of) the upper middle class. While admission to top colleges is ostensibly based on merit, the principle of merit is undermined both directly and indirectly. The most direct way in which merit is undermined is by affirmative action. No, not the kind that weighs race along with other factors when making admissions decisions. That sort of affirmative action is intended as best as possible to level the playing field and redress the historical lack of equal opportunity in preparing children for college (although the evidence of whether it is in fact working is far from conclusive).

The kind of affirmative action that gets far less coverage is the preferences shown for legacies and children of the wealthy who are perceived to be potential donors. While such direct influences are profoundly unfair, the indirect ways that merit is undermined are just as pervasive. These range from the far better preparation for college that affluent children receive in their schools to the extra measures taken by doting parents to ensure their kids have a better chance of being admitted. As Reeves puts it, "The main reason for upper middle-class dominance of good colleges is upper middle-class dominance of the top end of the measures that count most for college entry, including GPAs and SATs." Kids from affluent schools are more likely to be in contact with top college advisers, who can tell them exactly what scores they'll need to better their chances of getting into the school of their dreams. And those same kids are more likely to have parents who can invest in extra instruction to help get them those scores.

Because of this trend, it is all the more vital that there be a wide range of options available for kids from all kinds of backgrounds to get a quality college degree. The *New York Times* columnist Frank Bruni is well known for his criticisms of the madness around getting into college and of the rat race among top colleges to climb ever higher in the annual *U.S. News & World Report* college and university rankings. So I was delighted when, in a September 2016 column criticizing the annual rankings frenzy, he devoted more than half his space to writing about a nearby Maryland college, the University of Maryland, Baltimore County, or UMBC. Mr. Bruni's take on the school was eye opening. In addition to mentioning the mathematician and novelist Manil Suri, who teaches at UMBC and is a contributing columnist for the *Times*, he talked about meeting with a range of students and faculty, from a student filmmaker whose short film was selected for the Cannes Film Festival to a professor of biochemistry who told him he would never leave UMBC, in part because of the school's "almost unrivaled record for guiding African-American undergraduates toward doctorates and other postgraduate degrees in STEM fields." The school's success in recruiting and educating students of color and, importantly, students coming from economically disadvantaged families is impressive; fully a fourth of UMBC's students qualify for federal Pell grants for low-income families.

As it happened, I had a long-standing invitation to visit UMBC's well-regarded Dresher Center for the Humanities, so after making a date with Jessica Berman, its director, I got in the car and drove over. The campus of UMBC occupies six hundred acres in the town of Catonsville, Maryland, a mere twenty minutes from downtown Baltimore. Once I had deposited my car in one of the several parking garages that ring the campus, I made my way (with directions from a very helpful undergraduate student who saw me staring helplessly at a campus map and took pity on me) to the Dresher Center, which occupies a beautiful set of glass-walled offices in the campus's new and magnificent center for the performing arts.

After eating sandwiches with the center's fellows while discussing one fellow's work in progress in the field of Japanese history, Berman and I took a walk around campus, where I saw UMBC's center for the arts, in addition to its student union, with young people of every possible race and nationality working and eating lunch under a rainbow of flags representing the more than one hundred different countries the students hail from. The international makeup of the UMBC student body is a point of pride for its president, Freeman Hrabowski. Hrabowski is a civil rights icon who, as a kid, marched with Martin Luther King Jr. in his home state of Alabama. President Obama appointed him to chair the President's Advisory Committee on Educational Excellence for African Americans. While Hrabowski attended a historically black college, Hampton University, today he is a strong advocate for the kind of mixed population that UMBC represents. "I love saying that we can give students the kind of experience I had in Hampton in a multicultural setting, a place with students from a hundred different countries," he says in a deep, gravelly drawl, laughing.

Part of UMBC's success in attracting and graduating minority students is due to its well-known Meyerhoff Scholars program, which focuses on students in STEM fields (science, technology, engineering, and mathematics). Under Hrabowski's leadership, though, UMBC has insisted on a vision of education that is broad based, eschewing models that look like vocational training and instead encouraging students to educate themselves as human beings first and foremost. For this reason the school has been committed to attracting and training students in the arts and humanities as well as science and engineering, and that's where Berman and the Dresher Center come into play. "Reading and thinking are at the heart of success in any society," Hrabowski insists. "If we can get a child to read and think, we can teach her to do the math. In all the things we're doing in the city you'll see us focusing on the arts and humanities as well as math and science." As others are doing today, he speaks of STEAM fields instead of STEM fields, because "the arts are very important in helping us with creativity and getting the students to connect." For this reason, along with its Meyerhoff Scholars, UMBC has invested in a Humanities Scholars program to "attract a cohort of particularly talented young people who, over time, will have an impact on the intellectual atmosphere of the campus and will make significant contributions to the humanities in society."

Under the leadership of visionaries like Freeman Hrabowski, state colleges like UMBC have made extraordinary inroads into providing the kind of education that gives disadvantaged families a fighting chance. In 1960 less than 3 percent of blacks and 11 percent of whites had a college education. Today, in contrast, 20 percent of blacks and 37 percent of whites have completed college. But enormous challenges remain, and the current trend is in exactly the wrong direction. In fact, states are in the midst of defunding public institutions at an unprecedented rate, which has an outsize impact on minorities and the economically disadvantaged. The University of California system, which has led the nation in enrolling and graduating an economically diverse student body, has seen precipitous drops in its support of students who qualify for Pell grants. At UC San Diego, which five years ago led the nation with 46 percent of its students qualifying for Pell grants, the number saw a decline of 20 percent by 2017. Private universities have been using their endowments to try to pick up the slack, with 20 percent of the student body at a college like Pomona qualifying for Pell grants and, more important, paying a median seven thousand dollars in net tuition, far less than the median charge for students in the UC system. Harvard and Stanford, with the nation's largest endowments at around $1.5 million per student, are also the cheapest for the 15 percent of their students who qualify for Pell grants, with the median student paying around five thousand dollars. With an endowment around one tenth the size of those richest schools, Johns Hopkins lies in the middle of the bell curve, with 12 percent qualifying for Pell grants and the median student paying around thirteen thousand dollars.

Princeton University, with its long and hallowed reputation as one of the truly exclusive bastions of privilege in the country (which F. Scott Fitzgerald referred to in his novel *This Side of Paradise* as "the pleasantest country club in America"), has been leading the charge. As recently as 2003, a mere 6.5 percent of Princeton's entering class received Pells; but by 2017 this number had risen more than threefold, to 21 percent. Princeton's positive movement in this metric is part of its effort to diversify not just racially and ethnically, but socioeconomically across the board, by recruiting and graduating FLI students—"first-generation, low-income." Ultimately this strategy will only work if schools provide an adequate support network to make up for the gap between what these students can count on and the sorts of resources and family support networks that their wealthier peers take for granted. In Princeton's case, the strategy appears to be working, with the current FLI graduation rate of 93 percent only a few points lower than the overall average.

As terrific as these advances are, for the overall problem they are like a mouse trying to pull a locomotive. Uphill. As the columnist David Leonhardt writes in his coverage of these figures from the third iteration of the *New York Times'* College Access Index, "The United States is investing less in college education at the same time that the globalized, digital economy has made that education more important than ever. Gaps between college graduates and everyone else are growing in one realm of society after another, including unemployment, wealth and health. Given these trends, the declines in state funding are stunning. It's as if our society were deliberately trying to restrict opportunities and worsen income inequality." Even today, two thirds of Americans do not have anyone in their family who is going to college or has a degree, and where most people who went to college in the middle of last century graduated with a degree, today only about half do. In fact, today, people in the bottom 25 percent of the income spectrum have only a 10 percent chance of graduating from college.

These statistics point to an insidious trend in higher education. The rising costs of college are making it prohibitive for most families, whose real incomes have stagnated over the last decades. And tragically, federal money for college goes unused, because kids don't know about it and fail to apply by the deadline, March 1. This is the reason that Hrabowski's team preaches "deadline by Valentine's," a reminder in the form of a jingle to make sure kids have applied for aid by the March 1 cutoff. But support for students who are applying for federal aid is paramount, since the applications process is burdensome and has become more difficult to navigate. Indeed, the online function that allowed students to populate forms electronically with required financial information failed in 2016, leaving millions of kids with mountains of forms to fill out and little way of doing so before the deadline. As of this writing, the Trump administration's 2018 federal budget calls for the elimination of federal funding for loan programs that subsidize college education for the poor.

If going to college matters so much, that's in part because the kind of education that kids in the United States only start to get in college matters. That is, what matters is a quality engagement with ideas, with language, and with literature, as opposed to focusing exclusively on one field in the hopes of its leading to a specific career. While it's true that European societies don't have substantially higher university attendance rates than the United States does, what we call a liberal arts education has by and large already been attained by the time Europeans leave secondary education and either attend university, enroll in trade school, or begin to work. This is why I believe that well-meaning proposals like that of the sociologists Katherine Newman and Hella Winston to reinvest in trade schools in the United States to spur the growth of a non-college-educated middle class would not be effective here to the same extent as it is in Europe. For better or for worse, it is now the case that college has become the prerequisite for socioeconomic advancement in the U.S., and the answer is to invest in college and college preparedness—for everyone.

Community colleges are key in this process, and continuing the movement to make these as affordable as possible is essential. At present, more than 40 percent of the country's eighteen million college students are attending community colleges, not four-year institutions. This is in comparison to less than half of one percent who attend one of the Ivy League schools, as Gail Mellow, president of LaGuardia Community College, has reported. Despite this overwhelming plurality of students served, community colleges receive a relatively small proportion of the public resources allocated to higher education, at times because of state regulations requiring certain percentages of state and federal aid to be used on full-time students at four-year institutions. They also receive only a tiny fraction of the over forty billion dollars in charitable giving that colleges receive each year, further hampering their ability to fulfill their crucial social role.

Moreover, if we only invest in educational opportunity in urban areas, a major cause of inequality and divisiveness in the United States will only get worse. New legislation in Tennessee and several other states has now guaranteed that two years of community college will be free for anyone who cannot afford to pay, and it is making an enormous difference already. Enrollments in Tennessee's community colleges are up by more than 30 percent, and student debt is dropping. Across the state, counties are hosting Free Application for Federal Student Aid (FAFSA) workshops to help students fill out the applications for Pell grants. The state then kicks in whatever funding is still needed to ensure that the student pays no tuition at all until graduating from the two-year college. Tennessee now leads the nation in FAFSA applications, with almost three fourths of college seniors filling them out.

While the plan is plenty controversial, New York governor Andrew Cuomo recently signed into law New York's version of the plan, the first in the nation to offer free tuition at all public two- and four-year institutions. The hitches (there are several) in the New York plan are, first, that recipients of the "Excelsior Scholarships" must agree to stay in New York for the same number of years they have received the scholarship for; it is also limited to families making under $125,000 and only covers tuition, leaving aside the often-expensive fees and charges for room and board. What this means in practical terms is that New York's plan effectively only helps a certain stratum of middle-class families, since the poor are already receiving aid for tuition when they attend college, and the new scholarship doesn't help with the additional costs that can be so prohibitive.

Nevertheless, these changes are at least going in the right direction. Some form of quality college education should eventually be attainable for all students, no matter what their socioeconomic status is and, I would argue, no matter what their immigration status is. We all benefit from an educated populace. We will all benefit from a less divided, more equitable nation. This is not to say that universal access to college is a panacea. The factors that determine inequality extend far beyond access to college. Indeed, we can imagine a society in which the education needed to become a full-fledged citizen would be guaranteed by the end of secondary school; in which well-paying jobs that supported a family at a comfortable level were available for those who had attained this basic level; and in which college were simply one choice among others, leading to different and not necessarily better futures. In many ways and for many, but by no means all, Americans, this was an accurate description of society from after World War II to the early 1970s. Not anymore.

If we want to create that kind of a society, but this time without the exclusions that have marred our community, how we educate our citizens is a good place to start. The spread of education, and specifically college education, will not only redistribute wealth by giving those at the bottom a hand up the economic ladder. It will also help encourage the kind of civic participation that will help all of us have an increased stake in our community, and equip us with the cognitive and social tools to help change it for the better.

DIVERSITY IN HIGHER ED

I cannot say it often enough: the single greatest predictor of success in our society today is the four-year college degree, at least in part because of what that degree says about a student's socioeconomic status even before going to college. While there is room for debate about whether it makes more sense to address this problem by increasing the numbers of people who complete college or trying to reverse the trends that seem to make college indispensable—for example, by emphasizing trade schools rather than college—it remains a demographic fact that the college degree is today the clearest border between the haves and the have-nots. Given this state of affairs, we need to be asking what factors determine who gets a college degree and who doesn't.

Despite his Germanic name, Erwin Hesse is a U.S.-born Latino. His father is a construction worker from Peru, and his mother is a Salvadoran immigrant who cleans homes for a living. Hesse grew up in Wheaton, Maryland, a suburb of Washington, D.C., with a large Latino population. I was curious to hear his story. How did the son of working-class, Latin American immigrants who grew up in a blue-collar, immigrant neighborhood become the first person in his family to earn a college degree? More than that, Hesse is now finishing the research that will lead to his PhD at the Johns Hopkins School of Education. The topic of his research: how college admission officers can work to increase diversity on college campuses. In other words, here is someone who knows, both from the research and from personal experience, the challenges that face minority and immigrant children who are trying to get a college degree.

Hesse attended the public schools in his neighborhood and, like most of his friends, barely scraped the grades together to get from one year to the next. Far more interested in hanging out and playing basketball than in studying, he had no idea when he finally graduated what he would do next and had not even begun to think about looking for a job. One day on his way to the courts with his friends he was passing the local community college when the thought occurred to him—to this day he's still not sure why it did—to go in and ask some questions. He asked his friends to hold on while he went in, but they laughed and continued on their way to the courts. So he went inside on his own, found the admissions office, and asked what he needed to do to go to college.

Hesse had talked to people about college before. The previous year he, like all the other rising seniors in his school, had had a meeting with his school's college counselor. The man, whom Hesse had never met before, scanned his grades and told him that college was not an option for him. Hesse recalls not being particularly surprised. "I mean, the guy told me college was not for me, and I figured, he's probably right." But he also recalls feeling a flash of anger and the thought, "Why shouldn't it be an option for me?" Now he thinks that that feeling may have been hiding under the surface the day he opened the doors to his local community college.

The fact that so many students are dissuaded from applying or simply don't think of college as an option for them is one reason behind new programs such as the College Advising Corps. The CAC sends recent college graduates to poor, often rural school districts to work for two years as college advisers in schools whose own counselors are often so consumed by having to tend to the emotional needs of hundreds of students that they have little time left for advising students about college. CAC advisers find that often kids have very little idea of what applying to college entails, and with financial pressures at home, don't have parents who are particularly supportive of the idea in the first place.

Once he faced a college admissions officer, Hesse had a different experience. The man acted as though it was completely natural for Hesse to want to go to college. He explained to him that by paying a simple fee, at the time twenty-five dollars, he would be enrolled as a student. After that, he would need to select a course of studies, and then he could register for courses. The courses would cost something, of course. But then the admissions officer explained something else that Hesse didn't know. If he submitted the Free Application for Federal Student Aid he could qualify for federal Pell grants that would cover the tuition costs of the courses he took. The admissions officer showed him how to fill out the form and reminded him of the March 1 deadline.

Faced with the choice of what to study, Hesse chose a field that is surprisingly popular for young people in his situation: criminology. As he explains it now, he grew up watching the police assume that kids like himself and his friends were criminals, and he wanted to understand the law and see if there was something he could do about it. To illustrate what led him to make his choice, he told me a story about when he was in high school and was waiting at a bus stop with a friend of his, who was black. Although it was a warm day, the two of them were wearing bulky jackets. Suddenly a patrol car pulled up and two officers jumped out and demanded that they open their jackets. Hesse, terrified, did what he was told; but his friend, who had a more rebellious attitude, told the cops that he hadn't done anything wrong and to leave them alone. Within seconds they were on top of him, pinning him to the ground and hitting him, before pulling him into their car with a stern warning to Hesse to mind his own business. When Hesse saw his friend the next day he had a black eye and swollen lip but laughed off the whole experience, giving Hesse to understand that he must be pretty naïve not to realize that this was how cops behaved with kids like them.

Hesse took to his studies, applied himself, and excelled. Two years later he was accepted as a transfer student to the University of Maryland, College Park, where he was given a scholarship to cover the much more significant tuition he would be paying. After two more years he graduated and applied for the PhD program in the School of Education at Johns Hopkins, where he is now finishing his degree while working in the admissions office at the Johns Hopkins Carey Business School. In his doctoral work, Hesse is particularly focused on how to help undocumented students get a college degree. When I asked him why the specific focus on the undocumented, he put it this way: "Look, I was at best a mediocre student before I went to college. By sheer luck I pulled myself together just in time, and there were resources there for me to make this all possible. But what if I were undocumented? In my research I've come across kids who grew up as Americans, who are brilliant and hardworking, and who didn't even know they were undocumented until they got older and their parents had to warn them not to do this or that. But because of their status they don't qualify for federal funds and can't even get the education I managed to get. I am haunted by that injustice."

I met Hesse by chance when I invited Dan-el Padilla Peralta to lecture at Hopkins. While Padilla Peralta is a well-regarded classicist, I hadn't invited him to speak about ancient Latin texts. Instead, I asked him to talk about his personal story. You see, he arrived as a child from the Dominican

Republic and grew up in New York City homeless shelters after his mother decided to raise her two sons in the United States. Through no fault of his own, he spent his entire youth as an undocumented immigrant. He was one of those kids whom Hesse talked about as brilliant and hardworking. Without the benefit of the video games his friends at school were always playing in the afternoons, Padilla Peralta got lost in the few books that had been left behind when the shelter he was living in was converted from a school. For years, after curfew but before the lights were turned out at the end of the day, he would spend countless hours reading and feeding his voracious appetite for knowledge.

As it turned out, Padilla Peralta benefited from an extraordinary stroke of luck. A volunteer in a publicly run after-school program, recognizing his intelligence, took a liking to him and became a kind of mentor. He eventually got the attention of one of New York City's most prestigious private schools, which invited him to apply and then gave him a full scholarship. From there Padilla Peralta went on to Princeton, where he was the salutatorian. A few weeks before giving his address in Latin at graduation, he revealed his immigration status in an interview with the *Wall Street Journal*, and his story became public. He went on to tell his story in his acclaimed memoir, *Undocumented: A Dominican Boy's Odyssey from a Homeless Shelter to the Ivy League*. From Princeton, he went to get his PhD in classics from Stanford University and is now back at Princeton as an assistant professor. He has since gotten married and, for the first time, he is a legal resident of the United States.

Padilla Peralta's and Hesse's stories raise important questions about access to education in the United States. As Hesse points out, they are separated by nothing more than the caprice of fate. Like Padilla Peralta or so many of his friends in Wheaton, Maryland, Erwin could have grown up undocumented and never would have had the chance to reform himself and become the educator he is now becoming. On the other hand, Padilla Peralta, despite his brilliance, could far more likely *not* have been discovered and mentored, *not* been accepted with scholarships to the best private schools, and *not* become a professor at one of the world's finest universities.

Padilla Peralta's story also brings up vital questions about prejudice and how we think of merit in higher education. Padilla Peralta, who is black, recalls a conversation with a white, wealthy classmate from his prep school in New York that took place as the two of them were vying for acceptance at top schools. As they shared an elevator ride the white classmate looked at him and told him he was lucky. "Why?" Padilla Peralta wanted to know. "Because of this," the classmate said, pinching the skin on Padilla Peralta's arm. Astoundingly, a young, white, privileged man, whose family's wealth all but guaranteed him the best in life at every stage of his education, could think that Padilla Peralta—poor, undocumented, and only at that school by dint of his brains and hard work—was more fortunate than he, *not* because of the undeniable luck that led to his having been discovered and mentored, but because of the color of his skin.

If we're serious about diversity, we have to consider more than race and ethnicity. Increasingly colleges are recognizing the importance of emphasizing economic factors in considering the makeup of their admitted classes. A 2016 study funded by the Jack Kent Cooke Foundation found that little to no progress had been made since 2000 in increasing the representation of economically disadvantaged kids at top colleges, where those from the lowest socioeconomic quartile still amounted to less than 3 percent of student populations. Such "undermatching" of qualified students from poorer families often leads to them paying more to attend less prestigious schools that in turn don't have the resources to support them in the way that better-endowed colleges could have. In the words of the report, "Hidden within these numbers are thousands of students from economically disadvantaged households who, despite attending less-resourced schools and growing up with less intellectual stimulation and advantages, do extremely well in school, love learning, are extraordinarily bright and capable, and would do very well at selective institutions if offered admissions. They are just being ignored."

Often the kids who are undermatched simply don't know that they could be eligible for an Ivy League school, and furthermore have no idea that they could potentially attend such a school entirely tuition-free. Kids who grow up in rural school districts with fewer resources, for instance, might be in a school served by a single college counselor who herself isn't aware that a given student could be a good match for a distant elite college. As Caroline Hoxby, the Stanford economist whose work first brought national attention to this issue, put it, "Your typical guidance counselor in the United States has about 400 students with whom he or she is trying to deal." Getting the word out to rural kids can be particularly challenging, given that it often depends on admissions officers going places in person. As Bruce Poch, then dean of admissions at Pomona College, said in 2010, the "reality of college recruitment until this time has been largely based upon school visits and alumni attending college fairs to broaden awareness of our college brands. And, that reality, affected by efficiency needs and budget limits, has meant college admission and recruitment staffs visited more urban centers to achieve geographic goals."

Sometimes it just comes down to cultural differences. Emily Steele, a senior at Fleming County High School in northeastern Kentucky, is applying to colleges and wants to study biology. She would have been eligible for a number of major state schools, including the universities of Michigan, Alabama, and Kentucky, but her parents worried about her safety and felt strongly she should stay nearby. So, in place of the hour-and-forty-minute drive to the University of Kentucky's flagship campus in Lexington, she applied to Morehead State University, which she can get to in about half an hour. For Steele, Lexington is a big city. "There are shootings," she says. "I would rather be safe and close." In her family, in which she is the fourth of five kids, Steele is the first to even apply for college. As she puts it about her community, "There are a lot of kids that don't think they are good enough for college."

The combination of these factors has been particularly pernicious for rural whites. A study by two sociologists, Thomas Espenshade and Alexandria Walton Radford, showed that while for minority applicants, being socioeconomically disadvantaged helped their admissions prospects, for whites, "it was the reverse. An upper-middle-class white applicant was three times more likely to be admitted than a lower-class white with similar qualifications," as conservative columnist Ross Douthat wrote. Already in

2010, Douthat observed that "The most underrepresented groups on elite campuses often aren't racial minorities; they're working-class whites (and white Christians in particular) from conservative states and regions."

In retrospect his concern was prophetic, given the kind of political sea change that brought Donald Trump into the White House in 2016. As Douthat went on to write in that same column: "This breeds paranoia, among elite and non-elites alike. Among the white working class, increasingly the most reliable Republican constituency, alienation from the American meritocracy fuels the kind of racially tinged conspiracy theories that [Glenn] Beck and others have exploited—that Barack Obama is a foreign-born Marxist hand-picked by a shadowy liberal cabal, that a Wall Street-Washington axis wants to flood the country with Third World immigrants, and so forth." Better late than never, colleges have heard this message and are responding. A poll conducted by the website *Inside Higher Ed* and Gallup in the fall of 2017 showed that just over 30 percent of public colleges and around 25 percent of private colleges have decided to increase recruitment of lower-income white students.

FROM INEQUALITY TO DIVISIVENESS

I live in a wooded area of northern Baltimore. Where dwellers of other parts of the city might be awoken by traffic noises in the night, in my house it is just as often the sounds of nature that keep us up. Take one recent night when my wife and I were awoken by an almost otherworldly screeching, a sound you might imagine coming from the gullet of a Ringwraith from J. R. R. Tolkien's *Lord of the Rings*. It clearly freaked our dogs out as well, and before I was fully awake I was stumbling down the stairs vainly trying to shush two canines in thrall to their instincts to protect the domicile from alien intrusion. As some readers will have immediately recognized, the alien in this case was small and red with a bushy tail, and was on the prowl for rabbits or rodents. I've seen the neighborhood fox in the lingering twilight before, but only occasionally have I heard his soul-wrenching screech.

The fox finally moved on and I calmed the dogs and made my way back to bed. But after all the commotion I found I was unable to get back to sleep. As I lay awake reflecting on the intruder and the tumult he caused, my mind jumped unexpectedly to a radio interview I had heard at some point during the prior week and then forgotten, until now. The interview was with a Nicole Humphrey, who voiced her opposition to a plan to build a housing complex in her neighborhood in Frisco City, Texas, that would have some units set aside for holders of Section 8 housing choice vouchers, intended to allow low-income families to pay their rent and stay off the streets. "In this neighborhood, most of us are stay-at-home moms with young kids," Humphrey told NPR. "The lifestyle that goes with Section 8 is usually working, single moms or people who are struggling to keep their heads above water. I feel so bad saying that," she added. "It's just not people who are the same class as us." What stuck with me most clearly, though, was what came next. When the reporter asked her about her views on the opportunities that living in her neighborhood could bring to a low-income mother, including, most obviously, access to a good school, she became audibly defensive: "The problem with that is I hear a lot of the unfair of: 'Oh, we haven't been given this or that, or we haven't been afforded things you have been afforded.' I don't look at multimillionaires and think, 'Why don't I have a yacht?'"

As I lay in bed unable to return to sleep, I wondered why my thoughts had come back to Nicole Humphrey. When I heard her compare a poor single mother's desire to get an education for her child to her desire to have the same yacht as a millionaire, implying that the one was as unreasonable as the other, I dismissed it offhand and forgot about the interview. But in the insomniac wake of the incident of the fox, in the newly quiet dark of my room, I suddenly grasped her strange and frightening logic. In one fell analogy, Humphrey had revealed an attitude about the common good that is most certainly held, at least unconsciously, by many Americans. According to this assumption, where one lives, including public space and services, from streets to public education, is a natural outgrowth of one's wealth, which in turn is a sign of self-worth, of effort, and of talent. According to this model we sort ourselves instinctually into enclaves according to our financial ability, and it is right that we do so, and someone who cannot afford to buy in my neighborhood has no more right to such public services than I have to a yacht that I couldn't afford to buy myself.

Key to this theory is that people who hold it are not, at least consciously, being elitist or, even worse, racist. As Humphrey insists, her concerns are not about race—she claims that her neighborhood is racially diverse already—but about being understood by those who live in her community. "People see that I'm upper middle class, that I'm a woman who stays at home, who is kept by her husband, and instantly there's no clout. My opinion doesn't matter," as she puts it. "They look at me and think, 'She has never experienced a problem we're having.'" According to this model, those who are of my class are fundamentally like me; the others, those who could only live in my neighborhood with the help of a voucher, well, they are different. Like a different species, they don't fit in. Their intrusion into our world upsets us; it feels uncanny. So we set up walls to keep them out.

This dynamic is at work in myriad ways in zoning policies that function to segregate even those cities that proclaim themselves the most deregulated in the country, like Houston, Texas. In the upper-middle-class Galleria district of Houston, a recent proposal to build affordable housing units with federal tax credits for more than two hundred families was met, as such proposals often are, with vociferous resistance from the neighborhood's mostly white residents. When a black fair-housing advocate defended the proposal at a public hearing, telling the nominally progressive audience that the time had come for them to "stop succumbing to misleading rhetoric, and begin practicing the inclusive lifestyles that many of you claim to lead," she was greeted by choruses of boos. As the *Times* later reported, "The outcome was familiar. Elected officials sided with the opposition. And an effort to bring affordable housing to an affluent, majority-white neighborhood failed in Houston, where low-income housing is overwhelmingly confined to poor, predominantly black and Latino communities."

Restrictive zoning laws are one of three strategies that the economist Richard Reeves has identified as ways the upper middle class ensure that their own children remain in the top socioeconomic quintile and that those below them aren't able to join them. What's important to grasp is that exclusionary zoning laws are entirely deliberate attempts of the upper middle class to safeguard their privileges and keep others from sharing them, not, as we may like to assume, "the result of the free workings of the housing market." Indeed, these restrictions are driven "democratically," by neighborhood associations mobilizing to prevent the construction of "high-density" housing in neighborhoods consisting of single-family homes. As law professor Lee Anne Fennell has argued, "With exclusionary zoning in place, the purchase of a large quantity of housing is effectively bundled with the opportunity to live in a 'good' neighborhood and to send one's children to the best public schools." She adds that "perversely, federal tax policy makes attainment of these sought-after houses easier for those making more money; they will be in a higher tax bracket and will enjoy larger mortgage interest and property tax deductions, and therefore lower real costs, than their lower-income competitors." Reeves puts this in a nutshell: "We are using the tax system to help richer people buy bigger houses near the best schools."

While zoning works on its own to support the increased impenetrability of the upper middle class's enclaves, it is thus inextricably intertwined with education, and education has a major role to play in all the mechanisms we use to build and maintain those walls. As Reeves puts it, "An upper middle-class income is almost always accompanied by more education." This remains true whether families opt for private school, which vastly more of this class do (18 percent of upper-middle-class families, in contrast with 9 percent of middle-class and only 4 percent of poor families), or if they remain with public schools—for the simple reason that they can afford to live where the excellent public schools are, and most public schools continue to admit students based on where they live: "Schools that admit students based on geography become more socially segregated. Geography also has a strong influence on the development of social capital—the ties and institutions of civic life, from community associations, clubs, and churches to informal networks and groups."

Social capital, in turn, is reinforced by the clustering of kids from upper-middle-class families into the same schools. Part of what private schools are selling their prospective clients is, as the colleague who had moved from France, Marion, noted, that your kids will only be surrounded by the kids of "parents like you." Nowadays, "parents like you" is ostensibly purified of racial connotations. Indeed, private schools tend to go out of their way to talk about diversity, and will use tuition assistance when possible to ensure that some children from black and Latino families attend. But almost by definition the families with the knowledge and wherewithal to seek admittance to these schools and apply for financial aid are those that have started to amass the social capital that allows them entry to that world in the first place. They have implicitly become "parents like you." In other words, the framework of "diversity," while ostensibly inclusive and certainly a worthwhile goal, tends to hide the structural inequalities that schools continue to reproduce.

It is instructive in this light to recall the 1978 Supreme Court decision that permitted affirmative action policies only insofar as they were intended to augment a school's diversity as a positive good, and not if they were intended to redress specific historical wrongs. In his searing dissent, Justice Thurgood Marshall implicitly predicted the effects of this logic of diversity, a logic that inundates colleges and the workplace today, as an allowance to disregard historical inequality. In his words, "The position of the Negro today in America is the tragic but inevitable consequence of centuries of unequal treatment. Measured by any benchmark of comfort or achievement, meaningful equality remains a distant dream for the Negro." The logic of diversity, insofar as it allows us to turn a blind eye to a history of discrimination and prejudice, effectively permits any group to claim the same right for its representation to be protected and affirmed. In some cases these protections are justified, but as we are seeing today, even white supremacists have learned to justify hatred on a spurious claim to being a threatened cultural group. Likewise, the masculinist and often abusive culture of Silicon Valley has openly embraced natural outgrowths of diversity, like cognitive diversity, to argue that a bunch of white guys thinking different thoughts is as valuable an expression of diversity as the inclusion of people of different cultures, races, or sexual orientations. When we allow history rather than diversity to be our beacon, we are forced to remember that inequality has real causes, and that to rectify that, we might have to do more than just celebrate stuff.

THE REVENGE OF THE MIDDLE CLASS

In the summer of 2012 a Houston-based drilling company, disregarding the advice of one of its own engineers, pierced the top of a massive salt dome more than a mile beneath the town of Bayou Corne, Louisiana, about an hour's drive to the west of New Orleans. The dome's implosion caused tremors that damaged some 350 houses, among them the home of Mike Schaff, who felt the earth shake as he stepped through his front door and watched as his concrete floor split down the middle.

The company, Texas Brine, denied culpability and then proceeded to request permission from the state of Louisiana to dump its waste water into the sinkhole, which in the years since has spread into a thirty-five-acre underground toxic stew, leaking enough methane and other gases that locals avoid lighting matches for fear of erupting into a spontaneous fireball. Schaff, his house and neighborhood destroyed, has since become an environmental activist, organizing protests and petitions, marching on the state capitol, and writing scores of letters. He also continued to be an active citizen—voting for Republican and Tea Party candidates in local and state elections, all of whom promise to decrease the environmental regulations and taxes that burden companies like Texas Brine. Schaff hopes his political engagement will hasten the abolition of the EPA, which to his mind "was grabbing authority and tax money to take on a fictive mission: lessening the impact of global warming."

The sociologist Arlie Hochschild has a parable to explain the emotional drive behind voters like Mike Schaff. In that parable, there is a long line of people marching up a hill toward a promised land of wealth and dignity. Schaff and the men around him have been marching for a long time, respecting those who are ahead of them, trusting they will get there in their own time. Then, from well behind them, come new groups: blacks, women, immigrants, refugees, even animals, and the government holds back Schaff's part of the line to let them in. "I live your analogy," Schaff tells her when she recounts her parable to him. If this story captures your worldview, can a platform based on racial and gender equality change your mind?

Since the beginning of the 1970s the U.S. economy has stretched into an exponential curve, meaning that wherever you fit on the income ladder, the difference between you and the people just ahead of you seems far greater than between you and those right behind you. Everyone knows that "they" make too much, but everyone wants to draw that line right above where he or she currently is. They all share an interest in flattening the line and raising their common standard of living, but instead they struggle among themselves and hand over all power to those at the very top.

For Thomas Frank, Schaff and his fellow voters would be the classic example of working folks who are fooled by cultural politics to vote against their own economic interests. But as the moral psychologist Jonathan Haidt has shown, our political judgments, like our moral ones, are primarily intuitive and only secondarily reasoned out: "Moral intuitions arise automatically and almost instantaneously, long before moral reasoning has a chance to get started, and those first intuitions tend to drive our later reasoning." As Hochschild sees it, agreeing with Haidt against Frank, people like Mike Schaff are not being fooled into voting against their interests by cultural politics or fake news sites; rather, their embrace of cultural politics and attraction to fringe websites *are the very expression* of their interests, of their identity, their culture.

The current culture in what we now call red states, rural and deep suburban areas in the Midwest and the South, is one of siege and revolt. The numbers are in for white, middle-class families in these areas, and they aren't good. In Hochschild's recounting, "Across the country red states are poorer and have more teen mothers, more divorce, worse health, more obesity, more trauma-related deaths, more low-birth-weight babies, and lower school enrollment." The life expectancy gap between a typical blue state like Connecticut and a southern red state like Louisiana replicates that between the United States and a developing country like Nicaragua. And overall economic depression correlates with school performance, such that Louisiana ranks in the bottom three states in math and reading scores, and sends only 7 percent of its population on to professional or postgraduate degrees, while nearly 40 percent of Connecticut's citizens attain a bachelor's degree.

These statistics represent a significant downward trend for white families, who had enjoyed relatively uniform economic security prior to 1970. Between 1970 and 2000 the percentage of white children living in high-poverty neighborhoods increased from 25 percent to 40 percent. A 2011 Brookings Institution study found that "compared to 2000, residents of extreme-poverty neighborhoods in 2005–9 were more likely to be white, native-born, high school or college graduates, homeowners, and not receiving public assistance." This change most often occurs as a result of longtime local employers either moving, shutting down, or downsizing, leaving a community with few employment opportunities. This is what happened in Middletown, Ohio, when the local steel producer, Armco, merged with the Japanese firm Kawasaki. Without high-paying jobs to keep them, some locals opt to leave, if they can. Those who remain, perhaps because they owe too much on their house to sell, face not only declining job prospects, but fewer opportunities for social enrichment of any kind.

As J. D. Vance reports on Middletown, his hometown, "The last I checked, there was only an Arby's, a discount grocery store, and a Chinese buffet in what was once a Middletown center of commerce." These changing circumstances can be slow to sink in as a new generation reaches school age. In the words of local high school teacher Jennifer McGuffey, "A lot of students just don't understand what's out there . . . You have the kids who plan on being baseball players but don't even play on the high school team because the coach is mean to them. Then you have those who aren't doing very well in school, and when you try to talk to them about what they are going to do, they talk about [Armco-Kawasaki]. 'Oh, I can get a job at AK. My uncle works there.' It's like they can't make a connection between the situation in this town and the lack of jobs at AK." The result is, in some respects, a lost generation of students, only 80 percent of whom will even graduate high school; only a small minority of those high school graduates will make it through college.

The dearth of college opportunities for students like these is partly due to state universities closing their doors on the people they were intended to serve. Take a flagship state school like the University of Michigan. Despite the words of its third and longest-serving president, James Angell, that the university existed to provide "an uncommon education for the common man," Michigan now caters largely to the upper crust both from Michigan and around the country, with 10 percent of its student body coming from the top 1 percent of wealthy families, and only 16 percent coming from the bottom 60 percent. While the university has recently begun efforts to increase its economic diversity along with its racial and gender diversity, the median income of its students' families is still three times the statewide average. As the superintendent of schools from a nearby low-income school district puts it of the students in his schools, "It's ingrained at an early age—'You're not going to go there.'" University of Illinois at Chicago English professor Walter Benn Michaels puts it just as succinctly: "If you're a poor person in Michigan and you don't hate the University of Michigan, you deserve to."

Hate may seem like a strong word, but it resonates today. In fact, there is overwhelming evidence that middle-class anger at stagnating economic conditions and the perceived dismissive attitudes of the political establishment was responsible, more than any other single factor, for putting Donald Trump into the presidency. As one economist has written, "Donald Trump won the American presidential election because the middle class was disgruntled with the joint Democratic and Republican party establishment." Steven Rosefielde, who wrote these words, believes that "the common people's grievances are not figments of their imaginations," and goes on to list some of them: "It is no longer possible for middle-class workers to support their children's many desires, and other state-imposed obligations and intrusions have diminished the quality of family life. A worker who started his/her career 40 years ago is substantially worse off today than when he/she began. There are no prospects for a brighter tomorrow. Ordinary people sense the threat of technological displacement and flooded labor markets. This is hardly the stuff of the American Dream. The future for the middle class seems grim enough to have put Donald Trump over the top."

The reaction against the establishment entails a rejection of the political establishment's preferred educational policies, as embodied in federal public education programs like No Child Left Behind and Common Core, a universally despised symbol on the right of big government overreach. Rosefielde again: "The establishment is wedded to its No Child Left Behind/Common Core educational agenda that attempts to use education to solve both America's sociological and economic problems. It does not want to hear that it cannot have it all, without grasping that 'having it all' shortchanges the majority of students and is shallow."

While it is true that political divisiveness has had a large role to play in cultivating the kind of society and economy that breeds inequality, it is equally true that inequality helps foster the resentments and even hatred that have become a hallmark of today's political climate. The rich and the upper middle class in America live starkly different lives than the rest of the country. In some measurable ways, different also means better. While the top quintile obviously can afford more stuff, they also are healthier, live longer, and maintain more stable families. While divorce rates are high for most Americans, the upper middle class tend to get married and stay married. They also tend to marry people like themselves, which has the secondary effect of further concentrating their wealth and earning power.

Children who come from economically disadvantaged families are also far more likely to die at war, for the simple reason that our military is made up of kids from this class, with very little representation from the rich or upper middle class. The military, as Bill Bishop reports, "finds the highest proportion of its recruits among good kids who have few prospects for decent jobs or further education." He goes straight to the source in support of this contention, quoting from the Department of Defense: "propensity to enlist is lower for high-quality youth, youth with better-educated parents, and youth planning to attend college." The identification of some youth as "high-quality" is remarkably frank, and decidedly chilling.

The attitude that implicitly or explicitly derides kids from lower economic strata as something other than high quality pervades class consciousness in the United States. It also leads to high levels of resentment among those who have been excluded from the higher echelons. Vance forcefully describes the kinds of attitudes that develop among those excluded from the upper crust. While many liberal commentators saw conservatives' distrust and even hatred of President Obama in purely racial terms, Vance's recollections complicate that narrative, showing how racial resentment could be intertwined with something along the lines of envy.

As he puts it, "Barack Obama strikes at the heart of our deepest insecurities. He is a good father while many of us aren't. He wears suits to his job while we wear overalls, if we're lucky enough to have a job at all. His wife tells us that we shouldn't be feeding our children certain foods, and we hate her for it—not because we think she's wrong but because we know she's right." Granted, such class resentment is not always free of racial bias; generations of hillbillies likely had no problem with white men wearing suits while running the U.S. government. But there is a case to be made that envy and resentment run far deeper than skin color in this case, which might explain the otherwise curious fact that Trump may well have won in 2016 on the strength of voters who had previously voted *for* Obama. They were hoping for a change in status that simply never came.

The resentments that come from the starkly different levels of military service and the risks they entail can be even more visceral. Vance recounts in vivid detail an experience he had in a college class after he had served in the Marine Corps for four years, including a stint in Iraq:

During an undergraduate seminar in foreign policy, I listened as a nineteen-year-old classmate with a hideous beard spouted off about the Iraq war. He explained that those fighting the war were typically less intelligent than those (like him) who immediately went to college. It showed, he argued, in the wanton way soldiers butchered and disrespected Iraqi civilians . . .

As the student prattled on, I thought about the never-ending training on how to respect Iraqi culture—never show anyone the bottom of your foot, never address a woman in traditional Muslim garb without first speaking to a male relative . . . I thought about my friends who were covered in third-degree burns, "lucky" to have survived an IED attack in the Al-Qaim region of Iraq. And here was this dipshit in a spotty beard telling our class that we murdered people for sport.

Vance's account is powerful in part because, even now, from the vantage of a successful law and publishing career, and an upper-middle-class life in San Francisco, he still seethes at the injustice of the attitudes he perceived at the time. His account catches and to a certain extent helps explain the mutual "repulsion" that the radio exchange I detailed earlier between Michelle Goldberg and caller Scott evinced. It helps explain why the walls we have spent a generation building are so hard to break through.

What is it that makes people decide where the limits of their bonds to others should lie? Richard Rorty once argued that ethnocentrism, that label so often tossed around by the multicultural left, was in fact a universal attribute of human communities. What he meant is that each of us is born into a network of values and identifications that are determined by our particular clan. That clan can be relatively broad—a religious or ethnic group, for instance—or restricted—just those who are related by blood or marriage, say. Recognizing the universality of ethnocentrism was, for Rorty, essential to overcoming it. Nothing could be less realistic than assuming that it would be natural or easy for everyone in the world to love his neighbors as much as himself or his own family, much less someone in another part of the world with a language and culture utterly different from his. Instead, Rorty argued, we should conceive of our actual and potential loyalties as an almost infinite number of concentric circles. The goal of a liberal society, he believed, is to gently expand those circles, to enlarge our sense of community by creating a culture and ethos that supports identification and empathy with those beyond our most proximate neighbors.

It seems to me that the emphasis in American culture since the 1970s has moved away from this liberal ideal. The idealization of the individual, his or her racial, ethnic, or gender identity, and his or her desires and rights as a consumer, has been strengthened by the current extremes of income inequality, by way of a they-have-theirs-so-I-should-have-mine-too attitude. This means that our natural tendencies toward ethnocentrism have become even harder to overcome. How do we as a society stretch the border between providing for our families and thinking about a larger community that may include other people's families, too, even people we have not traditionally imagined as part of that community? How do we envision a society that reflects the reality that my family's well-being is interdependent with that of others? There is a fundamental problem with the very language we are using to stretch those boundaries now, and our education system is not helping.

It may be that we have lost sight of the original purpose and motivation of our education system, one that preceded even the founding of this country and that informed and led the framers as they set forth to create the world's first democratic nation-state. The philosophers and statesmen who declared the right of a people to take their equal place among the nations of the earth, and who set as their guiding principle the self-evident truth that all men are created equal, were steeped in a form and theory of education that had been known for two centuries as the liberal arts. Those founders knew that the citizens of the nation they were building would need a similar grounding if their experiment were to succeed, to fulfill its promise, and to become a better realization of those ideals than they could ever bring about themselves.

PART THREE

COMMUNITY

LEARNING TO THINK

When the political scientist Charles Murray took the stage at Middlebury College in the early spring of 2017, he was greeted by a crowd of jeering students who shouted and banged so loudly it was impossible for his talk to continue as planned. When he and the faculty member who had been asked to respond to his lecture tried to leave the lecture hall to go to a different venue, they were physically assaulted by a crowd that followed them to the car they were to leave in, pounding and jumping on it before they could drive away. Murray is the coauthor of highly controversial research that argues that cognitive ability as measured by IQ tests can explain social inequalities between races. The students who assaulted him and his respondent were expressing their outrage that someone who had espoused racist theories would be allowed to speak at their university.

The riot was widely condemned in the mainstream media, and the students were disciplined by the university, although none was expelled. While colleagues on my campus and others I spoke to were generally in agreement that the students' behavior was inappropriate, their opprobrium was usually accompanied by a slight pause, followed by a caveat that universities really had no business permitting authors of such discredited research to speak on campus—the implication being that while violence is lamentable, in cases of such profound offense it's also to be expected.

Putting aside for a moment the question of the status of Murray's claims—I believe that his claims in that book are flawed and invite racist interpretations—the issue becomes how best to *respond* to ideas that one believes are wrong and dangerous. On the day of the Middlebury riot, it bears mentioning, Murray had come to speak on another topic entirely, namely, working-class alienation, the subject of his later book, *Coming Apart*, an analysis of how economic inequality has led to the collapse of working-class and poor communities. But on that day the students came out to show their outrage against the sociopolitical order they felt stacked the deck against blacks, and to demonstrate solidarity for those who had been put in an inferior position by society and then made to feel as if it were their own fault by research like that of Charles Murray. These are noble goals; how much braver and more dignified would it have been, though, if the students motivated by those goals had come prepared with arguments and hard-driving questions and engaged Murray? How much more effective, as well, given that their violent behavior was so easily co-opted into a long-established narrative of privileged, left-wing intolerance on college campuses?

Perhaps the most infamous of such campuses at present is that of Reed College, in Oregon. As ranked by the *Princeton Review*, Reed's student body is the most left-leaning in the country. At the beginning of the 2016–17 academic year, students at Reed formed the group Reedies Against Racism (RAR), in response to the killings of young black men that had led to massive protests around the country. At Reed, RAR decided its main target would be the required introduction to the humanities called HUM 110. As the group's leaders explained in a letter to all incoming freshmen, "We believe that the first lesson that freshmen should learn about Hum 110 is that it perpetuates white supremacy—by centering 'whiteness' as the only required class at Reed." From the start of that semester, RAR staged in-class protests of every lecture given in HUM 110, leading to the great distress of some of its teachers.

One of those, Lucía Martínez Valdivia, who describes herself as a mixed-raced, gay woman with PTSD, decided to speak out. After trying to lecture over a phalanx of shouting students holding signs, some printed with obscene messages, and after having her microphone taken from her, she eventually published an op-ed in the *Washington Post* calling on faculty at Reed and elsewhere to end the current strategy of silently accepting the protests in the hopes that the moment will pass. As she put it, "In the face of intimidation, educators must speak up, not shut down. Ours is a position of unique responsibility: We teach people not what to think, but how to think."

Martínez Valdivia is right. It is the responsibility of humanities faculty to teach how to think. Unfortunately, the tenor of campus protest, like much of what passes for debate on cable news today, is in some ways the very suppression of thought. Rather than advancing arguments on the basis of evidence, students are pressured on social media to align themselves on one side or another, with no nuance allowed. At Reed, students could find themselves called out by name on Facebook if they demurred from attending rallies. As one student put it, trying to convince another to get over his qualms, "Hey man, everyone getting called out on here, me included, is getting a second chance tomorrow to wake up and make the right decision."

While the Reed protests and others like them stem from real feelings and are reactions to real social and political injustices, the form of expression they adopt does not change minds or raise consciousness. Instead, it exacerbates divisiveness and undermines potentially constructive dialogue, thought, and ultimately action on those very same injustices. One reason for this is that the extremists on the other side of the same issues use the specter of "liberal intolerance" to fan their own followers' flames. That two can and do play at this game was demonstrated in May 2017, when the Muslim American activist Linda Sarsour came to speak at CUNY in New York and was picketed by a group of right-wing activists led by none other than Milo Yiannopolous, himself famously the target of the Berkeley unrest earlier the same year. Sarsour was the target of a barrage of violent messages leading up to the event, including multiple death threats. Yiannopoulos encouraged the crowd at the protest, calling Sarsour a "Sharia-loving, terrorist-embracing, Jew-hating, ticking time bomb of progressive horror." As the Berkeley law professor Fred Smith Jr. pointed out in the wake of the hullabaloo, "There are a few people who have been very effective in branding the left as shutting down free speech, but the moment they are confronted with leftist speech they don't like, they are equally outraged and poised to suppress that speech."

Ironically, what is needed to defuse outrage and create a basis for dialogue are precisely the values taught in courses like HUM 110. As Martínez Valdivia put it, "I ask one thing of all my first-year students: that they say yes to the text. This doesn't mean they have to agree with or endorse anything and everything they read. It means students should read in good faith and try to understand the texts' distance, their strangeness, from our historical moment. Ultimately, this is a call for empathy, for stretching our imaginations to try to inhabit and understand positions that aren't ours and the points of view of people who aren't us." Sadly, the liberal arts, the intellectual ground out of which our democracy grew, has been outflanked by two powerful and opposed forces: on the one hand a growing neoliberal ethic that positions students not as citizens but as future earners, and on the other the focus on individual identities at the expense of thinking how these identities emerge from and depend on their place in the larger community.

As one campus protest led to another, I decided to return to where I had first become aware of the campus culture wars. As I walked across Dartmouth's campus, thirty years after seeing it for the first time, I was struck at how much it had changed. Today Dartmouth seems to have the same cafés, large and shiny student facilities, and multicultural food courts as all other elite schools do. The entrance to the stacks of Baker Library, where I had spent countless hours working on my senior research project, now opened onto an indoor thoroughfare that looked for all the world like an airport terminal. Some gems had been maintained, though. I was desperately relieved to walk into the miniature, wood-paneled Sanborn Library at four P.M. and find that they were preparing the same Earl Grey tea as they did thirty years before—still for a dime, and still in what may have been the same chipped cups.

After finishing my tea, I made my way across the street to Parkhurst Hall, home to the paper that had been ridiculed by conservatives as the Parkhurst *Pravda,* and to the office of the school's current president, Phil Hanlon. Hanlon, who has been president since 2013, knows quite a bit about student activism, but he draws a bright line between the kind of hooliganism that characterized the protests at Middlebury and Berkeley in 2017 and the normal expression of constitutionally sanctioned, political speech that he feels campuses and society at large have a duty to allow and even cultivate.

About a year after he took office, student protesters occupied his office. Hanlon had no problem relinquishing his office for a few days. Since then his administration has worked with student groups to come up with a more effective policy for handling sexual assault cases, and took the further step of banning hard alcohol on campus and shuttering some repeat-offending fraternity houses. Indeed, strolling past the Alpha Delta Phi house of *Animal House* fame, I saw boarded-up windows. In 2015, the college derecognized the fraternity for "violating the school's standards of conduct" after a hazing incident. No longer affiliated with the college, the house quickly lost its zoning permit and was forced to close.

Activism, for Hanlon, is a vital outlet for students' natural desire to have an impact, to change the world for the better. From his perspective, the normal expression of this drive is much more valuable than the extreme examples that garner all the press attention. The real change he notes between student activism in the 1970s and '80s and now is that the new generation's expectations are primed by the ubiquity of social media. A generation that has the ability to get its message out by blog or tweet expects to make an impact far more quickly than previous generations. For Hanlon, campus activism, no matter the specific politics of it, is an indicator of civic health and robust dialogue. Extreme cases, whether the antics of the *Dartmouth Review* from the 1980s or the recent examples from Middlebury and Berkeley, are outliers that shouldn't be taken as representative of what is in fact an exercise in civic engagement.

In fact, it's no coincidence that the prevalence of student activism correlates with access to the liberal arts. As the Harvard professor of government Danielle Allen has shown, propensity for political engagement has a high correlation with educational attainment and, ultimately, with exposure to humanities classes, the core of the liberal arts. One unforeseen consequence of the educational divide we now live in is that active civic engagement, which has always involved university students but used to have a wide base provided by unions, has dwindled and is largely confined to college campuses, where it can be more easily pigeonholed and dismissed as the rantings of privileged brats.

Today, sadly, a liberal arts education has become the icing on the cake of an expensive education, available only to the wealthiest few and, even then, seen as a luxury that kids on financial aid should think twice about allowing themselves. As such it both exacerbates inequality, because its undeniable advantages are monopolized by those who need them the least, and fails to do the work of promoting democratic participation for which it was originally envisaged. When a group of teenagers in a small Virginia community were convicted of having defaced a historic African American schoolhouse with racist and anti-Semitic slurs and images, the judge in the case sentenced them to a year of reading and writing reports on literary and philosophical classics, choosing from a list that ranged from the African American author Richard Wright to the German Jewish philosopher Hannah Arendt—an inspired decision that raises the question of why we should wait for kids to spew hate before feeding them great literature. To borrow a metaphor from medical policy, isn't it far better for a society— less costly, more humane—to prevent disease in the first place than to rush to treat it after the fact?

Reorienting our public education system to its original purpose of producing engaged citizens is a necessary step in redressing the socioeconomic imbalances and cultural disconnects that have brought us to the dead-end state of civil war we find ourselves in. To this end we must reverse the insidious trend whereby civics education is quickly becoming a thing of the past. As Erika Christakis notes, "Civics education has fallen out of favor partly as a result of changing political sentiment. Some liberals have come to see instruction in American values—such as freedom of speech and religion—as reactionary. Some conservatives, meanwhile, have complained of a progressive bias in civics education." The results of such a circular firing squad have been predictably disastrous for our democracy. At present, "three-quarters of Americans can't identify the three branches of government. Public-opinion polls, meanwhile, show a new tolerance for authoritarianism, and rising levels of antidemocratic and illiberal thinking."

While a revival of civics education is sorely needed, however, we also must grasp that simply teaching civics in school is not sufficient to the task. To some degree, we must work to make all education an education in civics. We must, in other words, reexamine why we have an education system in the first place; recommit to equal and high-quality education for all, regardless of income; and restore the liberal arts to the center of the educational experience. But to truly heal as a nation, greater steps are required than innovations within our educational institutions, as vital as those are. We also need to take steps toward creating a national community capable of incorporating and cultivating the vast network of individual, political, cultural, ethnic, and sexual perspectives that make up our society today.

This is the primary challenge we face today in our expanding world. We need to update our national myths by returning to their source in history and explaining their continued relevance and urgency today. Today our culture has elevated, and in some quarters even appreciates, formerly vilified identities. But those same groups, almost by virtue of the effort needed to defend them, have defied inclusion into a newly defined and more inclusive national community. This dispersion is echoed in the liberal arts curricula on campuses, where we have lots of new fields of study devoted to ethnicity, gender, and sexual orientation, but relatively few courses that are devoted to our evolving national community and how to maintain and nurture it. What would such a curriculum look like? What would be the effects of a new focus, not just on college campuses but in secondary education as well, on the stories that unify us as a nation? Over the last half century great strides have been made in undermining the cheap patriotism that for generations painted over real oppression and discrimination with an ersatz veneer of unity. But these critical perspectives, true and needed as they were, have combined with rising economic inequality to form a noxious brew of distrust and tribalism. It is time to forge new bonds of community in place of the faulty ones we have demolished.

The embrace of a profusion of sexual and ethnic identities on campus is a great thing, the culmination of a tradition of liberal thought and values.

We need to recognize that, among other things, the same spirit led philosophically to the creation of the United States as an experiment in self-governance by a pluralistic people. The problem, as we saw in the previous part, was that the embrace of diversity has taken place on a foundation eroded by devastating inequality. And instead of drawing attention to and combating it, colleges were and are actively promoting that inequality even as they are busy celebrating diversity. Our culture and our colleges have been complicit in the growth of inequality, and as a result we have intensified the conflict between individual and community, the very conflict that, as we will see below, the liberal tradition emerged to address in the first place. As educators, as humanists, we must learn again to see our jobs as primarily about teaching democratic values—free and open inquiry, unfettered debate, and the critical evaluation of evidence—that is to say, teaching students how to think.

THE WALRUS AND THE CARPENTER

My grandmother was born in 1912. Two decades later she graduated from Smith College, where she studied English literature. When she died, I was in graduate school, studying literature. I spoke at her funeral, and recited by heart some lines from Lewis Carroll's poem "The Walrus and the Carpenter," in which a group of young oysters are said to keep their shoes "clean and neat," to which the poet adds, "And this was odd, because, you know, / They hadn't any feet." I had to fight through tears of laughter and loss to get the words out. I had learned them as a child when she read to me from her leather-bound edition of *Through the Looking-Glass*. Later, as we had tea in her apartment among the material vestiges of her time on earth, my father and his brothers asked if there was anything of hers I would like to have. I replied without hesitation: her books.

I grew up looking at the spines of those self-titled Great Books and still have some of the editions today. I don't know how she collected her various titles, but the Modern Library was one among many publishers that offered subscriptions that catered to middle-class families eager to have their children become educated citizens of the world. When students protest the courses that teach these books, they are rightly pointing out that the great majority of authors canonized in such series were white men, members of a race and gender that placed itself on a pedestal of cultural, racial, and gender superiority while keeping everyone else either excluded or enslaved. What gets lost in the shouting, though, is the power that a common group of books can have to create and sustain a community—perhaps, even, the very community out of which the principles of equality and diversity can arise.

Recall my student Katy's response on the first day of our Great Books at Hopkins course, when she observed that there were two ways to read the kind of books we were reading for the class. One way, she said, was to read them so as to "have other people think of you as someone who knows a lot of classical references." Katy was being more insightful perhaps than she even knew. The French sociologist Pierre Bourdieu calls what Katy was describing "social capital." According to Bourdieu, a large part of what we are aiming to obtain through our education is not so much inherently valuable as it is valuable for how it positions us in our social circles. Families in positions of power automatically bestow social capital on their children, in the way their children learn to speak and to dress, and in the references they have for casual conversation. Children from families with less social capital find they are almost in a foreign country when they try to enter the more powerful circles.

J. D. Vance describes vividly the discomfort and even humiliation that can come from entering high-social-capital circles when coming from a low-social-capital milieu. When he arrived at Yale Law School he became entirely dependent on his then girlfriend, now his wife, for hurried instruction on such social niceties as how to use the array of different utensils splayed across his place setting at a fine restaurant, or that the color of his belt was supposed to match that of his shoes. The *New York Times* columnist David Brooks struck a nerve when he dedicated a column to observing how decisive social barriers are for segregating classes and helping generate the ocean of discontent and mistrust dividing America today. The column recounted him taking a friend to a panino shop where she froze up "as she was confronted with sandwiches named 'Padrino' and 'Pomodoro' and ingredients like soppressata, capicollo and a striata baguette." As he continues, "I quickly asked her if she wanted to go somewhere else and she anxiously nodded yes and we ate Mexican." The column went on to become the most shared and commented on in *Times* history.

One week later he explicitly drew on Bourdieu to explain the phenomenon: "Bourdieu reminds us that the drive to create inequality is an endemic social sin. Every hour most of us, unconsciously or not, try to win subtle status points, earn cultural affirmation, develop our tastes, promote our lifestyles and advance our class. All of those microbehaviors open up social distances, which then, by the by, open up geographic and economic gaps." What Katy was suggesting in making her observation about the two ways that we can go about reading Great Books is that one powerful—if, for her, spurious—motivation was simply the accumulation of social capital. We were reading these books as freshman at Johns Hopkins precisely to distinguish ourselves as the kind of people who went to Johns Hopkins (or Yale, or Stanford . . .) and who show this in subtle ways like happening to know that Boethius wrote *The Consolation of Philosophy.*

But this was only one of two reasons Katy saw for reading the Great Books. The other was "to read them for all those moments that make you stop and circle a phrase, and just be amazed that someone could have put something in just those words, and in a way that means so much to you, here, today." This is the way that Maynard Mack, one of Yale University's most legendary English professors, described Yale's version of Great Books, its Directed Studies programs. As he wrote almost seventy years ago, Directed Studies "is an effort to recapture, in a modern framework, what many educational theorists now feel was a signal virtue of the old classical curriculum—a community of intellectual experience." In this sense, programs like Directed Studies, Great Books, or the Core Curriculum at Columbia should be seen as doing something more fundamental than simply accruing social capital for their students; they should be understood as an act of resistance against what Roosevelt Montás, who directs the Center for the Core Curriculum at Columbia, calls the "professional intellectual environment" in much of higher education, the endemic hyperspecialization of universities that discourages and even implicitly looks down on the sort of general, liberal arts curriculum that great-books programs entail. As he puts it, "These programs provide a kind of antidote to the disintegration of knowledge that has characterized higher education for the past 50 years." They are also, I would add, an antidote to authoritarian and fundamentalist thinking. As the *New Yorker* staff writer David Denby put it in his memoir about taking Columbia's Core, "the ethos of religious totalitarians and suicide bombers is a negation of everything that such courses as Columbia's would hope to inculcate in its students."

All of this is another way of saying that, while a high-quality liberal arts education can certainly have the effect of driving social inequality, it also can work to expand and strengthen community and strengthen democracy, and it is incumbent on those of us who teach, not only college but at all levels, to promote precisely this aspect of the liberal arts. As Danielle Allen has forcefully argued, there is nothing more essential to the functioning of our democracy than the ability for people from different communities to cross over their walls and engage in conversation. For "only a political system built out of conversation—where multitudes share what they have come to understand with others—has even a scintilla of a chance of making good on the fundamental human truth that none can judge better than I whether I am happy." This, to me, is what we are trying to encourage when we teach Great Books. But it is also the basis of other college programs, like the increasingly popular "common read."

Each summer, thousands of incoming college freshmen are sent a book. These books, chosen by faculty committees at many of the nation's top universities, are intended to provide a common text that all new students will have read before attending their first classes. Professors then volunteer to lead groups of students in discussing these texts. Inevitably, perhaps, the large majority of texts assigned by colleges today are contemporary, and focus on hot-button issues. Many of these, books like Ta-Nehisi Coates's *Between the World and Me* or Bryan Stevenson's *Just Mercy*, deal specifically with questions of diversity. This year Loyola University, just up the street from Hopkins, chose Stevenson's book. The committee responsible for the choice justified it in terms of Loyola's mission to encourage its students to "think of themselves as part of something larger, as responsible for the betterment of our shared world; as men and women who think and act for the rights of others, especially the disadvantaged and the oppressed." But beyond this general appeal, they also draw attention to the city we live in: "As citizens living and learning in Baltimore in 2017, we must grapple with the gritty realities that contribute to systemic inequality in our city and beyond."

Predictably, the flavor of colleges' choices has provoked the ire of conservative commentators like David Randall, director of the National Association of Scholars, which each year publishes a list criticizing these books. According to Randall, these choices are based on the assumption "that diversity is defined by race or gender or what have you. It doesn't actually stretch your mind remotely to continue to think and talk about that," he adds. "It stretches your mind to read Aristotle, Austen." But Randall's complaint misses the point of the common read, even if his intuition about the power of certain books to "stretch the mind" is right. Our minds are stretched when we are challenged to expand our implicit definitions of community. One of the telltale marks of great literature is its ability to create a commonplace from which people from one world can experience and empathize with those of another. The greater the work's ability to bridge such divides, the more likely it will resonate across time and cultures, and gain the status of a "classic." It is precisely for this reason that great works of literature can and should be called upon to help students "think of themselves as part of something larger."

The practice of summer reading assignments is hardly new; nor is the tendency to try to use the assignment to engage politically timely questions of inclusiveness. When I arrived at Dartmouth some thirty years ago, my fellow freshmen and I had (presumably) just finished reading Alice Munro's *Lives of Girls and Women*. Not coincidentally, Dartmouth was experiencing a distillation of the culture wars particularly focused on women's historical exclusion from the college and the growing pains of their integration. Last year, Hopkins, located in a Baltimore that had only recently reeled from the unrest following the death of Freddie Gray and that was a focal point of the Black Lives Matter movement, had its incoming freshmen read another book by Ta-Nehisi Coates, this one about the civil rights movement—*The Beautiful Struggle*.

This year, in the wake of Donald Trump's election to the presidency on a platform dominated by the idea of cracking down on illegal immigration, it's perhaps not surprising that the book our faculty committee chose deals with the plight of undocumented children in the United States. So I duly purchased Joshua Davis's *Spare Parts: Four Undocumented Teenagers, One Ugly Robot, and the Battle for the American Dream* in preparation for meeting with my assigned group of freshmen on the Tuesday before classes started.

There can be no doubt that the stories Joshua Davis recounts are compelling, just as his characters, especially the four undocumented teenagers mentioned in the subtitle, are inspirational. As is well known by now, those four, Lorenzo, Cristian, Luis, and Oscar, with the extraordinary mentorship of two of their teachers and almost no resources, designed and built an underwater robot that beat out the entries of some of the top engineering universities in the country. By the time I sat down with my group of freshmen, some of the passages about immigration enforcement in the book had begun to seem eerily prescient. Two days before our first meeting, in fact, Donald Trump had pardoned former Arizona sheriff Joe Arpaio, who had recently been convicted of abusing his position to terrorize families on the basis of their perceived ethnicity. Davis, writing about him while he was still in power, notes that, for Arpaio, "Mexican immigrants were unlike any immigrants that had come before them. They were often disease-carrying criminals and didn't have the same values as American citizens."

The students in my common read group were quick to focus in on the topicality of the book to today's politically divided landscape. More pressingly, though, many of them were drawn personally to the four kids' stories of fighting against great odds to make it in a new country. As I looked around the room, I realized that this identification shouldn't surprise me. The room was a veritable rainbow coalition of ethnic origins. As they introduced themselves, that impression was confirmed by a United Nations panel's worth of names: there was Noor, wearing a black hijab; Franz, who spoke confidently in a richly accented English; and Nethra, whom I sheepishly had to ask to spell her name. As they spoke about their reactions to the book, those names and first impressions were supplemented by their personal stories. I quickly learned that even Sarah, who had at first blush seemed so, well, white, had a mother who had emigrated from Cuba; while Muna, who I had assumed from her unaccented English was African American, had a Nigerian father and a Russian mother.

If these kids were identifying with the book's protagonists, they were also savvy enough to know where to draw the line. While they may have come from a multitude of cultural backgrounds, their parents had sacrificed and struggled to give them every privilege. Nethra's parents went to the equivalent of a community college in a small town in southern India before emigrating to the States, where her father attended the University of Chicago's Booth School of Business. She wrestles with how her friends' progressive values caused them to disparage her parents' parochial worldview, when she recognizes that her parents sacrificed everything for her and her brother to be able to attend schools like Johns Hopkins. David pointed out that his identification could only go so far. As a Colombian American he felt solidarity with the Latino youth; but his own family in Colombia thinks of him as a "gringo" who grew up in privilege in the States. This sentiment was echoed by Janet Gomez, a second-generation graduate student at Hopkins. Recently she did a bit of stand-up comedy about her experience living in and leaving Miami. While she had always considered herself white in Miami, since everyone around her was more Cuban, at college she "discovered" she was an exotic Latina. As she said in her show, "Damn! I wish I had known about that when they were handing out those scholarships!"

It certainly didn't escape these kids either that they represented, in some ways, the very worst fears of the people who had voted Donald Trump into office. A solid majority of Republicans, and virtually all of those who continue as of this writing to make up Trump's base, believe that whites are today the most discriminated-against group in America. And it is scenes like my classroom that they have in mind when they assert that belief: an international, multihued elite that has taken over the seats of power and privilege in what used to be a majority-white nation. And yet, the data shows that even while colleges and universities have been diversifying their student bodies, and doing so, indeed, in a way that has reduced the proportion of white students, the percentage of African Americans and Hispanics among the student bodies of top schools, public and private, has failed to keep up with their population as a portion of the general public. In other words, despite universities' ostensible efforts to increase the representation of traditionally underrepresented groups, they have become even more underrepresented.

All these groups—people of color as well as suburban and rural whites from lower income families—need to feel that the American story is their story too. One of the bedrocks of American identity is the notion of equal opportunity. Americans as a rule don't like the idea of social democracies as they have developed in western Europe because they believe that competition is to some degree healthy, both for societies and individuals, and that states that do everything for the individual end up depriving those individuals of motivation, curiosity, and drive. Americans do, however, very much approve of the idea of the "level playing field," and are repelled by the kind of inborn privileges that Thomas Jefferson and his fellows rejected in Europe's monarchical societies.

Today, however, we have increasingly lost any semblance of a level playing field, even as we are coming to realize that the very idea of equality of opportunity was a myth for women and minorities. To the extent that we can cultivate new American stories in which to embed and celebrate the diversity of identities that comprise this nation, those stories need to point to a common heritage and emphasize a common principle. The heritage is our shared history, in all its pain and all its glory. That principle is equality, because for all our failures in getting there, and they have been legion, the core American ideal, the one that constitutes the fellow feeling or glue that binds our community together, is that no one is born better than her neighbor.

As the philosopher Adam Smith understood it, a society had to inculcate the ability to empathize with our neighbors, what he called the "fellow-feeling of the misery of others," and the way to do that was through sharing stories. As he wrote in his monumental *Theory of Moral Sentiments*, "Even our sympathy with the grief or joy of another, before we are informed of the cause of either, is always extremely imperfect. General lamentations, which express nothing but the anguish of the sufferer, create rather a curiosity to inquire into his situation, along with some disposition to sympathize with him, than any actual sympathy that is very sensible. The first question that we ask is, What has befallen you? Till this be answered, though we are uneasy both from the vague idea of his misfortune, and still more from torturing ourselves with conjectures about what it may be, yet our fellow-feeling is not very considerable." Since how we perceive the world is walled off from the perceptions of our fellows by our body and its senses, we need stories to conjure a different space, for "it is by the imagination only that we can form any conception of what are his sensations." These are the stories we need to function as a society; without them, we will never be more than solitary souls, obsessed with the satisfaction of our own basic needs.

EDUCATION AND FELLOW FEELING

Our discussion of the common read, as it turned out (or perhaps as it was envisioned), turned into a discussion about identity and national community. Given the rhetoric that has abounded about privileged "special snowflakes" playing up their victim status and complaining about every perceived slight to their identities, I was moved and somewhat surprised to find myself in a multicultural setting where the students were both aware of their privilege and, perhaps most disarmingly, concerned about how that privilege was impacting the possibility and future of community in the United States. These students had gotten the memo about how Trump's movement was reacting to them, and they were actively concerned with how the two sides of the rapidly widening breach could communicate with one another. Where I had been taught to expect anger and recrimination, I was hearing understanding and a desire for rapprochement.

Programs like our common read are almost ubiquitous on college campuses these days, and the choices often are, like ours was, oriented toward questions of identity and current political debates. Critics like Randall claim that these choices are of middling literary value, and that the students' time would be better used reading time-tested classics. Advocates of including books like these argue that it is a valuable opportunity to open the minds of young people, often privileged, who may never have had much occasion to meet people from different and less privileged backgrounds. They also emphasize that these assignments "can help nonwhite and first-generation college students feel more comfortable on campus."

While this back-and-forth may strike us as drearily familiar by now, it also goes to the heart of what diversity is, and why colleges should or shouldn't strive to teach it. Baked into Thomas Jefferson's notion of the purpose of public education was that it should not merely serve for personal advancement, but rather lead to the strengthening of the nation's civic culture and the protection of democratic values. For Jefferson, one side of this role was ensuring the development of a citizenry capable of warding off the tyranny of the few, the oligarchs who would seek to return the people to their former state of enslavement. Indeed, his most passionate missives from his years in France were always about the vast advantages enjoyed by free Americans over their counterparts in Europe, who, in the years of mounting discontent prior to the storming of the Bastille during the last summer of Jefferson's appointment as minister plenipotentiary to France, were suffering "under physical and moral oppression," reduced to one of "several stages of degradation," wherein "the many are crouched under the weight of the few."

But while freedom from such a tyranny of the few was always at the front of Jefferson's mind, the other side of the balance was equally pressing: namely, freedom from the tyranny of custom, the "ignorance and prejudices" that enabled "kings, nobles, or priests" to shackle the "minds of their subjects," but could just as easily push most of a nation's people to deprive smaller groups and individuals of their unalienable rights to life, liberty, and the pursuit of happiness. The key to protecting these rights from the encroachments of custom and prejudice was the idea of toleration that stemmed from the liberalism of thinkers like John Locke. In fact, unlike most moral traditions that have developed systems of rules that privilege community coherence over the individual, the liberal tradition distinguishes broadly between such truly unalienable rights as those described by Jefferson in the Declaration and mere social conventions, the ways a culture goes about expressing what is specific to it. This distinction accepts and protects a far greater toleration of cultural difference between subcommunities than is the rule for most other traditions.

The toleration that was on the minds of Locke and Jefferson was primarily religious toleration, which resonates with us today, even if the examples that burned for them were of sectarianism within Christianity as opposed to the interreligious strife that characterizes our times. In Locke's famous *Letter Concerning Toleration*, he famously gave pride of place to the importance of tolerating others' religious beliefs. Exempting atheism, which he believed would lead humans to be unable to respect any covenant, his version of civil society, so influential to Jefferson, would allow for total respect of all other "practical opinion," so long as "they do not tend to establish dominion over others." In his words, "neither Pagan, nor Mahumetan, nor Jew, ought to be excluded from the Civil Rights of the Commonwealth because of his Religion." Even differences of religious belief and custom should not be enough to inhibit fellow feeling. Locke's view on toleration would thus become the first page in a new story about a particularly American form of community based on a commitment to mutual toleration.

For Jefferson this meant forging a community of Americans out of Quakers, Puritans, and mainstream Anglicans. It meant that loyalty to the idea of being an American had to be at least as strong if not stronger than loyalty to one's specific sect. And this required in turn that, as detestable as the teachings of one sect might be for any member of another, the members of any sect must respect and hold dear the right of others to follow their own preferred teachings, precisely to ensure that their own culture would be granted the same respect. Jefferson also knew that any sect that found itself in the majority would suffer a strong temptation to establish itself and its customs as the default, and curtail the rights of others. It was precisely because he knew this to be a danger that he advocated from the beginning for a Bill of Rights to be included in the Constitution, and said repeatedly that freedom of speech and religion were the central tenets of a liberal democracy. In the end his concerns were heard, and James Madison drafted the Bill's list of amendments, which were adopted in 1791, already three years after the ratification of the Constitution.

The Bill of Rights, including the First Amendment, continues to shape American democracy in profound ways, setting it apart even from some of its European counterparts. Not long ago, riding the subway with my then eight-year-old son to his school in Vienna, Austria, I noticed a headline in a newspaper left on a nearby seat: SCHOOLTEACHER SUES MUSLIM FATHER FOR REFUSING TO SHAKE HANDS WITH HER. The story of the schoolteacher captured my attention because it raises difficult questions about the legal and philosophical foundations of the liberal democratic project that Europe seeks to embody, as well as its American alternative.

In the United States, the schoolteacher's suit would have very little likelihood of succeeding. As offensive as it may be to have a man refuse to shake hands with her based on her gender, the First Amendment does not permit mere offensiveness of behavior to override the freedoms of belief and the expression it guarantees. In many European countries, in contrast, the schoolteacher would at least have a case, because their constitutions provide for a far more thorough enumeration of specific rights. In the Austrian schoolteacher's case, a Muslim man's right to follow the teachings of his religion does not automatically trump her right to be treated with the same respect a man could expect.

In the United States the bar for justifying the curtailment of liberty to practice one's religion is set rather high. The First Amendment is a vital bulwark against the majority imposing its values or beliefs on minorities, and is the reason why Americans have tended to tolerate even extreme expressions of intolerance. In Europe, where a constitution like Germany's was crafted after the horrors of the Second World War and Austria's was reinstated in 1945 with many amendments following, a justified fear of intolerance in its most extreme form led to the creation of civil societies that more expressly enforce the boundaries of acceptable expression. This is why you can go to jail for denying the Holocaust in Germany and Austria, but the Unite the Right rally that took place in Charlottesville in August 2017, with its torches and Hitler salutes, is allowed to take place.

In essence, what liberal societies are saying is "Tolerate others' beliefs (except when doing so contradicts this very principle)." For a liberal society to ensure that its members continue to enjoy the liberties it guarantees, the glue of its community must be focused on the idea of toleration and not on a set list of acceptable beliefs or identities. This is what the First Amendment to the U.S. Constitution does when it prohibits Congress from making any law "respecting an establishment of religion, or prohibiting the free exercise thereof; or abridging the freedom of speech, or of the press; or the right of the people peaceably to assemble, and to petition the government for a redress of grievances." Notice that the amendment says nothing about what kind of laws Congress should make; rather, it focuses on limiting the content of its legislation. The German constitution, in contrast, which runs to over 140 articles, each with multiple clauses, is essentially an exhaustive enumeration of positive rights (Austria's is actually longer).

But tolerating others' differences is just the first step in establishing a liberal community. The next, even more crucial step is learning to cherish others' freedom of expression as a necessary guarantee of one's own freedoms. This is what the civil rights lawyer Pauli Murray meant when she wrote a letter to Yale University's provost Kingman Brewster in 1963, urging him *not* to rescind Yale's invitation to the segregationist Alabama governor George Wallace in the wake of the Sixteenth Street Baptist Church bombing that killed four African American girls and wounded some twenty-two others. "This controversy affects me in a dual sense, for I am both a lawyer committed to civil rights including civil liberties and a Negro who has suffered from the evils of racial segregation," Murray stated. And yet despite her long and principled stance against the violence of segregation, despite having called it in her legal writings "a monster, dividing peoples, thwarting personalities, breeding civil wars," Murray was unequivocal in her defense of the right that she and Wallace shared as Americans. This freedom, to hold and express one's beliefs even when the larger society disapproves, she wrote, "has been the principle behind the enforcement of the rights of the Little Rock Nine, James Meredith and others to attend desegregated schools in the face of a hostile community and threats of violence. It must operate equally in the case of Governor Wallace."

In some cases, instead of insisting on this fundamental freedom and thus keeping the bounds of its community open and subject to contestation, a liberal society may try to define what groups, behaviors, or beliefs are acceptable occupants of it. This is what I believe is happening to Europeans as they face the challenge of assimilating a new wave of immigrants from the Middle East, many of whom are Muslim. But filling the idea of community with a specific ethnic or religious content, as Trump's movement is working hard to do, undermines the very basis of American democracy. As Barack Obama put it in his famous Cairo address of 2009, "we can't disguise hostility towards any religion behind the pretense of liberalism." To put it another way, we must avoid filling the open space guaranteeing tolerance with a specific image of what tolerance looks like, one that, unsurprisingly, may have a specific national image and thus infringe on the equal rights of those not sharing in that image to pursue their own happiness. This is why Germans of Turkish descent or French citizens of North African descent, born in Germany or France and speaking no other language than German or French, can still struggle to consider themselves German or French. In contrast, even recent immigrants to the United States commonly embrace an American identity along with that of their own ethnic and national origins. Indeed, it is a common joke among the youth of the Paris banlieues that they need a passport and vaccination card to attempt to take the metro into downtown Paris.

As we will see in what follows, the kind of fellow feeling that binds America's community cannot be an ethnic, racial, or religious one. The American democratic project was from the outset of a different stripe entirely. While the framers may not have envisioned a population as diverse as the one we have built, it was their *idea*—the equal opportunity among those of wildly different provenances to define and pursue their own vision of happiness—that enabled that diversity to arise in the first place. Today, as we are confronted by raging tribalism on all sides, it may very well be that returning to this original idea is the only chance we have to salvage a civil society organized not on the image of a specific ethnic, religious identity, but on the promise of a self-governing community of diverse peoples, each permitted to pursue their own vision of happiness while protecting the right of others to do the same.

DEMOCRACY AND THE LIBERAL ARTS

Ten years after their upstart declaration, and only three years after the last British soldiers sullenly departed from American soil, the mood among many of the Founding Fathers was decidedly grim. The young confederation's secretary of foreign affairs, John Jay, lamented in a letter to George Washington that the nation's future lay in the hands of men who were "neither wise nor good." Washington's reply offered little in the way of consolation, admitting, "I do not conceive we can exist long as a nation."

An exception among such pessimists was the one whose pen had drafted the young nation's founding declaration ten years earlier, and indeed one of the most avid students of the Enlightenment currently brewing across the ocean. Thomas Jefferson sought to ease Washington's concerns in a series of letters from his post in Paris, reminding the great general of "the good sense of the people" in the United States, which "enjoys a precious degree of liberty and happiness." Washington didn't respond to Jefferson's sentiments, but he clearly wasn't convinced by the younger man's optimism, or by his faith in the ability of the people to govern themselves. The nation could only survive, he had written in August 1786, if the general population were led by "the more discerning part of the Community," without whose benevolent guidance the people would almost certainly fail to accept "measures the best calculated for their own good."

After the signing of the Declaration of Independence in July 1776, Thomas Jefferson had returned to the Virginia assembly to work on a number of bills expressive of his commitments to equality and access to education. While he successfully passed legislation limiting the entailment of hereditary estates, a tradition which had led to the concentration of property into fewer and fewer hands, he failed at his efforts to pass laws providing for free public primary and college education. As he would complain, his efforts ran up against the resistance of, in the words of one historian, "the wealthy class . . . unwilling to incur [funding] the education of the poor." He feared his failure would perhaps undermine the great democratic experiment that the United States would become. There is substantial evidence that his fear is currently being realized, with middle-class and working-class Americans looking on as a billionaire president, the most gilded cabinet in history, and a Congress stacked with millionaires pass changes to the tax code intended to redistribute wealth up the economic ladder.

Jefferson's most famous attempt to pass a general education bill in Virginia, Bill 79, "A Bill for the More General Diffusion of Knowledge," begins with this extraordinary preamble:

> Whereas it appeareth that however certain forms of government are better calculated than others to protect individuals in the free exercise of their natural rights, and are at the same time themselves better guarded against degeneracy, yet experience hath shewn, that even under the best forms, those entrusted with power have, in time, and by slow operations, perverted it into tyranny; and it is believed that the most effectual means of preventing this would be, to illuminate, as far as practicable, the minds of the people at large, and more especially to give them knowledge of those facts, which history exhibiteth, that, possessed thereby of the experience of other ages and countries, they may be enabled to know ambition under all its shapes, and prompt to exert their natural powers to defeat its purposes.

While his bill failed in 1778, his dedication to the idea of public education as the best defense of liberty lived on in the project that he would deem his most important achievement, the founding of the University of Virginia, where he instituted a curriculum of classical learning founded on the proposition made explicit in his earlier bill that it becomes expedient for promoting the publick happiness that those persons, whom nature hath endowed with genius and virtue, should be rendered by liberal education worthy to receive, and able to guard the sacred deposit of the rights and liberties of their fellow citizens, and that they should be called to that charge without regard to wealth, birth or other accidental condition or circumstance.

Between these two statements on the value of education there lies a tension. On the one hand, Jefferson believed that it was vital for democracy that education should, as far as is practicable, illuminate the minds of people at large. On the other hand, he also believed that there were people especially endowed by nature, regardless of wealth or social stature, with genius and virtue, and that these were the ones who should receive the kind of liberal education that would permit them to "guard the sacred deposit of the rights and liberties of their fellow citizens." Jefferson's philosophy, in other words, was explicitly elitist, but it was a new kind of elitism. While committed to sloughing off the crusty injustices of hereditary privilege in all its forms, Jefferson still believed that some citizens would naturally rise above others, and that these had the responsibility to lead. A liberal education was above all important for these citizens, but it was vital that the opportunity to prove themselves be universal.

It is hard to overemphasize how radical Jefferson's fundamental idea was: an intellectual and moral virtue that was not limited to a hereditary aristocracy but could show itself in any human being so long as a society were imbued with a free spirit of inquiry. This stance was both revolutionary in its own right and utterly essential to his vision for the United States. It was, in his mind and that of his fellow revolutionaries, a principle worth risking everything for, a reason to "mutually pledge to each other our Lives, our Fortunes, and our Sacred Honor," in the resounding final words of the Declaration. It was, and is, the core of the American idea of citizenship. Today we know that principle as that of equal opportunity, and we are committed, at least in theory, to a version of it that extends to every American, regardless of gender, race, or national origin. Even in the abrogated, truncated form it took in the eighteenth century, this idea had the power to overturn established political orders and to cause an upstart nation to rebel against its monarchical fatherland.

The foundation of the American model of democracy was radical, yet it wasn't born in a vacuum. The founders had taken a set of ideas that had been circulating among intellectuals in England, France, and Germany, and put them into action on a national scale that had been so far impossible on the continent because of the entrenched power of the aristocratic and monarchical orders. What Washington and his foreign secretary were struggling with was what political thinkers as different as Thomas Hobbes, an apologist for a strong centralized state, and the Scottish philosopher David Hume had puzzled over, namely, how to safeguard community while allowing for individual freedom.

In locating education at the heart of liberty, Jefferson was evoking ideas that were being debated contemporaneously in Europe and had been the subject of philosophical inquiries for much of the preceding century. Key in his formulation is the balance between the "genius and virtue" that "nature hath endowed" and "the sacred deposit of the rights and liberties of their fellow citizens." Building balance out of this potential conflict at the heart of every democratic society was, for Jefferson as it was for thinkers like John Locke, Jean-Jacques Rousseau, and Jefferson's contemporary Immanuel Kant, the ultimate goal of education. George Ticknor, a prodigious scholar of classical and modern languages who had graduated from Dartmouth College at the age of sixteen, exemplified this spirit. Jefferson shared a love of book collecting with Ticknor, and also hoped to appoint him to a professorship in his new university. Ticknor, who eventually accepted the chair of modern languages at Harvard instead, wrote to Jefferson of the philosophical spirit in which he saw the Germans practice humanistic scholarship, arguing that this spirit should be "transplanted into the U. States, in whose free and liberal soil I think it would, at once, find congenial nourishment."

Jefferson was more than convinced. His faith in the ability of common people to self-govern was not blind. In fact, there was plenty of evidence for the inherent *in*equality of men, given the conditions and behaviors that had been causing Washington and his government so much grief. His faith, in other words, was not a naïve, counterfactual faith in the *actual* equality of people despite the myriad abilities and talents they might show. Rather, contrary to what had been passed down by centuries of aristocratic certainty in the superiority of certain classes over others, he believed in their equal status as citizens and in the equality of the opportunity they should have to find and express their talents.

The cornerstone for such a philosophical spirit, he felt, could only be the availability of a classical education to all who could show themselves worthy, the kind of education from which he himself had benefited. At the age of seventeen, Jefferson had enrolled in the College of William and Mary in Williamsburg, Virginia. There the young man who had been studying Latin, Greek, and French since he was nine dedicated himself to the study of "mathematics, science, philosophy, and rational inquiry" under the tutelage of William Small, a man well known for his "liberality of sentiment." Jefferson never wavered in his conviction that such an education was essential to any republican system and should be the birthright of all citizens of a democratic nation. As he later wrote, "A nation [that] expects to be ignorant & free . . . expects what never was & never will be."

Jefferson's words and convictions transcended and belied the blinders of his own customs, and their power proved contagious even in his own lifetime. A free black man living in Baltimore, Benjamin Banneker, would write a letter to Jefferson in 1791 that caught him in his own hypocrisy even while it proved the truth of his convictions about the universality of human potential for intellect and virtue. In that letter Banneker challenged Jefferson to be true to his own words: "Sir, if these are Sentiments of which you are fully persuaded, I hope you cannot but acknowledge, that it is the indispensible duty of those who maintain for themselves the rights of human nature, and who profess the obligations of Christianity, to extend their power and influence to the relief of every part of the human race, from whatever burthen or oppression they may unjustly labour under, and this I apprehend a full conviction of the truth and obligation of these principles should lead all to."

The philosophical tradition that led from Thomas Jefferson through Banneker and eventually to Martin Luther King Jr. both entails and is entailed by a liberal arts education. While contemporary campus debates at times seem to suggest the opposite, in fact there is no antagonism between that liberal tradition and cultural diversity, because the liberal tradition—which developed out of European humanism into a political philosophy dedicated to balancing the rights of individuals against the needs of community cohesion, and to disseminating tools for discerning truth against a backdrop of superstition and misinformation—guarantees that diversity, just as diversity requires the liberal tradition. Today more than ever, Jefferson's impassioned defense of democracy and "the good sense of the people" has been sharply challenged by America's demographic complexity and the emergence of a technological and media landscape that he could never have imagined. With today's proliferation of multiple and wildly divergent sources of information and propaganda, an educated citizenry is more important than ever to the functioning of democracy.

MEDIA LITERACY

The liberal tradition didn't burst full grown from the minds of Enlightenment thinkers, like Athena from the head of Zeus; it grew slowly and painfully of age in an intellectual garden that had been fertilized by a rediscovery of the arts and letters of classical antiquity, whose transmission via the translations of Arab intellectuals forced open a European mind that had been closed by centuries of isolationism and religious fanaticism. Gradually a new spirit enveloped the old continent, a spirit that would pave the way for the liberties we take for granted in the modern world. That new spirit was tolerance: the practice and principle of accepting the equal freedom of others to hold and express different values and beliefs. The Czech novelist Milan Kundera once wrote that the "imaginative realm of tolerance was born with modern Europe." Indeed, all that is most precious about the liberal tradition—in his words again, "respect for the individual, for his original thought, and for his right to an inviolable private life"—depends on and grows from that imaginative realm. The liberal arts developed to preserve and enhance this imaginative realm; it is this realm that we have abandoned in the misguided conviction that education is only or primarily a private resource and tool for economic self-improvement; and it is this realm that we must revitalize as part of a national project to revive our civic culture.

Within two centuries of the first glimmers of the humanist tradition in the middle of the fifteenth century, the very idea of the purpose and breadth of education had changed radically. With the first humanists, their rediscovery of classical texts, the depth of their knowledge of Latin, and the brilliance of their lectures had all been expressions of unique intellects. The next generation, men like Erasmus of Rotterdam, created a method of education that could be replicated and extended throughout Europe, independent of the talents and abilities of individual teachers.

By the sixteenth century, in other words, humanism had definitively "changed from an active emulation of great scholarly teachers . . . into a 'liberal' arts course—an all-purpose substitute for other forms of basic education." Men like Erasmus now believed in such a liberal arts education as "a methodical programme for the moral regeneration of European civilisation and culture." At the core of this vision was a shift in the very notion of who would be the target of such a program. While earlier humanism had largely been focused on distinguishing the aristocracy by lavishing on it the tools of erudition, the new humanism envisioned its methods as cultivating a new kind of aristocracy born of the fruits of its own talents and efforts. Given this history, it is worth mentioning that Erasmus is now the name of a pan-European study-abroad program that is instrumental in opening students to new perspectives.

The core of Erasmus's own program was the construction of a set of exercises with which any teacher could give practice to a group of students in the arts of debating, arguing, declaiming, or even composing their own poetry on classical models. Central to these exercises was a body of "commonplaces," texts from the classical tradition that all students would be expected to read and know. The point of knowing these particular classical texts, however, was not the assumption that they contained a specific, eternal wisdom that could not be gleaned from any other texts; rather, the idea was that they create a common ground, the basis of an international community of thinkers able to communicate and argue among themselves, a common denominator enabling a productive exchange of differing ideas. This exchange, conducted in the medium of rhetoric, would be "the basis of all civilised discourse."

As the historians Anthony Grafton and Lisa Jardine tell it, no matter how "classical" the commonplaces were—that is, however distant in time and culture from the contemporary political, social, and cultural concerns of the day—the system of "literary training" devised by the new humanists was very much intended to hone skills and abilities of students so as to enable "significant intervention on the most challenging intellectual issues of the day, both temporal and spiritual."

What the humanists thought about the rationale behind providing their students with a common set of texts for study and debate should enlighten our own thinking today about the relation between what we call the canon and a liberal arts education. Too often, both politicians and educators frame debates about the liberal arts as a political conflict around which texts ought to be taught. Conservatives bellyache about liberals desecrating the classics in favor of newfangled, multicultural texts of lesser quality, while liberals defend expanding the canon by pointing to the oppressive reign of "dead white men" in the curriculum. But from the perspective of those who first promoted the liberal arts as a method of educating an unprecedented swath of citizens, what was essential was not the specific texts chosen but *that there be common texts in the first place.*

There can be no doubt that behind this movement was a new commitment to the universality of education, even if one constrained by the prejudices of the time. The civilization the new humanists sought to develop was no longer to be limited to the elites, leaders, and churchmen who had been the individual beneficiaries of the brilliance of early Italian humanists. And while it would be too early to speak of a true democratization of education given the numbers of people who were effectively excluded from educational institutions by means, gender, and social standing, the new program extended both in practice and theory to sectors of society that never before would have thought education of this kind to be useful.

In part for political reasons, the Erasmian system of humanistic training quickly gained a foothold in England, whose king, Henry VIII, had an interest in undermining the church lawyers and the scholastic education system that perpetuated their power. The result, however, was an educational program whose implicit aim was, in the words of the Oxford historian James McConica, "an international society of men—and women—clerical and lay, who were steeped in a common cultural discipline derived from the ancient worlds." In the philosophy of this program, the works selected to study were great, but not by virtue of a specific cultural content and national character that they conveyed to the reader. Their greatness lay rather in what twentieth-century critics and teachers like F. R. Leavis and Eliot would recognize as their usefulness for training students in "delicacy of perception, in supple responsiveness, in the wariness of conceptual rigidity that goes with a Blakean addiction to the concrete and particular, and in readiness to take unforeseen significances and what is so unprecedented as to be new." Such training would be "useful for life, but useful here means permeating every aspect of human activity." What was great about the commonplace works, in other words, was the way they could be used to foster precisely the kind of open, philosophical spirit of inquiry that George Ticknor effused about in his letter to Jefferson.

What attracted men like Ticknor and Jefferson to this philosophical spirit was its conduciveness to the kind of open and informed debate that was essential to democracy. But democracy per se was not yet on the horizon for the method's originators. Erasmus and his humanist followers were instead concerned with truth. Specifically, he was convinced that "close reading" could weed out the "corrupt and spurious" passages that clouded men's understanding of historical texts and would thus lead to improved ability to discern the truth. Vitally, this discernment could be taught to any and all, regardless of their station in life: "By keeping the contact always in view, by bearing in mind the speaker's and writer's situation, the student will be able to avoid the doctrinal errors and evasions that the scholastics— those insensitive readers—have committed." As Erasmus writes about his model reader, "Let him not consider it adequate to pull out four or five little words; let him consider the origin of what is said, by whom it is said, to whom it is said, when, on what occasion, in what words, what precedes it, what follows. For it is from a comprehensive examination of these things that one learns the meaning of a given utterance."

It should not escape a reader living in today's tumultuous media world that the skilled and discerning reading urged by the humanists is all the more important today. The inflationary explosion of media proclaiming biased or outright false claims as "news" or "fact" has deeply undermined the underpinnings of modern democracy. Today conspiracy theories flare up and are difficult if not impossible to put to rest. Individual lives and reputations are ruined by spurious connections made on the basis of a picture circulated on social media, or a misspelling of a person's name. It is a sign of the times and likely a necessary step for all modern democracies to follow that Italy, itself awash in a politics of conspiracy and innuendo, is adopting as of this writing a new program in media literacy for its schools, intended to defend Italians against the "fake news" that, in the words of Laura Boldrini, the member of parliament who is spearheading the new program for some thirty thousand Italian schoolchildren, "drips drops of poison into our daily web diet and we end up infected without even realizing it."

The dangers of propaganda and the importance of education for checking it are not new, by any stretch. In an early essay penned while he was a student at Morehouse College in Atlanta, Martin Luther King Jr. wrote, "To save man from the morass of propaganda, in my opinion, is one of the chief aims of education. Education must enable one to sift and weigh evidence, to discern the true from the false, the real from the unreal, and the facts from the fiction." We are, however, entering a new age in the diffusion of propaganda. With today's proliferation of multiple and wildly divergent sources of information and propaganda, an educated citizenry is more important than ever to the functioning of democracy.

In fact, while specific programs of media literacy are laudable, the skills these programs teach—verifying claims, checking sources and evidence—are staples of the humanistic education developed by Erasmus a half a millennium ago. This is one of the reasons that Danielle Allen has been so vociferous in arguing for the centrality of the humanities today to civic engagement. As she puts it, "Writers and thinkers need skills of careful, authentic writing; readers and listeners needs the skills of slow reading and close listening, skills very much endangered in contemporary culture. With such skills, citizens can understand and choose among political positions even when those are too often conveyed in sound bites." Today more than ever these skills of discernment are desperately needed, as huge swaths of the electorate are swayed by both fake news and the false claims that true news is fake.

If we take these admonitions seriously, it would appear that our education system is failing to stem inequality in ways more fundamental than we've recognized so far. Yes, education prepares children for economic success. When you are ill prepared by your school, you have a lesser chance of succeeding, and this perpetuates and exacerbates the inequalities that led to your getting a lesser education in the first place. This is what Daron Acemoglu and James A. Robinson mean when they write, in their critique of the economist Thomas Piketty's book *Capital in the Twenty-First Century*, that education has an impact on inequality by affecting "how technology evolves, how markets function, and how the gains from various different economic arrangements are distributed." But as recent research has shown, our unequal education system may be abetting inequality in an even more pervasive and insidious way: namely, by failing in its essential mission of preparing citizens for full participation in a democratic society. Allen adds, commenting on the same point,

> the preparation of citizens through education for civic and political engagement supports the pursuit of political equality, but political equality, in turn, may well engender more egalitarian approaches to the economy. An education that prepares students for civic and political engagement brings into play the prospect of political contestation around issues of economic fairness. In other words, education can affect income inequality not merely by spreading technical skills and compressing the income distribution. It can even have an effect on income inequality by increasing a society's political competitiveness and thereby impacting

"how technology evolves, how markets function, and how the gains from
various different economic arrangements are distributed."

Humanistic education, that is to say, is crucial for American civic society
because it inculcates and upholds the specifically American values of equal
opportunity and democratic participation.

Another way to put this is to say that access to equal education is only
part of the problem; what gets taught is equally crucial. To live up to the
ideal our nation set for its public education system of cultivating a citizenry
capable of self-governance, primary and secondary curricula need to include
a robust program in civics. In 2010, a report by the National Center for
Education Statistics scored less than a quarter of students nationwide as
proficient in civics. The Campaign for the Civic Mission of Schools argued
that this shocking lack of understanding of the basic operation of our
democracy be rectified by including controversial issues and current events
in class discussions, as well as debates about public issues and role-playing
exercises, among other strategies.

But while such recommendations are admirable and should be implemented, the "factual knowledge about government processes" that is the
core of civics education will always sound hollow if divorced from the ideas
that our country is founded on, the literature that narrates our common
experience, and the sense of community that underlies the commitment to
our democratic ideals. To benefit from or even understand the basics of a
general civics program, students at all levels must be exposed to a liberal
education—that is, they must learn to read great literature and discuss big
ideas, study the facts and narratives that comprise our history, and be
exposed to the humanistic values that are the foundation of our democracy.

This is what Allen proposes when she suggests that a liberal arts education is the essential ingredient in what she prefers to call "participatory
readiness." The fact that the liberal arts are still the cornerstone of college
education is the main reason that Allen can state that "it's clear that college
provides something useful there that our K-12 system generally does
not," and that "something is happening on our campuses that engenders

'participatory readiness.'" While it remains true that higher income, property ownership, and hence economic stakes in the system correlate with greater degrees of civic participation as measured by voting, it is also the case that the correlation between civic participation and education is closer than that between civic participation and economic attainment. Furthermore, and this is key, "there is a statistically significant difference between the rates of political participation that we see from those who have graduated with humanities majors and those who graduated with STEM (science, technology, engineering, and mathematics) majors." To put it clearly, the more humanities courses you have taken in your life, the more likely you are to participate in and have an impact on your society.

JEFFERSON'S WORDS

In the aftermath of the 2016 presidential election, Teresa Sullivan, president of the University of Virginia, sent an e-mail to the school's students, faculty, and staff. In the e-mail, which she had planned to send whatever the outcome of the election, she called for a spirit of unity and civility to prevail on campus, despite the divisiveness that had surfaced on both a national and a local scale during the election year. She further impressed on her colleagues and students the importance of not withdrawing from the political process, and she buttressed her words with a quotation from the university's founder and America's third president, Thomas Jefferson.

Shortly after she sent the e-mail, Sullivan received a letter signed by more than 450 UVA students and faculty, objecting to her using Jefferson's words as a moral compass, since, given his active participation in slavery, "many of us are deeply offended by attempts of the administration to guide our moral behavior through their use." The letter went on to point out that Jefferson "was deeply involved in the racist history of this university" and to cite "other memorable Jefferson quotes," such as that blacks "are inferior to the whites in the endowments of body and mind."

In her response to the letter, Sullivan stated that "quoting Jefferson—or any historical figure—does not imply an endorsement of all the social structures and beliefs of his time, such as slavery and the exclusion of women and people of color from university life." She also added that, while she disagreed with the letter's arguments, she fully endorsed the right of the signatories to express their views about "UVA's complicated Jeffersonian legacy."

Less than a year after Sullivan sent her e-mail, I went to UVA as the campus was preparing to commemorate the laying of the university's cornerstone two hundred years earlier. John Lyons, a professor of French at UVA, took me to see the building whose construction began on October 6, 1817. As we stood before the door of Pavilion VII, the central building on the west wing of UVA's famous Lawn, university personnel were busily setting up thousands of seats on the grass behind us, where the audience for the next day's festivities would sit to hear several hours of speeches before finally getting what they had come for: a concert by the Goo Goo Dolls.

I came to Charlottesville with my colleague Nathan Connolly, a distinguished historian of race in America, to hear him take part in a live session of the NPR history program *BackStory* that was also to be part of the weekend's events. Like the cornerstone celebration, the live session had been planned long before, and yet by the time we left Baltimore on a warm October morning, the name Charlottesville had taken on a new, sinister meaning in American political life.

The events of the weekend of August 11, 2017, began darkly enough, as throngs of white men carrying tiki torches marched through the darkening streets late Friday evening. Some of the marchers raised their hands in Hitler salutes and yelled anti-Semitic slogans like "the Jews will not replace us." The images were frightening enough that the CEO of the company that makes the torches felt obligated to issue a statement disavowing any relation to right-wing movements. The next day, however, things got much worse.

As the sun rose and the white supremacists marched through the streets again, this time they were met by lines of counterprotesters, arms linked.

Shouts and slogans flew back and forth, and before long there were blows as well. To the outrage of many present, the police appeared to be under orders not to interfere; acts of violence went unchallenged, even if they took place right before the eyes of officials. Then, outrage turned to panic, and people started to scream and run away as a car plowed into the crowd of counterprotesters. When the melee had finally settled and the driver had run off, there were more than a dozen injured, and Heather Heyer was dead.

Charlottesville—a city that had been known for its idyllic setting near Virginia's Shenandoah National Park and for its historical significance as the home of Thomas Jefferson and seat of the United States' first public university—quickly became a synonym for racial and political hatred and violence. In the days that followed it would furthermore become the symbol of the political divisions that continued to plague the nation, as the president's comments on the violence pulled his administration ever further into controversy and turmoil. As soon became clear, the attitude of Trump and many of his followers toward the events was that while some "bad elements" may have infiltrated the protesters, their movement as a whole was not evil, and the issue that unified them was a justifiable desire to protect their heritage and history. There were "very fine people," he said, on "both sides," just as "both sides" were to blame for the violence that ensued. It was a shame, Trump said, that liberals were forcing cities to take down "beautiful statues." Where would it end? Once the Confederate generals came down, "is it George Washington next week, and is it Thomas Jefferson the week after? You know, you really have to ask yourself, where does it stop?"

Compared with what everyone there now calls "the events of August 11th and 12th," the controversy over Sullivan's letter may have been little more than a tempest in a teapot. When I asked John Lyons for his thoughts on the matter, the thirty-year-veteran professor raised his eyebrows in surprise and admitted that he had no idea what I was referring to. He seemed mildly chagrined and joked that he must have been too caught up in his work to notice, but it was clear that what had been so widely reported in the press and bounced around in conservative echo chambers as yet another example of left-wing academic excess had barely registered here on campus.

The deadly standoff between the white supremacists and their counter-protesters was another thing entirely. The violence and the reactions to it on the part of the president and the press are symptoms of a tension that has lain at the heart of the American project since its very beginning, a tension between the bonds of community and the exclusions that such bonds at times seem to require. And while that tension is clearest in the pitched battle between racists and defenders of equality, the truth is, even the teapot tempest exhibits some strains of it. On the one hand are the faculty and students who are so offended by the historical reality of Jefferson's actions as a slaveholder that they demand his words not be used as a moral compass; on the other, the outraged voices that call for the resignation of the "idiots" who would protest the quoting of one of the most important of the nation's founders.

At first glance the conflict seems to be about whether a person's words can still have value even when some of their actions are despicable. Perhaps the most important words in this specific debate are from the second sentence of the Declaration of Independence, which Jefferson drafted in June 1776 and submitted to the Continental Congress, where it was subjected to multiple revisions before being ratified on July 4. That famous sentence reads:

> We hold these truths to be self-evident, that all men are created equal, that they are endowed by their Creator with certain unalienable Rights, that among these are Life, Liberty and the pursuit of Happiness.—That to secure these rights, Governments are instituted among Men, deriving their just powers from the consent of the governed,—That whenever any Form of Government becomes destructive of these ends, it is the Right of the People to alter or to abolish it, and to institute new Government, laying its foundation on such principles and organizing its powers in such form, as to them shall seem most likely to effect their Safety and Happiness.

The most stunning phrase of the sentence, "that all men are created equal," is also the one that in some ways hinges on how we understand Jefferson today. As a slave-owning patriarch who clearly condoned and profited from a system of government that did not grant suffrage to women or blacks, the word "men" may well have meant white males, not all human beings. If this were the case, then Jefferson's words would indeed be seriously devalued.

Danielle Allen, who has studied and taught the Declaration for many years, does not think this is an accurate reading of Jefferson's words. As she points out, at the outset of the Civil War, the leaders of the Confederate States of America understood perfectly well what Jefferson's words meant and how revolutionary they were. Alexander Stephens, the vice president of the Confederacy, argued that the original Union was based on the "assumption of the equality of races." In response, he and his fellows insisted that their "new Government is founded on exactly the opposite ideas; its foundations are laid, its cornerstone rests, upon the great truth that the negro is not equal to the white man; that slavery . . . is his natural and moral condition." Furthermore, in a passage from Jefferson's original draft criticizing the slave trade, which was edited out by Congress, Jefferson refers to King George III as having "waged cruel war against human nature itself, violating it's [sic] most sacred rights of life & liberty in the persons of a distant people who never offended him." He then refers to these "persons" as "MEN," in capitals, knowing full well that men, women, and children were all victims of the slave trade.

If it is true that Jefferson meant what we today have taken his words to mean, namely, that all *human beings* are created equal—that is, that we have a right to an equal status as citizens even if our circumstances and abilities are myriad and unique—we are certainly right to ask how it is that a person can hold such an idea even while engaging in a practice that so blatantly and violently contradicts that ideal. To claim to believe that all men are created equal while still holding slaves is certainly an example of hypocrisy. At the same time, the impulse to discount ideas when they are undermined by hypocrisy may be epically self-defeating. After all, changes in attitude and ultimately behavior must come from somewhere; and often the ideas that lead the way are first expressed in contexts that contradict them, and by persons who do not yet live up to them. As Allen puts it regarding this same contradiction in Jefferson's person, "When we observe a person who says one thing and does another, we might be looking at a liar, but we might also be looking at a person who hasn't yet been able to turn her ideas into a script that is concrete enough to guide her actions . . . Yet we can reasonably hope that our ideas, which wait up ahead, will make a clearing for desire."

It is precisely the idea that is embodied in Jefferson's words that embodies the second, more pressing meaning of the conflict, the one that conjoins the violence of Charlottesville with the controversy around its founder. For Jefferson's words were, famously, a call to arms, the justification of an act of violent disruption against the law. His justification depended on the articulation of rights as well as the articulation of equality. The two poles, in other words, must remain in balance. We declare independence, we rebel against a government, when we perceive that government to have illegitimately impinged upon our right to define and pursue our happiness as we see fit. At the same time, how we define our happiness must have internal limits, since we cannot so define it as to impinge upon the same right held by others. Where one draws that line, the line separating those who are *within* our community and share our pursuit of happiness, and those who are *outside* it and whose own pursuit may come into conflict with our own—this is the fundamental question of democracy.

The historians who gathered for the live taping of *BackStory* were there to debate exactly this question. The title of the event, "Who Speaks for America?," raises it explicitly. The group—my colleague Nathan, along with Joanne Freeman, Ed Ayers, Peter Onuf, and Brian Balogh—bantered amiably and wittily as they looked at that question though the eyes of eight Americans: Thomas Jefferson, Alexander Hamilton, Abraham Lincoln, Frederick Douglass, Ida B. Wells, Theodore Roosevelt, Ronald Reagan, and Oprah Winfrey. While the selection may seem a bit haphazard, the idea was to show how, again and again, that question has been posed, challenged, and posed again. At the end the members each took a shot at answering a question about what they—and we—were doing there that night. In other words, why do history at all? Nathan's response was electrifying. History, he argued, is the metric we use to decide what gets counted as legitimate debate in a changing democracy. We are called to judgment, he said, and knowledge of history is what can justify us in arguing that some perspectives are simply "beyond the pale."

Resolving the question of this line, of the borders of what counts as a community as it changes along with the changing demographics, technologies, and interests of the people gathered within a democracy, requires the civic engagement of an educated public. That public need not agree on all topics—and in fact they will not. But given the urgency of the questions we are debating, this is absolutely not an area about which we can simply agree to disagree—not when the issues are fundamental to how our society is organized and who is included in its reach. Therefore—and this is the only option left—we must agree upon the groundwork for articulating our disagreement. This is what the founders were striving to create as they designed the world's first modern democratic state. And while far, far from perfect, their ideas provide the common ground on which we strive to work out our differences as a society. History, as Ed Ayers put it at the end of the session, "does give us common ground." It is only through staging our debates in a way that is informed by history that, as he put it, "the idealism of our founding documents will have their day as well."

Jefferson's words matter because words are the basis of action and plant the seeds that grow into history. Long before Teddy Roosevelt acted against the entrenched interests of the plutocrats, Jefferson undermined the very basis of traditional privilege by attacking the institutions of primogeniture that permitted wealth and privilege to be passed unchecked from generation to generation. Liberals today would do better to claim that history than reject it, and should call out efforts to repeal the estate tax for what they are: un-American. Yes, American history is a history of slavery, oppression, and extermination. But it is also a history of redemption, of coming to terms with our nation's sins, and of overcoming them on the way to a better future, on the way to, in Abraham Lincoln's words from the blood-soaked battlefield at Gettysburg four score and seven years later, "a new birth of freedom."

As David Brooks movingly argued in a column he wrote to mark Thanksgiving 2017, it was another speech, one given toward the very end of the war and only a month before Lincoln was murdered, that best sets the tone for the new narrative America needs. Brooks argues that those who have come of age since the 1970s have been taught, justifiably, an American history that emphasizes the injustices suffered by marginalized groups and their heroic efforts to overcome them. This has led to the predominance today of narratives "predicated on division and disappoint-ment." These include a "multicultural narrative, dominant in every school-house, [that] says that America is divided into different biological groups and the status of each group is defined by the oppression that it has suffered," and a "populist narrative, dominant in the electorate, [that] says that America is divided between the virtuous common people and the corrupt and stupid elites." As he stresses, this is a bipartisan problem. Conserva-tives like to blame liberals for the rise of a divisive identity politics, but the small-government movement on the right has equally been about the deni-gration of institutions that claim to act on behalf of the greater commu-nity. While it is thus true that the left learned to look on institutions as repressive, the right has done so, too, perhaps with even greater consequence for the fate of American community.

Lincoln's Second Inaugural Address, Brooks feels, is the model for what our new narrative should say. On a rain-soaked day in early March 1865, Lincoln spoke to a nation traumatized by the most violent conflict in its history, and one it had wrought on itself. Rather than berate the Confed-erates or crow over the Union's impending victory, Lincoln used his char-acteristic brevity to urge Americans to see the war as the price paid for "the wealth piled by the bond-man's two hundred and fifty years of unrequited toil." He wanted to repaint the suffering all Americans were mired in as a painful penance, to be borne "until every drop of blood drawn with the lash, shall be paid by another drawn with the sword." He acknowledged that both sides of the conflict "read the same Bible, and pray to the same God; and each invokes His aid against the other," and thus urged that, while "it may seem strange that any men should dare to ask a just God's assistance in wringing their bread from the sweat of other men's faces . . .

let us judge not, that we be not judged." For Brooks, the Second Inaugural is a kind of acid that can eat away at the rock-hard righteousness that bolsters today's divided politics. As he puts it, "In one brilliant stroke, Lincoln deprives Christian politics of the chauvinism and white identitarianism that we see now on the evangelical right. He fills the vacuum of moral vision that we see now on the relativist left. He shows how American particularism always points to universalism—how the specific features of our settler's history and culture point to [a] vision of communion for all mankind."

The point is that our history, as full as it is of examples of depravity and corruption, oppression and discrimination, is equally full of stories of altruism and redemption, of the triumph of community over selfishness. These are the stories we need now. When the markets crash and thousands lose their homes and savings, we need to recall how it was the selfishness of the gilded class that led to the Great Depression, and look to how Americans came together under Franklin Roosevelt to rebuild the country by investing in programs and causes meant to benefit all. When the scourge of racism persists and black people continue to suffer disproportionately from police violence and poverty, we need to look to the advances of the civil rights movement as a model, not just for how a particular community helps itself, but for how the American community should respond to its own failings and improve. Rather than point to "special snowflakes" who whine for safe spaces as the outcome of identity politics, we should recognize, in the generation of gay and transgender people who fought against horrific legal persecution to transform how they are viewed and accepted in society today, the very model of how America learns ever again from its epic failures, led on by the ideal claimed in those other immortal words, "We the People of the United States, in Order to form a more perfect union . . ."

WHAT ARE PEOPLE FOR?

In the words of a well-known joke, the science major asks, "Why does it work?"; the engineering major asks, "How does it work?"; the business major asks, "How much will it cost?"; and the liberal arts major asks, "Do you want fries with that?" Given the seemingly limitless growth in college tuition from year to year, it's hardly surprising that every spring I face roomfuls of fretful parents whose main concern is how a Hopkins degree is going to help their child get a well-paying job upon graduation, especially if she majored in a fun but frivolous subject like history, English, or philosophy.

Regrettably, if understandably, the question I don't get from parents at these events is how studying at Hopkins will help mold their children into better citizens, or how education will strengthen our community. The sad truth is that it makes sense that parents aren't asking those questions. They are getting ready to pony up some sixty thousand dollars a year for the next four years for their child to study with us, or open their personal finances to thorough review in the hopes of having the school give them at least some discount on that bank-breaking tuition. Such conditions are enough to make the most idealistic among us think about the costs and benefits of education in very practical terms. But the precipitous rise in the cost of higher education isn't just a damper on our ability to think about the higher purpose of education, it's equally a symptom of our society's failure to grasp the essential link between education and community.

The idea that we need to get more students to study STEM fields—science, technology, engineering, and math—became the paradoxical dogma even under President Obama, who credited his own humanistic training and love of literature for preparing him to run the free world while calling ceaselessly for more training in math and science. But while science and math are vital in their own right, the urge to study them exclusively in order to better prepare young people to be productive participants in the economy is reflective of the tensions that are straining our social fabric. When we conceive of education as a way of turning our children into more effective cogs in the machine, we forget that cogs don't think and that society is more than a collection of producers and consumers. We forget that all of us, urban and rural dwellers, liberals and conservatives, talk-radio personalities and college professors, are in the same boat, one we are busy pulling apart while afloat on the high seas.

It was just as manufacturing started declining and higher education was becoming more essential for the new economy that college started becoming more difficult to afford. Instead of bridging the gap and bringing more people into the middle class, education began its free fall into privatization, and a generation of students began taking on more debt than all previous generations combined. Over the last quarter of a century, while the inflation-adjusted wages of college graduates have increased just 1.6 percent, the amount of debt carried by graduates has increased 163 percent—one hundred times the increase in their earning capacity.

Given these scary trends, I have to take parents' financial concerns seriously. So I usually point them to the accumulating data showing that employers are just as likely to hire humanities majors as graduates with STEM degrees, and that students who show a balanced curriculum including a humanities major end up earning on average five thousand dollars more per year than their peers who focused solely on math or engineering. All of these points are valid, but these days my thoughts turn more and more to the fact that we appear to be entering an age when the presumption that there will be enough work for everyone is no longer a safe one. In the University of Warwick economist Robert Skidelsky's estimation, within twenty years, up to a third of jobs in the Western world could be automated, a development that, more than any other, is beginning to undermine the correspondence between work and human worth that has dominated and in some ways driven the extraordinary success of the West's twin engines of market capitalism and liberal democracy.

In 2016 Switzerland held a national election that was rather different from the other one that rocked the United States and the world. Theirs included campaign posters that sported questions like this one: "What would you do if your income were taken care of?" That campaign message was in support of the "yes" side of a referendum that would have guaranteed all Swiss citizens a basic minimum income (BMI). As it happens, the Swiss apparently thought that the answer of many of their fellow citizens would be "not much at all," since they voted decisively against the initiative. But in other countries around the world, trial tests of a BMI are going forward. On the first day of 2017 Finland began a program that provides two thousand unemployed citizens with a BMI of just over five hundred euros a month; Utrecht, in the Netherlands, will provide several test groups of citizens with just under one thousand euros a month under different conditions; and the Italian city of Livorno started last year by giving its one hundred poorest residents a monthly BMI of five hundred euros, a group that will double in size this year.

BMI movements are an extreme example of national communities starting to ask how people are going to value themselves in an age when we can no longer count on work to define that value. Indeed, there are signs that modern society has left us precariously dependent on our careers for our identities, as one by one the other pillars of communal life surrounding individual workers have been stripped away. As Harvard sociologist Robert Putnam showed in his influential 2000 book *Bowling Alone*, Americans' involvement in clubs, churches, and other forms of community organizations started declining precipitously after the 1970s, and this movement has never slowed down. And it has been abundantly clear that declining participation in clubs and organizations is not an isolated phenomenon but part of an overall, potentially devastating trend surrounded by conveniences and technologies that previous generations could only have dreamed of, Americans have never been lonelier.

Today, most of us would be surprised by such an assertion, pointing to the enormous number of friends we are in contact with on social media. It may be, however, that ersatz digital communities are exacerbating the problem of a culturewide epidemic of solitude rather than helping alleviate it, according to Hilarie Cash, a psychotherapist who founded reSTART Life, a rehabilitation center for Internet and gaming addicts. While Cash refocused her practice more than a decade ago to try to help the "tsunami" of people coming to her with serious Internet dependencies, she is convinced that the problem goes well beyond a few isolated cases. She believes that we are living in a culture in which people are not "getting the connections that they need in order to be healthy human beings." Social media, which we turn to as a way of filling that void, isn't helping, because what we need are real, physical connections, "face-to-face, where we are able to see, and touch, and smell, and hear each other . . . We're social creatures. We're meant to be in connection with one another in a safe, caring way, and when it's mediated by a screen, that's absolutely not there."

The British author Ruth Whippman sees the trend as part of modern life's overall emphasis on the individual and the growing conviction that happiness is something we generate internally. Unfortunately, the research is showing that we are getting it exactly wrong. As she puts it, "While placing more and more emphasis on seeking happiness within, Americans in general are spending less and less time actually connecting with other people. Nearly half of all meals eaten in this country are now eaten alone. Teenagers and young millennials are spending less time just 'hanging out' with their friends than any generation in recent history, replacing real-world interaction with smartphones." It turns out that this trend is insidious for personal well-being, carrying "a risk of premature death comparable to that of smoking, and . . . roughly twice as dangerous to our health as obesity." But if isolation is bad for our individual health, it may be even worse for society.

In fact, research into social loneliness suggests that isolation from community cultivates precisely these kinds of thoughts and feelings at a broader societal level. As Johann Hari puts it in his recent book about depression and the loss of social connections, "Protracted loneliness causes you to shut down socially, and to be more suspicious of any social contacts. You become hypervigilant. You start to be more likely to take offense where none was intended, and to be afraid of strangers. You start to be afraid of the very thing you need most." Suspicious, hypervigilant, and taking offense are pretty good descriptions of how broad swaths of the American public view each other these days. And while causality is probably at the very least a two-way street, it stands to reason that decades of declining engagement in organizations, along with declining civic engagement all round, has a lot to do with increasing acrimony in the public sphere.

This picture is disturbingly reminiscent of the dystopian future portrayed in the movie *The Matrix*, in which humanity is glued to a giant virtual reality machine: thousands of isolated brains, each plugged into its own screen, all feeding a system none of them is aware of. In many ways our own knee-jerk political responses—in voting, in how we watch NFL games, and in whom we block on Twitter—are benefiting a class of invisible over-lords who feed on how distracted and angry we are. Should we not ask ourselves how much money Papa John's is getting for being the pro-Trump pizza? How much is Lyft getting for being the anti-Trump ride-hailing app? Recently Les Moonves, the chairman of CBS, was caught on tape saying how good Trump was for business—not because people love him but because people love to hate him. In a sense, such signs of the sociopolitical times as the rise of right-wing, xenophobic parties and candidates in the United States and Europe; the apparently ubiquitous threat of terror attacks, often committed by homegrown extremists; or the dramatic rise in school shootings in the United States since the nineties, are themselves symptoms of this very predicament.

Think about how the terror organization the Islamic State supports disparate acts of terror around the globe. More often than not, it recognizes an assailant after the fact and "claims responsibility" for the death and destruction wrought by his actions. But in truth what ISIS most resembles is an online community dedicated to some noxious, violent perversion—like those frequented by the so-called cannibal cop who fantasized online about killing and eating women. The difference in this case is that the alienated young men it inspires and claims as its own have taken the next step and carried out the grim fantasies they encourage in one another.

This phenomenon, whereby group dynamics permit the overriding of borders determined by widely accepted social norms, was theorized by the Stanford psychologist Mark Granovetter in the 1970s. Granovetter was trying to explain why otherwise law-abiding citizens would, in the context of a riot, commit acts of violence that they would find appalling as indi-viduals acting under normal circumstances. He claimed that the "thresh-olds" separating members of the group from such actions could be collectively lowered when these members were surrounded by others whose own thresh-olds were respectively lower. In other words, a few agitators with extremely low violence thresholds could influence a next layer, who in turn would influence a larger group with far higher thresholds. But whereas the phenomena Granovetter was describing were localized, the endless possibili-ties of virtual space have liberated that process.

Malcolm Gladwell has argued that this is what explains the dramatic increase in school shootings since the nineties, and in particular since the tragedy at Columbine High School in Colorado in 1999. At the time, I can recall how news of the massacre by duster-wearing outsiders Eric Harris and Dylan Klebold of twelve of their fellow students and one teacher was interspersed with television ads for *The Matrix*, with a duster-sporting Keanu Reeves as a kung-fu-wielding member of a cyberrevolutionary group intent on freeing humanity from the all-encompassing virtual reality program that has it in its grips. Who could have foreseen the irony that these two figures would become Internet legends themselves, inspiring dozens of lonely, angry young men over the next two decades to act out their revenge fantasies?

In some ways, school and other mass shootings are similar to the acts claimed by ISIS, regardless of the intent the perpetrators may declare. That's because the young men who commit them have become islands in a sea of solitude, meeting in a virtual space to commiserate and share their fantasies. What Gladwell writes of the two-decade-long epidemic of school shootings is thus equally true of the growth of Internet-inspired terrorism: they are like "slow-motion, ever-evolving" riots unfolding over years instead of hours, and over the whole globe instead of a few city blocks.

This idea may also help explain why radicalization fails to track accurately with socioeconomic oppression. Many of the young men who kill others and blow themselves up come from well-established middle-class families. Their allegiance to radical groups recalls the veneration of other, isolated young white men to the cult of the black duster they created around Harris and Klebold. They may believe it is about history, religion, and culture, but it is not; it is about an entirely constructed identity whose online proponents proffer it as a solution to all their pain. As David Brooks puts it, "These days, most fanatics are not Nietzschean supermen. They are lonely and sad, their fanaticism emerging from wounded pride, a feeling of not being seen."

This is not to say that there aren't real social and culture factors underlying the fragmentation of groups according to ethnic and religious identity. France's failure to offer equal opportunity for the full economic integration of its citizens is central to the sense of exclusion that so many young men of African and Middle Eastern descent growing up in the banlieues feel. Nevertheless, the alienation of the banlieues is not based on a positive, historical identity. As the cultural historian Andrew Hussey has put it, "The kids in the *banlieues* live in this perpetual present of weed, girls, gangsters, Islam . . . They have no sense of history, no sense of where they come from in North Africa, other than localized bits of Arabic that they don't understand, bits of Islam that don't really make sense." Such models of identity, removed from their historical context, provide neither lasting solace nor a real basis for social cohesion. Instead, they are like tiny seams in the fabric of the larger community, primed to rip apart at the first signs of tension.

GROWING COMMUNITY

At their heart, "humanities" and "arts" are the names we give to the ways we have developed to connect with different people across the abyss of time and culture. It is for this reason that they have so often been seen as ends in themselves rather than means to other social ends. Philosophers and economists from John Stuart Mill to John Maynard Keynes believed that, as productivity rose, workers would have more time to devote to noble pursuits such as art and philosophy. It was Karl Marx, who saw that profit comes from excess labor, who also realized that capital would be loath to return gains in productivity in the form of leisure time for workers, a prediction that has been borne out. As Michael Higgins, president of the Republic of Ireland, recently put it, explaining Ireland's move to include philosophy in the public school curriculum, "The dissemination, at all levels of society, of the tools, language and methods of philosophical enquiry can, I believe, provide a meaningful component in any concerted attempt at offering a long-term and holistic response to our current predicament."

The Catholic theologian John Henry Newman understood that the primary goal of education was not merely learning the specifics of an individual field of study, but understanding how input from disparate fields connected to form a greater picture. As he put it, "The mind never views any part of the extended subject-matter of Knowledge without recollecting that it is but a part . . . It makes everything in some sort lead to everything else." As such, the institution dedicated to cultivating the mind, liberal education, was responsible for nothing less than the very fabric of community, aiming as it did at "raising the intellectual tone of the society, at cultivating the public mind, at purifying the national taste, at supplying true principles to popular enthusiasm and fixed aims to popular aspiration, at giving enlargement and sobriety to ideas of the age, at facilitating the exercise of political power, and refining the intercourse of private life."

The problem now is that this fundamental ethos is becoming more and more limited to a tiny substrate of the population, those who attend elite colleges. And even among those students, there is increasing pressure not to allow their minds and interest to "wander" into precisely those realms and areas that provide the kind of impetus to expanding one's interests and connecting with others, or "making everything in some sort lead to everything else." A community of equals is the very condition of possibility of our democracy, but that community is unthinkable without citizens capable of connecting beyond the myopic limits of their own self-interest. To this end we must strive to spread the ethos of the liberal arts beyond their traditional home in our most elite schools. Like the community Ticknor described to Jefferson, that ethos needs to become the foundation of public life, not the birthright of a select few.

From Socrates's claim that the unexamined life is not worth living to the rapid growth of scholarly reflection on the products of human culture that led to the Renaissance, what we now call humanities are those fields of inquiry and creation that are unified by the belief that, in the words of Bryan Doerries—whose Theater of War project uses classical tragedy to help veterans heal from the ravages of PTSD—"we are not alone across time." The Theater of War project has performed ancient Greek tragedies for upward of eighty thousand soldiers, veterans, and their families, in an effort to use classical literature, and specifically the war plays of Sophocles, to "de-stigmatize psychological injury, increase awareness of post-deployment psychological health issues, disseminate information regarding available resources, and foster greater family, community, and troop resilience." Key to their method is that the plays are not simply performed for inert, merely receptive audiences. Rather, those audiences are invited to engage with the performers and each other in town-hall-style discussions after performances. They are thus able to bring their own stories to others and compare what they have seen in their own experience with Sophocles's reflections on the trauma of war.

Stories, perhaps especially those works that have proved most enduring, seem to have a special ability to connect far-flung people and show them that they are not alone across time and culture. In 1981 a young Somali man named Mohamed Barud was accused by the government of Siad Barre, the country's military dictator, of treason, for having written a letter complaining of the conditions in the hospital where he worked. Despite being recently wed, he was sentenced to life in prison, where he was confined to a tiny cell and ordered not to speak to anyone, ever.

Living in total solitary confinement, Mohamed began to develop paranoid suspicions about everything and everyone, including his young wife. He began to assume the worst of her: that she had moved on, and was enjoying her life and freedom, while he was wasting away in captivity. Consumed by the torturous thoughts, he was surprised one day to hear a man's voice whispering to him from the cell next to his. Whenever the guard was far away enough not to hear, he heard the man repeat the same phrase: "Learn ABC through the wall." And so began a lengthy communication. After learning a tapped code from the man in the neighboring cell, he soon learned who he was: the director of the hospital, who had been arrested and confined as a result of Mohamed's letter. But far from seeking revenge, the doctor, Adan Abokor, was trying something out that he hoped would alleviate Mohamed's suffering.

Over the next seven years, Adan patiently tapped out, letter by letter, the entirety of Tolstoy's great novel *Anna Karenina*, with Mohamed translating it into words on the other side of the wall. Tolstoy's novel tells the story of a young Russian noblewoman who falls in love with a young soldier and leaves her husband. As the journalist Gregory Warner tells it, "Instead of having a secret affair like others in her social set, she leaves her husband, makes her love public. And she's punished. She's isolated and alone. Anna stays in her room, wondering what her lover is up to when he's not with her, kind of like Mohamed was wondering what his wife was doing outside the prison walls." Listening to the novel, page by page, each of its roughly three million words tapped out by Adan over seven years, Mohamed learned to free himself of the mental bonds his physical confinement had imposed on him. He learned to empathize and identify with his wife instead of resenting and blaming her. As Mohamed puts it, "It definitely helped— definitely, definitely. In a place like that prison, people become very selfish. You think, everybody has forgotten about me, and nobody cares about me like that. But when you think about other people's situation, then you—it helped me survive."

Rebuilding a common sense of civic commitment in our country will involve investment and sacrifice from all sides, and we are sorely unused to sacrificing for anything other than ourselves or our immediate families. Since the 1970s, to take a particularly loaded example, we have depended on volunteer armed services to defend our country. What this has meant in practical terms is that most of those who enlist come from economically less advantaged backgrounds than those who do not—a difference that is most clearly seen in the fact that fewer than 7 percent of enlisted members have completed a bachelor's degree, compared with almost a third of the population at large. Our poorest citizens risk their lives while the rich benefit from their sacrifices while protecting themselves and their children. As has been well documented, less than 1 percent of U.S. congressmen and senators have children in the military. In fact, when John McCain's two sons enlisted in 2006, they increased the existing number by 50 percent. But graduates from elite colleges are no better, also averaging barely 1 percent enlistment.

A year of public service—in rural and urban school districts, retirement homes, food banks, or the military—would ensure that all citizens divert some portion of their energies from their private ambitions and commit to the commonwealth that secures their freedom in the first place. As a candidate in 2008 Barack Obama called for precisely such a reinvestment in the idea of public service. Recalling what he saw as the missed opportunity after the attacks of September 11, 2001, he said, "Instead of a call to service, we were asked to shop . . . Instead of leadership that called us to come together, we got patriotism defined as the property of one party and used as a political wedge . . . we ended up going into a war that should have never been authorized and should have never been waged."

In 2016 the former general and leader of the allied forces in Afghanistan Stanley McChrystal issued precisely such a call to service. As he wrote in a widely cited article in the *Atlantic*, "A year of service has the power to bring young people together from different races, ethnicities, incomes, faiths, and political backgrounds to work on pressing problems facing U.S. society today. In the process, they can build empathy by getting to know each other around something positive—the shared work of participating in a democracy—as they shape their views of their country and the world." It's important to note that while this call was coming from a general, it had almost nothing to do with war or even preparedness for war. Rather, what the general was emphasizing were the possibilities inherent in such a program for the reconstruction of American community. In his words:

> Imagine for a moment a large-scale commitment to offering young Americans who are black and white, rich and poor, Republican and Democrat, and Christian, Jewish, and Muslim opportunities to work side by side, serving their country together. The focus of their service year would be teaching, tutoring, and mentoring disadvantaged students; cleaning neighborhoods in need of renewal; renovating homes in blighted areas; and helping veterans reintegrate into their communities.

As McChrystal emphasizes, one virtue of the call to public service is that it has the potential to transcend our facile political categorizations. In the past public service was largely identified with the Democratic Party, with then senator John Ashcroft dismissing Bill Clinton's signature AmeriCorps program as "welfare for the well-to-do." But over the last two decades the idea has been championed by Republicans as well. John

McCain, whose life has been dedicated to the principle of service, is a major supporter of the idea. And President George W. Bush, while notably failing to galvanize a spirit of community and sacrifice after the September 11 attacks—calling on Americans to "go down to Disney World in Florida" and to "take your families and enjoy life the way we want it to be enjoyed"—did create the USA Freedom Corps and at least called on Americans to engage in public service.

The first thing to recognize in thinking about moving toward universal public service is that the infrastructure already exists. AmeriCorps already signs up more than eighty thousand Americans a year to its numerous service programs, ranging from education to environmental stewardship to disaster relief to fighting poverty. Since its creation in 1994, more than a million people have participated. Through the program, volunteers receive a small stipend and grants to be used toward higher education. For all its virtues, though, eighty thousand people a year is far from universal. Ideally we could institute an obligatory year of service, a duty of citizenship, but associated with excitement and patriotism rather than the dreaded inevitability with which Americans treat paying taxes or being called to jury duty. The problem is that, as one commentator has put it, "Americans don't like to be told what they have to do." But to make service nearly universal some serious carrots would have to be deployed, which, naturally, undercuts the very spirit of community that a year of national service is intended to bolster.

If obligatory universal service is truly politically impossible, we could make the carrot be a far more generous higher-education scholarship, to be used at any university that grants the candidate admission. Currently the maximum education grant from AmeriCorps is limited to just shy of six thousand dollars, an amount that, while significant for less-advantaged students, doesn't make much of a dent in the tuitions of many state or private schools. An agreement among universities to underwrite a year of tuition for every year of public service would be both fair and feasible. It would help solder together the goals of service and higher education in the public imagination. And to ensure compliance, universities' tax-free status and eligibility for public funds could be made contingent on participating.

The call to public service is right. It has been made before and will be made again. But it will fall on deaf ears if we cannot change the way we talk about community in this country. Can it be that we have forgotten something that our liberal tradition has long known, that our democracy cannot be taken for granted, that civil society doesn't emerge magically from a group of individuals pursuing their own interests, but rather that the individual freedoms we enjoy will disappear without a true community to nourish and protect them? Fortunately, there are signs that we are starting to catch on, that we are starting to realize that dozens or hundreds of friends on Facebook don't compensate for the desperately sad decline in the number of close friends Americans report having. One encouraging trend is the growing number of programs that use the arts and humanities to foster community engagement.

Lockerman Bundy Elementary School sits beside the Franklin-Mulberry Expressway, the thoroughfare that cuts through West Baltimore, pumping commuters into and out of the city's downtown without their having to see, much less interact with, the Sandtown-Winchester neighborhood a few blocks to the north, where Freddie Gray lived, which saw the worst of the 2015 unrest following his death in the back of a police van. The area is 97 percent African American. A fourth of its houses are vacant. A third of its residents live below the poverty line. Inside the elementary school's metal doors, the brightly mural-bedecked walls were a stark contrast to its bleak surroundings as I filed into the school's multipurpose gym among a dozen chattering boys and girls. The boys had just finished playing basketball and were downing bottles of water as the students gathered for afternoon rehearsal. In only two weeks they would be opening the Baltimore Symphony Orchestra's annual fall gala, accompanied by storied trumpeter Wynton Marsalis.

If these kids were nervous at the thought of performing under that kind of pressure, they didn't show it. The bustle and laughter slowly died down as they took their seats in metal chairs set up around the gym floor. Then, without a word, their conductor, the Peabody Conservatory instructor of music theory Eli Wirth, raised his right hand, and the percussionists and trombones kicked off the first measures of a lively New Orleans–style second line march. As the bass line repeated, one by one the sections stepped in, until finally the whole orchestra was alight with sound and movement, a wiry trumpeter named Kevin was on his feet blowing toward the ceiling, and my own feet were thumping up and down to the irresistible rhythms.

I was jolted out of a musical reverie when Eli closed his first with a brief flourish and the jamboree came to a sudden stop. "How big is the Meyerhoff?" he asked, referring to the BSO's music hall in the Mount Vernon district of Baltimore. "Is it bigger than this gym?" The kids nodded their assent and Eli continued, now talking to the clarinetist seated to his left. "That's right. It's much, much bigger than here. So, Asia, does that mean you need to be playing really soft and quiet"—he lowered his voice to a whisper—"like a little mouse?" "No," she giggled. "What was that?" he pretended not to hear her. "NO!" she shouted, at which point Kevin, the trumpeter, shouted from the back of the room, "We gonna play LOUD!"

Kevin, Asia, and the other kids in the room are in the OrchKids program, created about a decade ago by the BSO's music director, Marin Alsop, as "a school program that combines music and mentorship to have a positive impact on Baltimore City youth." As Alsop puts it, "I believe passionately that music has the power to change lives, and the BSO should lead the movement. By providing a strong foundation and developing the whole individual, we can position these students for lifelong success—a success not limited to music, but in all areas of their lives."

As Eli told me during a break at one of their rehearsals, the group of mostly high school kids I was spending the week with had all been with the program since its inception. They would be its first graduating class. But the two dozen or so musicians in the room were only a sliver of the more than one thousand kids around Baltimore who were now participating in the program at one of six elementary, middle, and high schools around the city. If Alsop's hope is for this program to have a positive impact on her students' lives beyond just learning to play music, it sure seems to be working. The kids I spoke with radiated confidence and poise. They were energized and enthusiastic, and spoke about the future with an irrepressible gleam in their eyes.

OrchKids is one of an ever-growing number of community-strengthening programs blossoming around the country that seek to invest in local community through the arts and humanities. I got a call from the director of one of those programs in New York City, asking me to come to Bushwick, an immigrant neighborhood that has largely been passed by in Brooklyn's rush to rival Manhattan in property values. On a cold, rainy afternoon a few weeks later I pulled up at the address he had given me. I looked around for the school I had come to visit. It took me a few moments to realize that I was standing right in front of it. In fact, it was more of a storefront than a school. Through the scratched glass window and door I could now see some long tables dispersed around a room filled with books stacked haphazardly on shelves but also scattered on tabletops or in apparently random piles. I pushed the door open and was immediately greeted by a white-bearded and beaming Stephen Haff, the director, teacher, and all-around force of nature behind Still Waters in a Storm.

A half an hour later, after meeting the kids and munching on the delicious potato tortillas with tomatoes and sour cream that one of the mothers had provided, we dove into two hours of translation and discussion of Cervantes's *Don Quixote* that could have been taking place in one of my seminars at Hopkins. As we worked out how to render into English the famous scene in which Don Quixote and Sancho disagree on whether what they are looking at are giants or just windmills, Jonathan, a shy twelve-year-old whose parents are from Ecuador, looked up and met my eyes. "They can't agree on what the facts are," he said. "That happens nowadays, too."

Still Waters is a radical experiment in learning that bucks the trend in education wherein every learning experience is evaluated in terms of its immediate and practical application. Stephen Haff presents his students with literary classics and asks them to translate them both into a different language and a different world. He challenges them, in other words, to find common ground across time and culture with a distant world, and to bring that world into their own. As they do so, these kids see their own worlds grow beyond the confines of family and the city blocks that seem to wall them off from the opportunities showered on the children in the increasingly gentrified neighborhoods of Brooklyn. They see them grow because they are connecting with other people across cultures and times.

Still Waters and OrchKids are just two examples of a narrative that is emerging to counter today's spirit of fragmentation and resentment. Where our daily political showdowns reveal tribalism at its worst, artists and teachers like Eli and Stephen exemplify the possibility that still lies at the core of the American project: to expand the reach of our fellow feeling to connect with people from different origins, backgrounds, and economic strata. They allow us to see in practice the kind of impact McChrystal's proposal could have at a national level, if we could only see our way to realizing it.

THE IDEA OF AMERICA

Too often today's contributions to the debate about the quality of our civic discourse have devolved into repeating the same pattern of divisiveness. We assume the world must be divided between red and blue, conservative and liberal, so we naturally categorize every contribution, every position, as falling along that spectrum. The right blames the left, the left blames the right, but everyone is doing it; and if you're not, if you criticize the practice, then you risk being dismissed as a wishy-washy moderate. A criticism of the spectrum itself then, paradoxically, gets placed on the same spectrum, just somewhere in the middle, where partisans of the extremes can make themselves feel good by quoting Dante's assertion, "The hottest places in hell are reserved for those who maintain their neutrality in times of moral crisis."

The heat of moral outrage, I'm afraid, infects the accuracy of their quotations as much as it blinds them to the possibility of other ways of conceptualizing political debate. The neutrals, as my students would quickly remind them, don't occupy any place in Dante's hell. They are forever locked outside its gate, in its vestibule, believing they would prefer the clarity of concrete suffering over an eternity of uncertainty. And yet, perhaps, that very illusion is what clouds us and leads us astray. As we have become more isolated, sorted into ever-smaller circles of loyalty, we have become ever more enamored of our own rightness and ever less willing to engage with those who dissent.

Everyone is divided. Republicans are divided into establishment neoliberals and white nationalists. Democrats are divided into identitarians and economic populists. Garrison Keillor rips into Congressman Keith Ellison, asking if "a lackluster black Muslim congressman from Minneapolis is" the person who will get the Democratic Party to "connect with disaffected workers in Youngstown and Pittsburgh." When Mark Lilla, calling for a revival of American civic engagement, writes that "this is a time when, precisely because America has become more diverse and individualistic in reality, there is greater, not less, need to cultivate political fellow feeling," I couldn't agree more. And yet, in the same book he criticizes the Black Lives Matter movement, calling it "a textbook example of how not to build solidarity." Lilla, a liberal, is criticizing the movement that David Brooks, a conservative, calls "the most complete social movement in America today, as a communal, intellectual, moral and political force." Why, I find myself asking, do we have to choose? Why do I need to have fellow feeling either for working-class whites *or* for the young black men who have never ceased to have their civil rights trampled on? Why can't we find common ground for both, for all?

Mark Lilla and Garrison Keillor would respond with pragmatic arguments. If progressives want to change things, they first need to win elections. To that end, Lilla cites Lincoln's dictum, "Public sentiment is everything. With it, nothing can fail; against it, nothing can succeed," and then goes on to argue that "the American right understands in its bones this law of democratic politics, which is why it has effectively controlled the political agenda of this country for two generations." But by blaming "identity liberalism" for the loss of public sentiment, Lilla and others have at least implicitly suggested a kind of course correction away from concern for racial minorities and toward an embrace of white, working-class voters—as if this itself weren't identity politics to exactly the same degree.

It seems to me that, of recent political commentators, Van Jones has said it best: "Should the party focus more on racial minorities, or should it focus more on working-class white voters? This is a stupid debate." As he says about progressives, "I think it is okay to admit that in recent years we have not known how to draw our circle big enough to include . . . white guys wearing hard hats." The point is not to acknowledge yet another identity group, but to find a way to generate that "fellow feeling" that seems to be so lacking today. That feeling doesn't come from claiming the status of victim: it comes from connecting with other people across cultural divides, from listening to each other.

Listening to each other isn't just some surface fix; it's foundational to the very idea of liberty that the United States claims to embody. Political philosopher Yuval Levin made this point brilliantly when he described the weakness of today's political culture as a bipartisan forfeiture of the "long way" to liberty. He writes of "the dangerous impoverishment of our political culture today: The idea of liberty that both progressives and conservatives generally articulate takes the person capable of freedom for granted without pausing to wonder where he might come from." We have forgotten that liberty is something we need to create by disseminating and upholding our fundamental values. As he puts it, "Our bipartisan, individualist language of liberty keeps us from seeing that the liberty that liberalism offers exists in large part to foster precisely the moral formation we need and the institutions that engage in it. Religious freedom, freedom of association, freedom of the press—these are liberties designed to protect our traditions of moral formation, and they do just that."

For our society to relearn the crucial role of our vaunted liberties, beyond the pleasures of just "doing what we want," the dissemination of a liberal arts education is key. Such an educational focus, however, has become, as Levin writes,

out of step with our times because it offers us not vocational skills but the shaping of habits of thought and practice. It forms our souls through exposure to beauty, to truth, and to the power of the sublime that we can only glimpse through the mediation of rare artistic genius. It is, in this sense, closer to an aristocratic idea of leisure than to the modern idea of training. It is decidedly not utilitarian. It is no short way to liberation. And it is therefore under fierce assault precisely in the academic institutions that should be havens for liberal formation.

If liberal education, one of the foundations of this redirection of liberty, is itself under attack from right-wing politics and market-oriented ideologies, another foundation has been widely pilloried by the left: religion. While religious institutions in the United States have, in recent times, clustered on the conservative side of the political spectrum, the left needs to learn to cherish moderate religious beliefs, and not just those stemming from non-Western cultures. Van Jones, an observant Christian, is effusive about the potentially progressive value of religious commitment, admonishing his leftist readers that "Democrats should never forget the contributions made by people of faith on the front lines during our most important battles for justice." The reason religion can inform progressive as well as conservative politics is because of its intrinsic relation to community. As Levin puts it, "Religious institutions are not just counterbalances but foundations of the liberal order. They command us to a mixture of responsibility, sympathy, lawfulness, and righteousness that align our wants with our duties. They help form us to be free. And what is true of religion in particular is true more generally of the institutions of the long way to liberty: They are foundational to liberalism not so much because they counteract its vices as because they prepare human beings to handle the burdens and responsibilities of being free."

David Brooks succinctly summarizes Levin's arguments when he argues that our political spectrum is dominated by liberals in the classical sense, that is, people who believe government exists to maximize liberty. The thing is, whether on the left or the right, today's liberals "assume that if you give people freedom they will use it to care for their neighbors, to have civil conversations, to form opinions after examining the evidence. But if you weaken family, faith, community and any sense of national obligation, where is that social, emotional and moral formation supposed to come from? How will the virtuous habits form?" In the absence of institutions like a liberal education or churches doing the hard work of cultivating a truly liberal community, other, market-driven institutions will happily step in, but without the same community-oriented goals.

Today, Fox News and other cable outlets occupy the role of religious leader for great swaths of the American public. After talking with evangelical Christians who have become disillusioned with and highly critical of the co-optation of Christians by right-wing media outlets like Fox, journalist Molly Worthen quoted one such believer: "The reason Fox News is so formative is that it's this repetitive, almost ritualistic thing that people do every night. It forms in them particular fears and desires, an idea of America. This is convincing on a less than logical level, and the church is not communicating to them in that same way." This realization is leading some evangelical Christians to withdraw further into their own religious communities. But, as Worthen points out, "at a time when many Americans live in economically and ethnically segregated communities, it seems doubtful that further withdrawal from the world will stimulate radical empathy. The urge to batten down the hatches may actually feed the cultural patterns that enabled the election of Donald Trump: the impulse to associate only with people like ourselves and grow even more certain that evil forces are persecuting us."

Perhaps the most vibrant debate in the postmortem year following the 2016 presidential election was between those who claimed that racism propelled Trump into the White House and those who argued that his voters were inspired mainly by economic injustice, even if they placed their faith in precisely the wrong man. In fact, the two factors can't be separated. Since Nixon and especially since Reagan, the right has achieved political success selling the myth of a federal government bloated by handouts to freeloading minorities while hardworking (read: white) Americans get the shaft. The first part of the story was a lie; minorities were and continue to be the victims of systemic discrimination. The second part was true; it's just that the right's purported solutions were never really intended to fix that problem. The election of Donald Trump was a historic reckoning,

as much for the Republican "establishment" as for the Democrats. What
unites those who voted for him is not racism, even if Trump caters to
racists and is a racist himself. No, Trumpism is driven by sorrow and rage:
sorrow for the loss of community, rage at those perceived to be the authors
and beneficiaries of what has come to take its place—cosmopolitan,
university-trained elites and the "special interests" they cater to.

We need to understand that the rage isn't going to dissipate if community isn't rebuilt. It isn't enough to win back seats, to undo tax policies, or
to appoint new justices, only to wait for the next election and have the tables
be turned again. To thrive, to even survive as a nation, America must
rebuild its splintered community; we must reach into our past for the ideas
and stories on which to found a common future. To do this, though, we
also have to learn to think of ourselves and each other as part of the same
project again. We need to learn to think of ourselves as Americans, bound
together by our faith in that project.

There's an extraordinary difference between being an American and
being a citizen of almost any other nation, and it's one that, no matter where
I go and with whom I speak, all people seem to recognize. In most countries, to truly become and feel like you belong, you have to speak or look
a certain way. Not in America. Unlike in most countries, being an American has nothing to do with accent or religion or skin color. Instead, it has
to do with our commitment to an idea. The idea is radical; in fact, it is so
revolutionary that it has almost never been realized. And yet, if we search
our souls, we still know it is our guiding light. The idea is simply this: If
you come here, where you came from doesn't matter. Here you start fresh.
No one gets a leg up. Here we are all equals.

Humans are social animals. Over eons we have developed the most
complex communication systems of any species on the planet, and used
them to exert ever more control over our environments. But we still orga-
nize ourselves into clans, much as our earliest ancestors did. Over time we
have proven that loyalty to clan can be expanded. We have learned to identify with townships, ethnicities, nations, and transnational religions. But
every expansion of our loyalty comes at a cost, as if we were tearing at some
primordial bond. When we become frightened, we are quick to withdraw

back into our most parochial clans, rejecting all and anyone who seems foreign and who might be a threat.

America—the idea, the project, more than its slow and painful realization—has always been a challenge to this baseline human tendency. It was this idea that the poet Emma Lazarus would evoke so fragrantly in 1883 in the poem she wrote in homage to the French Republic's gift to its sister democracy, which would be erected three years later. Unlike that Colossus "of Greek fame, / With conquering limbs astride from land to land," Liberty, the New Colossus, would have the name "Mother of Exiles," and from her "beacon-hand / Glows world-wide welcome." Of those people described so vividly in her most famous lines, "your tired, your poor, / Your huddled masses yearning to breathe free, / The wretched refuse of your teeming shore," perhaps the best description is one that comes a line later, "Send these, the homeless, tempest-tost to me." *Homeless.* For the idea of America, the idea embodied in the words of Jefferson and his fellows when they assumed "among the powers of the earth, the separate and equal station to which the Laws of Nature and of Nature's God entitle them," was that of a people defined not by their home—their blood and soil—but by their devotion to the idea of equality.

As Danielle Allen writes, "If we abandon equality, we lose the single bond that makes us a community, that makes us a people with the capacity to be free collectively and individually in the first place." If we are to solve the catastrophes facing the world today—from the rise of fundamentalism to the rise of the seas—we can only do so by learning to come together as a community of equals. Our schools, once the guarantors of our equality, and hence of the single bond that joins us, have, along with society as a whole, lost their way. We must work together to find it again. Our democracy, our freedom itself, is at stake, and time is running out.

Acknowledgments

This book is the product of an intense, yearlong dialogue with my editor, Anton Mueller. Without his skeptical questions, keen insights, and at times exasperating prodding, it might never have taken shape, and certainly not the shape it currently has. The production team at Bloomsbury, especially Barbara Darko, have been nothing short of extraordinary, and copyeditor Greg Villepique and proofreader Nora Nussbaum were able to catch a host of errors and infelicities I had passed over. I am also deeply grateful to my agent, Michael Carlisle, who was the first to encourage me to pursue the idea, and who is a perpetual source of support. Troy Tower was an indispensable resource, as he always is, both as a second set of eyes and for compiling the back matter in record time. I have benefited tremendously from intense conversation on many of these fronts with Nathan Connolly. Bernadette Wegenstein, my wife and partner in all ways intellectual and emotional, immeasurably enriched early drafts with her incomparable sense of character and narrative. Finally, my oldest son, Alexander, now at an age and place in life where he is deeply engaged in many of this book's central questions, provided compelling feedback from a freshness of perspective I have lost through age and professional experience. Despite my great debt to them all, only I am to blame for any errors or inaccuracies that may remain.

Notes

Introduction

2 **In Thomas Jefferson's powerful words**: Thomas Jefferson to Charles Yancey, January 6, 1816, in *1 September 1815 to 30 April 1816* (2012), vol. 9 of *The Papers of Thomas Jefferson: Retirement Series*, ed. J. Jefferson Looney (Princeton, NJ: Princeton University Press, 2004–), 328–31, 331 (italics added).

2–3 **Indeed, as he said of the university**: Thomas Jefferson to William Roscoe, December 27, 1820, in *Letters Written After His Return to the United States, 1789–1826* (1903), vol. 15 of *The Writings of Thomas Jefferson*, ed. Andrew A. Lipscomb (Washington, D.C.: Thomas Jefferson Memorial Association, 1903), 302–4, 303.

3 **as Cardinal John Henry Newman**: See section 1:7.10 of John Henry Newman, *The Idea of a University: Defined and Illustrated in Nine Discourses Delivered to the Catholics of Dublin in Occasional Lectures and Essays Addressed to the Members of the Catholic University*, ed. Martin J. Svaglic (Notre Dame, IN: University of Notre Dame Press, 1982), 134.

3 **As Columbia professor**: Mark Lilla, "The End of Identity Liberalism," *New York Times*, November 18, 2016, https://www.nytimes.com/2016/11/20/opinion/sunday/the-end-of-identity-liberalism.html.

3 **Donald Trump capitalized**: Beverly Gage, "How 'Elites' Became One of the Nastiest Epithets in American Politics," *New York Times Magazine*, January 8, 2017, https://www.nytimes.com/2017/01/03/magazine/how-elites-became-one-of-the-nastiest-epithets-in-american-politics.html.

6 **By 1991 even a left-leaning**: Arthur M. Schlesinger Jr., *The Disuniting of America: Reflections on a Multicultural Society*, rev. ed. (New York: W. W. Norton, 1998), 22.

7 **forcing Sullivan to issue**: Sullivan's e-mail is quoted in Kate Bellows, "Professors Ask Sullivan to Stop Quoting Jefferson," *Cavalier Daily*, November 13, 2016, http://www.cavalierdaily.com/article/2016/11/professors-ask-sullivan-to-stop-quoting-jefferson.

9 **New York's City College**: David Leonhardt, "America's Great Working-Class Colleges," *New York Times*, January 22, 2017, https://www.nytimes

.com/2017/01/18/opinion/sunday/americas-great-working-class-colleges
.html. Leonhardt's data is drawn from a 2017 report published by the
Equality of Opportunity Project; see Raj Chetty, John N. Friedman,
Emmanuel Saez, Nicholas Turner, and Danny Yagan, "Mobility Report Cards:
The Role of Colleges in Intergenerational Mobility," http://www.equality
-of-opportunity.org/papers/coll_mrc_paper.pdf. On the nicknames City
College has earned, see "Our History" on their website, https://www.ccny
.cuny.edu/about/history.

10 **its masthead read**: For the masthead of the *Revolution* and its revisions,
see Jennifer Chambers, *Abigail Scott Duniway and Susan B. Anthony in
Oregon: Hesitate No Longer* (Charleston, SC: History Press, 2018), 54–56.

10 **The long title of the Civil Rights Act**: The text of the Civil Rights Act of
1964, Public Law 88-352, can be found at the website of the Clerk of the
House of Representatives, http://library.clerk.house.gov/reference-files/PPL
_CivilRightsAct_1964.pdf.

10 **These phrases refer to rights implicitly**: Citations of the U.S. Constitu-
tion follow the online edition of *Constitution of the United States of America:
Analysis and Interpretation* published by the U.S. Congress, last updated
August 26, 2017, https://www.congress.gov/constitution-annotated.

10 **He defined equality as a state**: See paragraph 4 of the *Second Treatise of
Government*, in John Locke, *Two Treatises of Government*, 2nd ed., ed. Peter
Laslett (Cambridge, UK: Cambridge University Press, 1967), 283–446,
287. For the philosophical and political legacy of Locke's social contract,
see Michael Lessnoff, *Social Contract* (New York: Macmillan, 1986); see also
Hans Aarsleff, "Locke's Influence," in Vere Chappell, ed., *The Cambridge
Companion to Locke* (Cambridge, UK: Cambridge University Press, 1994),
252–89.

11 **in Rawls's famous formulation**: See chapter 46 of John Rawls, *A Theory of
Justice*, revised ed. (Cambridge, MA: Harvard University Press, 1999),
266.

11 **As he once put it, borrowing**: In *Contingency, Irony, and Solidarity*
(Cambridge, UK: Cambridge University Press, 1989), xv, Richard Rorty
paraphrases Judith Shklar's claim that "liberal and humane people . . . would
choose cruelty as the worst thing we do"; see her *Ordinary Vices* (Cambridge,
MA: Harvard University Press, 1984), 44.

11 **what Adam Smith called**: See chapter 1.1.1.3 of Adam Smith, *The Theory
of Moral Sentiments*, corrected ed., eds. David Daiches Raphael and Alec
Lawrence Macfie (Oxford, UK: Clarendon Press, 1979), 10.

12 **"common vocabularies and common hopes"**: Rorty, *Contingency, Irony,
and Solidarity*, 86.

13 **One popular news site**: The Nashville foreman is quoted in Deirdre Reilly,
"Vanderbilt's Gender-Neutral Nonsense," *MomZette*, September 6, 2016,
http://www.lifezette.com/momzette/vanderbilt-gender-neutral-nonsense.

I. Identity

Undoing History

17 Katrin Schultheiss, the chair: Schultheiss is quoted in in Lily Werlinich, "History Department Changes Major Requirements to Draw in Students," *GW Hatchet*, November 14, 2016, https://www.gwhatchet.com/2016/11/13 /history-department-changes-major-requirements-to-draw-in-students.

17–18 In a statement put out in 2016: ACTA's press release, dated July 1, 2016, is available at https://www.goacta.org/news/top_u.s._colleges_fail _to_require_history_majors_to_take_u.s._history. For the ACTA mission statement, see https://www.goacta.org/about/mission.

19 whose research into the young men: Stephen Orgel, *Impersonations: The Performance of Gender in Shakespeare's England* (Cambridge, UK: Cambridge University Press, 1996), xiv.

19 Until the 1960s: For figures on educational attainment by race and gender before the 1990s, see the National Center for Education Statistics' 1993 survey *120 Years of American Education: An Educational Portrait*, ed. Thomas D. Snyder, https://nces.ed.gov/pubs93/93442.pdf. The U.S. Census Bureau has published data from as recently as 2016 at https://www.census.gov/data /tables/2016/demo/education-attainment/cps-detailed-tables.html.

22 As Harvard president: Drew Gilpin Faust, "Don't Defund American History," *New York Times*, March 9, 2017, https://www.nytimes.com/2017 /03/09/opinion/killing-a-program-that-brings-history-to-life.html.

A First Volley in the Culture Wars

22 released a report authored: William J. Bennett, "To Reclaim a Legacy: A Report on the Humanities in Higher Education" (Washington, D.C.: National Endowment for the Humanities, 1984), 1, https://files.eric.ed.gov/ fulltext/ED247880.pdf.

23 she and her committee declared the principal: Lynne V. Cheney, "Humanities in America: A Report to the President, the Congress and the American People" (Washington, D.C.: National Endowment for the Humanities, 1988), 17–18, https://files.eric.ed.gov/fulltext/ED303408.pdf.

24 In the very first words: William F. Buckley, Jr., *God and Man at Yale: The Superstitions of "Academic Freedom,"* new ed. (Washington, D.C.: Regnery Gateway, 1986), lvii, lix–lx, lxii.

24 Those to follow him: For an overview of the notion of "culture wars" in recent American politics, see, among others, Gerald Graff, *Beyond the Culture Wars: How Teaching the Conflicts Can Revitalize American Education* (New York: W. W. Norton, 1992); and Irene Taviss Thomson, *Culture Wars and Enduring American Dilemmas* (Ann Arbor: University of Michigan Press, 2010).

24 **As the literary biographer**: James Atlas, *The Book Wars* (Knoxville: Whittle Direct Books, 1990), 86.

25 **As the novelist and essayist**: Cynthia Ozick, "T. S. Eliot at 101," *New Yorker*, November 20, 1989, 119–54, 119, 152. The essay is reprinted under the title "T. S. Eliot at 101: 'The Man Who Suffers and the Mind Which Creates,'" in *Fame & Folly: Essays* (New York: Alfred A. Knopf, 1996), 3–49.

Making the Personal Political

26 **In 1970, three years before**: Carol Hanisch, "The Personal Is Political," in Barbara A. Crow, ed., *Radical Feminism: A Documentary Reader* (New York: New York University Press, 2000), 113–16, 114.

28 **a countermovement led by an alliance**: For a history of politically correct discourse, see Richard Feldstein, *Political Correctness: A Response from the Cultural Left* (Minneapolis: University of Minnesota Press, 1997). For critiques, see Michael S. Cummings, *Beyond Political Correctness: Social Transformation in the United States* (Cincinnati: University of Cincinnati Press, 2001); and Robert Maranto, Richard E. Redding, and Frederick M. Hess, eds., *The Politically Correct University: Problems, Scope, and Reforms* (Washington, D.C.: AEI Press, 2009).

28 **Buckley himself weighed in**: William F. Buckley describes Professor William Cole in a 1988 column entitled "The Great Purge," reprinted in his collection *Happy Days Were Here Again: Reflections of a Libertarian Journalist*, ed. Patricia Bozell (New York: Random House, 1993), 91–93, 92.

31 **As Carter put it**: Stephen Carter is quoted in Dinesh D'Souza, *Illiberal Education: The Politics of Race and Sex on Campus* (New York: Free Press, 1991), 5.

31 **when blacks are imprisoned**: Figures on racial disparities in incarceration rates, based on 2001 data from the Bureau of Justice Statistics, are available from the Sentencing Project; see "Criminal Justice Facts," http://www .sentencingproject.org/criminal-justice-facts.

31 **one in five women report**: A 2015 survey by the *Washington Post* and the Harvey J. Kaiser Family Foundation confirmed on a national scale the contested statistic that 20 percent of women college students experience sexual assault; see Nick Anderson and Scott Clement, "1 in 5 College Women Say They Were Violated," *Washington Post*, June 12, 2015, http://www.washing tonpost.com/sf/local/2015/06/12/1-in-5-women-say-they-were-violated. The same statistic had been presented in a 2014 report prepared by the Obama White House off a 2007 finding by the Justice Department, studies that have both been critiqued for their methodology. A 2015 report by the American Association of Universities reported that 23.1 percent of female students at twenty-seven American universities experienced sexual assault; see David Cantor, Bonnie Fisher, Susan Chibnall, Reanne Townsend, Hyunshik Lee,

Carol Bruce, and Gail Thomas, "Report on the AAU Campus Climate Survey on Sexual Assault and Sexual Misconduct," revised October 20, 2017, https://www.aau.edu/key-issues/aau-climate-survey-sexual-assault-and -sexual-misconduct-2015. For a discussion of the crisis of college sexual assault, see Laura Kipnis, *Unwanted Advances: Sexual Paranoia Comes to Campus* (New York: HarperCollins, 2017).

The Best That Has Been Thought and Said

31   **the ostensibly eternal list**: On the Western canon see Harold Bloom, *The Western Canon: The Books and School of the Ages* (New York: Harcourt Brace, 1994). For a critique of canon-making, see, among others, E. Dean Kolbas, *Critical Theory and the Literary Canon* (Boulder, CO: Westview Press, 2001); and, more recently, Philipp Löffler, ed., *Reading the Canon: Literary History in the 21st Century* (Heidelberg, Germany: Universitätsverlag Winter, 2017).

31   **She also reaffirmed her commitment**: Ozick, "T. S. Eliot at 101," 124–25.

32   **As he wrote in his famous essay**: T. S. Eliot, "The Metaphysical Poets," in *The Perfect Critic, 1919–1926*, eds. Anthony Cuda and Ronald Schuchard (Baltimore/London: Johns Hopkins University Press/Faber and Faber, 2014), vol. 2 of *The Complete Prose of T. S. Eliot: The Critical Edition*, gen. ed. Ronald Schuchard (2014–), 375–85, 381.

32   **rank artistic contributions**: T. S. Eliot, "William Blake," in *The Perfect Critic*, 187–92, 191.

33   **Richard Rorty when he writes**: Richard Rorty, *Achieving Our Country: Leftist Thought in Twentieth-Century America* (Cambridge, MA: Harvard University Press, 1998), 136.

The Rise of Theory

35   **In 1966, a group**: The proceedings of the conference are in Richard Macksey and Eugenio Donato, eds., *The Languages of Criticism and the Sciences of Man: The Structuralist Controversy* (Baltimore: Johns Hopkins University Press, 1970). See also Elena Russo, "1966: Morning in Baltimore," *Romanic Review* 101, nos. 1–2 (January–March 2010), 167–80.

37   **the *New York Times* published**: Jonathan Kandell, "Jacques Derrida, Abstruse Theorist, Dies at 74," *New York Times*, October 10, 2004, http:// www.nytimes.com/2004/10/10/obituaries/jacques-derrida-abstruse-theorist -dies-at-74.html.

37   **the sentence that would be quoted**: See part 2.2 of Jacques Derrida, *De la grammatologie* (Paris: Les Éditions de Minuit, 1967), 227. The translation is my own.

38   **As the comedian George Carlin**: See George Carlin's 1996 HBO special, *Back in Town*, directed by Rocco Urbisci (MPI Home Video, 2003).

39 **for Spivak, the othering is twofold**: Spivak's paper "Can the Subaltern Speak?" was published in the proceedings of the 1983 conference where it was first delivered; see *Marxism and the Interpretation of Culture*, eds. Cary Nelson and Lawrence Grossberg (Urbana: University of Illinois Press, 1988), 271–313.

39 **As the novelist Richard Wright**: See part 2 of *White Man, Listen!* in Richard Wright, *Black Power: Three Books from Exile* (New York: Harper Perennial Modern Classics, 2008) 631–812, 704–6.

39 **Harvard professor of English**: Henry Louis Gates, *Loose Canons: Notes on the Culture Wars* (New York: Oxford University Press, 1992), 111 (with my slight emendations).

40 **As Gates puts it**: Gates, *Loose Canons*, 175, 35–36, xiii, 33 (italics his).

The Liberal Imagination

42 **In an important essay**: T. S. Eliot, "The Function of Criticism," in *The Perfect Critic*, 458–68, 459.

42 **the critic I. A. Richards**: I. A. Richards, *Practical Criticism: A Study of Literary Judgment*, 2nd ed. (London: Kegan Paul, Trench, Trubner, 1930), 313, 15.

42 **The great philosopher of liberalism**: See chapter 2 of *On Liberty*, in John Stuart Mill, *Essays on Politics and Society* (1977), vol. 18 of *The Collected Works of John Stuart Mill*, gen. ed. J. M. Robson (1963–1991), 213–310, 232. Some of the ideas and quotations in this chapter were brought to my attention by "Many-Sided Lives: Liberal Judgment and the Realist Novel," Mathew T. Flaherty's dissertation, submitted to the Johns Hopkins University in May 2017.

43 **In his critical essay on the Romantic**: "Coleridge," in *Essays on Ethics, Religion and Society* (1969), vol. 10 of *The Collected Works of John Stuart Mill*, 117–63, 163.

43 **This passage from Mill**: See Lionel Trilling, *The Liberal Imagination* (New York: New York Review Books, 2008), xvi, xxi.

44 **As Harvard professor of English**: Louis Menand, "Introduction," in Trilling, *The Liberal Imagination*, vii–xiv, ix (italics his).

44 **A university, Cardinal Newman wrote**: See section 1:6.6 of John Henry Newman, *The Idea of a University: Defined and Illustrated in Nine Discourses Delivered to the Catholics of Dublin in Occasional Lectures and Essays Addressed to the Members of the Catholic University*, ed. Martin J. Svaglic (Notre Dame, IN: University of Notre Dame Press, 1982), 103.

44 **Sure enough, these are**: Gates, *Loose Canons*, xv.

45 **he cobbled together under**: Rorty, *Achieving Our Country*, 78, 89–90, 80, 84.

47 **As the critic Gerald Graff**: Graff, *Beyond the Culture Wars*, viii.

A Contagion of Disapproval

48 Dolezal was called: Rebecca Tuvel, "In Defense of Transracialism," *Hypatia* 32, no. 2 (Spring 2017), 263–78, 263.

49 She had strictly limited herself: Tuvel, "In Defense of Transracialism," 264.

50 Specifically, the authors faulted: The open letter to the *Hypatia* board can be found at https://docs.google.com/forms/d/1efp9CoMHch_6KfgtlmoP Z76nirWtcEsqWHcvgidl2mU.

50 In an op-ed piece: Rogers Brubaker, "The Uproar over 'Transracialism,'" *New York Times*, May 18, 2017, https://www.nytimes.com/2017/05/18/opi nion/the-uproar-over-transracialism.html.

An Authoritarian Underbelly

51 In 2014, a self-described contrarian: Laura Kipnis's article "Eyewitness to a Title IX Witch Trial," later adapted into *Unwanted Advances*, was published in the *Chronicle of Higher Education* in 2017, https://www.chron icle.com/article/Eyewitness-to-a-Title-IX-Witch/239634.

51 A letter signed by twenty-eight professors: "Rethink Harvard's Sexual Harassment Policy," *Boston Globe*, October 15, 2014, http://www.bostonglobe .com/opinion/2014/10/14/rethink-harvard-sexual-harassment-policy/HFDD iZN7nU2UwuUuWMnqbM/story.html.

52 One of the conclusions: Kipnis, *Unwanted Advances*, 2.

52 a group of professors posted: The open letter following Kipnis's talk at Wesleyan was published by the Foundation for Individual Rights in Education, https://www.thefire.org/subject-facstaffdiscuss-statement-cere -faculty-re-laura-kipnis-freedom-project-visit-aftermath.

55 As the critic Kenan Malik: Kenan Malik, "In Defense of Cultural Appro- priation," *New York Times*, June 14, 2017, https://www.nytimes.com/2017/06 /14/opinion/in-defense-of-cultural-appropriation.html.

55 "That even the disfigured corpse": Hannah Black's letter is printed in full in Lorena Muñoz-Alonso, "Dana Schutz's Painting of Emmett Till at Whitney Biennial Sparks Protest," *ArtNet News*, March 21, 2017, https:// news.artnet.com/art-world/dana-schutz-painting-emmett-till-whitney -biennial-protest-897929.

55 to engage in what another critic: Adam Shatz, "Raw Material," *LRB Blog*, March 24, 2017, https://www.lrb.co.uk/blog/2017/03/24/adam-shatz/raw -material.

56 we should perhaps wonder along: Brubaker, "The Uproar over 'Transra- cialism.'"

Boutique Multiculturalism

57 the term was used to designate: Richard Bernstein, *Dictatorship of Virtue: How the Battle over Multiculturalism Is Reshaping Our Schools, Our Country, and Our Lives* (New York: Vintage, 1995), 4.

57 he chose as his topic: For Stanley Fish's critique, see "Boutique Multiculturalism, or Why Liberals Are Incapable of Thinking about Hate Speech," *Critical Inquiry* 23, no. 2 (Winter 1997), 378–95.

57 As one of these, Richard Bernstein: Bernstein, *Dictatorship of Virtue*, 6. For a history of the concept of multiculturalism and its political and philosophical legacy, see among others Sarah Song, "Multiculturalism," 2016 revision, in Edward N. Zalta, ed., *Stanford Encyclopedia of Philosophy*, Spring 2017 ed., https://plato.stanford.edu/entries/multiculturalism. For its impact on higher education, see James A. Banks, ed., *Handbook of Research on Multicultural Education*, 2nd ed. (San Francisco: Jossey-Bass, 2004). On the self-serving institutional embrace of multiculturalism, see Roderick A. Ferguson, *The Reorder of Things: The University and Its Pedagogies of Minority Difference* (Minneapolis: University of Minnesota Press, 2012).

58 U.S. history was cut down: Arthur M. Schlesinger Jr., *The Disuniting of America: Reflections on a Multicultural Society*, rev. ed. (New York: W. W. Norton, 1998), 72.

58 In 1989, New York: The report by the New York State Task Force on Minorities and its revisions are quoted in Schlesinger, *The Disuniting of America*, 72–73.

58 his theories, including one dividing: Leonard Jeffries is described in Schlesinger, *The Disuniting of America*, 73–74.

59 In defense of its decision: The announcement that Brandeis would rescind Hirsi Ali's honorary degree is available at http://www.brandeis.edu/now/2014/april/commencementupdate.html.

59 including calling the religion: Ayaan Hirsi Ali's remarks come from a 2007 interview; see David Cohen, "'Violence is Inherent in Islam—It is a Cult of Death': Islamic Faith Schools Must Close, Sharia Law Could Happen Here; Multiculturalism Has Failed; Islam is the New Fascism," *London Evening Standard*, February 7, 2007, 18.

59 as its president observed: See the 2006 interview with Jehuda Reinharz, then president of Brandeis, quoted in David Bernstein, "Brandeis University's Double Standard on Honorary Degrees," *Washington Post*, April 9, 2014, https://www.washingtonpost.com/news/volokh-conspiracy/wp/2014/04/09/brandeis-universitys-double-standard/?utm_term=.463e92920deo.

60 Unfortunately, as Greg Lukianoff: Greg Lukianoff and Jonathan Haidt, "The Coddling of the American Mind," *Atlantic*, September 2015, https://www.theatlantic.com/magazine/archive/2015/09/the-coddling-of-the-american-mind/399356.

A Presupposition of Incommunicability

63 **As underrepresented minorities**: For completion rates of bachelor's degree programs by race, see a 2017 report by the National Student Clearinghouse Research Center, Doug Shapiro, Afet Dundar, Faye Huie, Phoebe Khasiala Wakhungu, Xin Yuan, Angel Nathan, and Youngsik Hwang, "Completing College: A National View of Student Attainment Rates by Race and Ethnicity—Fall 2010 Cohort (Signature Report No. 12b)," 2017, https://nscre searchcenter.org/signaturereport12-supplement-2.

63 **"White privilege"**: For an early description of the "invisible weightless knapsack" of white privilege, see Peggy McIntosh's paper "White Privilege and Male Privilege," first published in 1989 and reprinted in Michael S. Kimmel and Abby L. Ferber, eds., *Privilege: A Reader*, 4th ed. (Boulder, CO: Westview Press, 2016), 28–40. For an account of white privilege in the wake of the Black Lives Matter movement, see Jim Wallis, *America's Original Sin: Racism, White Privilege, and the Bridge to a New America* (Ada, MI: Brazos Press, 2016).

64 **He recalled how in his first year**: Duwain Pinder's speech is quoted in Fred Thys, "Black Harvard Students Hold Their Own Commencement Ceremony," WBUR, Boston, May 23, 2017, http://www.wbur.org/edify/2017/05/23/harvard-black-commencement.

64 **At a similar celebration at Columbia**: Lizzette Delgadillo is quoted in Anemona Hartocollis, "Celebrations of Diversity in Distinct Ceremonies," *New York Times*, June 3, 2017, https://www.nytimes.com/2017/06/02/us/black-commencement-harvard.html.

64 **For anti-affirmative-action crusader**: Ward Connerly is quoted in Hartocollis, "Celebrations of Diversity."

65 **As Upton Sinclair famously said**: See chapter 20 of Upton Sinclair's 1934 booklet, *I, Candidate for Governor: And How I Got Licked*, ed. James N. Gregory (Berkeley: University of California Press, 1994), 109.

Hyperspecialization

65 **"socialistic eggheads of the professoriate"**: Gage, "How 'Elites' Became One of the Nastiest Epithets."

65 **Ronald Reagan's negative fantasy**: See the text of his 1964 speech, Ronald Reagan, "A Time for Choosing (The Speech—October 27, 1964)," in Eric D. Patterson and Jeffry H. Morrison, eds., *The Reagan Manifesto: "A Time for Choosing" and Its Influence* (New York: Springer, 2016), 131–41, 132.

66 **It all ends at the MLA**: See part 5.1 of David Lodge, *Small World* (London: Secker & Warburg, 1984), 314–15.

67 **symptoms of the hyperspecialization**: For a history and statistical survey of specialization in the academic discipline of history, which mirrors anecdotal

evidence about other disciplines, see Robert B. Townshend, "The Rise and Decline of History Specializations over the Past 40 Years," *Perspectives on History*, December 2015, https://www.historians.org/publications-and-direc tories/perspectives-on-history/december-2015/the-rise-and-decline-of-history -specializations-over-the-past-40-years.

68 **As Jamie Koufman, a clinical professor**: Jamie Koufman, "The Specialists' Stranglehold," *New York Times*, June 4, 2017, https://www.nytimes .com/2017/06/03/opinion/sunday/the-specialists-stranglehold-on-medi cine.html.

69 **As he once put it**: Rorty, *Achieving Our Country*, 128, 130.

The Trap of Relevance

70 **Tenure is a loaded word**: For an early history of tenure in American universities, see Richard Hofstadter and Walter P. Metzger, *The Development of Academic Freedom in the United States* (New York: Columbia University Press, 1955). For the variety of responses to academic tenure, see the considerations of the former president of the American Association of University Professors, James E. Perley, "Reflections on Tenure," *Sociological Association* 41, no. 4 (1998), 723–28.

70 **in the belief that**: Rick Brattin is quoted in Colleen Flaherty, "Killing Tenure," *Inside Higher Ed*, January 13, 2017, https://www.insidehighered .com/news/2017/01/13/legislation-two-states-seeks-eliminate-tenure-public -higher-education.

The Time to Think

74 **One of our founding documents**: "General Statements in Respect to the Plan of this University," from the 1877–1878 *Johns Hopkins Register*, is cited in Laurence R. Veysey, *The Emergence of the American University* (Chicago: University of Chicago Press, 1965), 149.

74 **For Newman, the object**: The passages from the preface to Newman's *Idea of a University*, xxxvii, are treated in Kevin Carey, *The End of College: Creating the Future of Learning and the University of Everywhere* (New York: Riverhead, 2015), 29–31.

74 **As he wrote in an article**: Charles William Eliot, "The New Education," *Atlantic*, February 1869, https://www.theatlantic.com/magazine/archive /1869/02/the-new-education/309049.

75 **As the historian Hal Lawson**: Hal Lawson, "Specialization and Fragmentation among Faculty as Endemic Features of Academic Life," *Quest* 43, no. 3 (December 1991), 280–95, 283.

75 **"The most pronounced effect"**: Veysey, *The Emergence of the American University*, 143–44.

75 **As Cambridge professor of English**: See Stefan Collini's foreword to Maggie Berg and Barbara K. Seeber, *The Slow Professor: Challenging the Culture of Speed in the Academy* (Toronto: University of Toronto Press, 2016), viii.

77 **As shown by one survey**: Heather Menzies and Janice Newson, "No Time to Think: Academics' Life in the Globally Wired University," *Time & Society* 16, no. 1 (March 2007), 83–98, http://journals.sagepub.com/doi/pdf/10.11 77/0961463X07074103.

77 **What has been widely described**: On the adoption of corporate practices by institutions of higher learning in the United States, see Benjamin Ginsberg, *The Fall of the Faculty: The Rise of the All-Administrative University and Why It Matters* (New York: Oxford University Press, 2011).

78 **the corporate model has**: Berg and Seeber, *The Slow Professor*, 14.

78 **professor Terry Eagleton's impression**: Terry Eagleton, "The Slow Death of the University," *Chronicle of Higher Education*, April 6, 2015, http://www.chronicle.com/article/The-Slow-Death-of-the/228991.

79 **Hunter Rawlings, a former president**: Hunter Rawlings, "College Is Not a Commodity. Stop Treating It like One," *Washington Post*, June 9, 2015, https://www.washingtonpost.com/posteverything/wp/2015/06/09/college -is-not-a-commodity-stop-treating-it-like-one/?utm_term=.9d3eec5db121.

A Neoliberal Ethic

81 **The current wave of "disinvitations"**: Passages of this section have been developed from arguments David R. Castillo and I make in *Medialogies: Reading Reality in the Age of Inflationary Media* (New York: Bloomsbury, 2017).

81 **According to a 2010 survey**: The survey, "Engaging Diverse Viewpoints: What Is the Campus Climate for Perspective-Taking?," was conducted by Eric L. Dey, Molly C. Ott, Mary Antonaros, Cassie L. Barnhardt, and Matthew A. Holsapple and published by the Association of American Colleges and Universities in 2010, using data from 2007, https://www.aacu.org/sites/ default/files/files/core_commitments/engaging_diverse_viewpoints.pdf.

81 **"There's no such thing"**: Stanley Fish, *There's No Such Thing as Free Speech: And It's a Good Thing, Too* (New York: Oxford University Press, 1994), 102.

82 **As Frank Fear, a professor emeritus**: Frank Fear is quoted in Castillo and Egginton, *Medialogies*, 115.

83 **"Neoliberalism" normally refers**: On the concept of neoliberalism and its political afterlife, see among others David Harvey, *A Brief History of Neoliberalism* (New York: Oxford University Press, 2005); Manfred B. Steger and Ravi K. Roy, *Neoliberalism: A Very Short Introduction* (New York: Oxford University Press, 2010); and Daniel Stedman Jones, *Masters of the Universe: Hayek, Friedman, and the Birth of Neoliberal Politics* (Princeton, NJ: Princeton University Press, 2012). For a critique, see, for example, Simon Springer, *The*

Discourse of Neoliberalism: An Anatomy of a Powerful Idea (Lanham, MD: Rowman & Littlefield, 2016).

84 **"decolonising" the university**: The School of Oriental and African Studies document is quoted in Kenan Malik, "Are Soas Students Right to 'Decolonise' Their Minds from Western Philosophers?," *Guardian*, February 19, 2017, https://www.theguardian.com/education/2017/feb/19/soas-philosopy -decolonise-our-minds-enlightenment-white-european-kenan-malik.

84 **The *Telegraph*, a popular London paper**: Camilla Turner, "University Students Demand Philosophers Such as Plato and Kant Are Removed from Syllabus Because They Are White," *Telegraph*, January 8, 2017, http://www .telegraph.co.uk/education/2017/01/08/university-students-demand-philoso phers-including-plato-kant.

85 **in this case the *Guardian***: "Soas Students Have a Point. Philosophy Degrees Should Look Beyond White Europeans," *Guardian*, January 10, 2017, https://www.theguardian.com/commentisfree/2017/jan/10/soas-stud ents-study-philosophy-africa-asia-european-pc-snowflakes.

86 **many in the United Kingdom**: Camilla Turner, "Universities Warned over 'Snowflake' Student Demands," *Telegraph*, January 8, 2017, http://www .telegraph.co.uk/news/2017/01/08/universities-warned-snowflake-student -demands.

Sounding the Alarm

87 **as a recent Pew survey**: The survey, "The Partisan Divide on Political Values Grows Even Wider," was released by Pew on October 5, 2017; see http://www.people-press.org/2017/10/05/the-partisan-divide-on-political -values-grows-even-wider.

II. Inequality

The Great Equalizer

94 **Aaron Hanlon, now an assistant professor**: Aaron Hanlon, "Advice for My Conservative Students," *New York Times*, February 16, 2017, https://www .nytimes.com/2017/02/16/opinion/advice-for-my-conservative-students.html.

95 **As the *New York Times*'s**: Nate Cohn, "Election Review: Why Crucial State Polls Turned Out to Be Wrong," *New York Times*, June 1, 2017, https://www.nytimes.com/2017/05/31/upshot/a-2016-review-why-key-state -polls-were-wrong-about-trump.html.

95 **On a call-in radio show**: Tom Ashbrook with Mark Lilla, Vann Newkirk, and Michelle Goldberg, "The Future—or End—of Identity Politics," *On Point*, WBUR, Boston, November 23, 2016, http://www.wbur.org/onpoint /2016/11/23/identity-politics-clinton-trump-voters.

96 **where the rural poor of Kentucky**: At a fund-raiser on September 9, 2016, Hillary Clinton categorized some of Trump's supporters as a "basket of deplorables"; see the transcript in Katie Reilly, "Read Hillary Clinton's 'Basket of Deplorables' Remarks about Donald Trump Supporters," *Time*, September 10, 2016, http://time.com/4486502/hillary-clinton-basket-of-deplorables-transcript.

96 **In the words of Larry Laughlin**: Larry Laughlin is quoted in Sabrina Tavernise, "As Fake News Spreads Lies, More Readers Shrug at Truth," *New York Times*, December 7, 2016, https://www.nytimes.com/2016/12/06/us/fake-news-partisan-republican-democrat.html.

97 **Barack Obama's famous speech**: See the transcription of Barack Obama's keynote address at the 2004 Democratic National Convention at *The American Presidency Project*, http://www.presidency.ucsb.edu/ws/?pid=76988.

97 **One daughter of a working-class family**: The midwestern student is quoted in Elizabeth A. Armstrong and Laura T. Hamilton, *Paying for the Party: How College Maintains Inequality* (Cambridge, MA: Harvard University Press, 2013), 27–28.

98 **The percentage of the federal budget**: For a history of federal education spending, see Matthew G. Springer, Eric A. Houck, and James W. Guthrie, "History and Scholarship Regarding United States Education Finance and Policy," in Helen F. Ladd and Margaret E. Goertz, eds., *Handbook of Research in Education Finance and Policy*, 2nd ed. (New York: Routledge, 2015), 3–20; see in the same volume Nora E. Gordon, "The Changing Federal Role in Education Finance and Governance," 317–35.

98 **Justice Lewis F. Powell, who authored**: See the opinion at "San Antonio Indep. Sch. Dist. v. Rodriguez, 411 U.S. 1, 18, 2 (1973)," https://supreme.justia.com/cases/federal/us/411/1/case.html.

98 **In a powerful dissent**: See Thurgood Marshall's dissent, "*San Antonio Independent School District v. Rodriguez* (1973)," in *Thurgood Marshall: His Speeches, Writings, Arguments, Opinions, and Reminiscences*, ed. Mark V. Tushnet (Chicago: Lawrence Hill Books, 2001), 328–46, 334.

99 **Prior to 1980, the poverty rate**: For poverty rates across various levels of education, see the 2014 study by the Pew Research Center, "The Rising Cost of Not Going to College," http://www.pewsocialtrends.org/2014/02/11/the-rising-cost-of-not-going-to-college. Pew also conducted a poll on the perceived negative impact of higher education; see Hannah Fingerhut, "Republicans Skeptical of Colleges' Impact on U.S., but Most See Benefits for Workforce Preparation," July 20, 2017, http://www.pewresearch.org/fact-tank/2017/07/20/republicans-skeptical-of-colleges-impact-on-u-s-but-most-see-benefits-for-workforce-preparation.

What Happened to the American Dream?

101　The historian James Truslow Adams: On the "American dream," see the epilogue to James Truslow Adams, *The Epic of America* (Boston: Little, Brown, 1931), 404. The concept is treated by Richard V. Reeves in *Dream Hoarders: How the American Upper Middle Class Is Leaving Everyone Else in the Dust, Why That Is a Problem, and What to Do About It* (Washington, D.C.: Brookings Institution Press, 2017).

101　As a reporter from *Time*: The 1953 *Time* article, Alvin Josephy's "The U.S.: A Strong and Stable Land," is quoted in Paul Krugman, *The Conscience of a Liberal* (New York: W. W. Norton, 2007), 37–38.

102　the portion of families owning: Home ownership figures by decade are available from the U.S. Census Bureau at https://www.census.gov/hhes /www/housing/census/historic/owner.html.

102　top marginal tax rates that peaked: For historical data on tax rates, see Kenneth Scheve and David Stasavage, *Taxing the Rich: A History of Fiscal Fairness in the United States and Europe* (Princeton, NJ: Princeton University Press, 2016). For a history of U.S. tax policy, see W. Elliot Brownlee, *Federal Taxation in America: A History*, 3rd ed. (New York: Cambridge University Press, 2016).

102　According to Krugman's analysis: Krugman, *The Conscience of a Liberal*, 129.

102　As the economist Richard V. Reeves: Reeves, *Dream Hoarders*, 3–4, 10–11.

103　what Anthony Carnevale, director: Anthony Carnevale is quoted in Karin Fischer, "Engine of Inequality," *Chronicle of Higher Education*, January 17, 2016, http://www.chronicle.com/article/Engine-of-Inequality/234952.

103　given that 90 percent of their benefits: Reeves, *Dream Hoarders*, 2.

104　"The empowerment of the hard right": Krugman, *The Conscience of a Liberal*, 7.

104　This is the situation that Thomas Frank: Thomas Frank, *What's the Matter with Kansas? How Conservatives Won the Heart of America* (New York: Henry Holt, 2005), 7 (italics his).

104　In 1970 only around a tenth: On national educational levels in modern U.S. history, see Bill Bishop with Robert G. Cushing, *The Big Sort: Why the Clustering of Like-Minded America Is Tearing Us Apart* (New York: Houghton Mifflin, 2008), 131.

106　by the year 2000: Bishop and Cushing, *The Big Sort*, 132.

107　As Mark Lilla describes: Mark Lilla, *The Once and Future Liberal: After Identity Politics* (New York: HarperCollins, 2017), 132 (italics his).

Toddler Trenches

111 In 1995, education researchers: Todd R. Risley and Betty Hart, *Meaningful Differences in the Everyday Experience of Young American Children* (Baltimore: Paul H. Brookes, 1995), 198.

112 In the view of Stanford: Larry Cuban is quoted in Alia Wong, "The Case Against Universal Preschool," *Atlantic*, November 18, 2014, https://www.theatlantic.com/education/archive/2014/11/the-case-against-universal-preschool/382853.

School Haze

113 Under Ronald Reagan in the 1980s: For a history of the major initiatives in U.S. educational policy, see the 2009 essay by the New York State Archives, "Federal Education Policy and the States, 1945–2009: A Brief Synopsis": http://www.archives.nysed.gov/common/archives/files/ed_background_overview_essay.pdf.

113 The preamble to that bill stated: The text of the Improving America's Schools Act is available through the digitized database of congressional legislation, https://www.congress.gov/103/bills/hr6/BILLS-103hr6enr.pdf.

113 But as early childhood educator: Erika Christakis, "Americans Have Given Up on Public Schools. That's a Mistake," *Atlantic*, October 2017, https://www.theatlantic.com/magazine/archive/2017/10/the-war-on-public-schools/537903.

115 the school choice movement: For a history of proposed and realized educational voucherizations, see Jim Carl, *Freedom of Choice: Vouchers in American Education* (Santa Barbara, CA: Praeger, 2011). For a recent study of the inconclusive economic outcomes of school voucher programs, see Dennis Epple, Richard E. Romano, and Miguel Urquiola, "School Vouchers: A Survey of the Economics Literature," *Journal of Economic Literature* 55, no. 2 (June 2017), 441–92.

115 As David Osborne, director: David Osborne, *Reinventing America's Schools: Creating a 21st Century Education System* (New York: Bloomsbury, 2017), 4.

116 with nearly "40 percent": Reeves, *Dream Hoarders*, 47, 48.

117 But as Reeves has shown: Reeves, *Dream Hoarders*, 47.

117 Journalist and now MacArthur Fellow: Nikole Hannah-Jones's comments come from a January 16, 2017, interview with Terry Gross on NPR's *Fresh Air*; see the transcript at https://www.npr.org/templates/transcript/transcript.php?storyId=509325266.

117 As the liberal commentator and Brookings Institution: E. J. Dionne is quoted in Reeves, *Dream Hoarders*, 17.

121 black families have often been: On the federally protected practice of redlining black families out of certain neighborhoods, see among others

Nathan Connolly, *A World More Concrete: Real Estate and the Remaking of Jim Crow South Florida* (Chicago: University of Chicago Press, 2014).

121 **while blacks today earn**: A 2016 Pew survey on racial wage gaps found that black men have earned 73 percent of white men's earnings since 1980, while black women earn 65 percent of white men's earnings, up from 56 percent in 1980; see Eileen Patten, "Racial, Gender Wage Gaps Persist in U.S. Despite Some Progress," http://www.pewresearch.org/fact-tank/2016/07/01/racial -gender-wage-gaps-persist-in-u-s-despite-some-progress. For data on racial disparities in wealth accumulation, see the 2015 study by Demos and the Institute on Assets and Social Policy, "The Racial Wealth Gap: Why Policy Matters," http://www.demos.org/sites/default/files/publications/RacialWealth Gap_1.pdf.

Educational Ecologies

123 **Public charters are one way of encouraging**: For an early history of charter schools in the United States, see Joseph Murphy and Catherine Dunn Shiffman, *Understanding and Assessing the Charter School Movement* (New York: Teachers College Press, 2002). More recently, see Osborne, *Reinventing America's Schools*, which also has figures on charter schools in New Orleans.

124 **Charter schools are, as David Osborne**: Osborne, *Reinventing America's Schools*, 5.

126 **The school has identified six**: See the program description at the Afya Public Charter School website at http://www.afyabaltimore.org/afya/ program.

129 **As Reeves has pointed out**: Reeves, *Dream Hoarders*, 47.

The College Bottleneck

131 **As the economist Richard Reeves has shown**: Reeves, *Dream Hoarders*, 53.

131 **The economist David Autor**: David H. Autor, "Skills, Education, and the Rise of Earnings Inequality among the 'Other 99 Percent,'" *Science* 344, no. 6186 (May 23, 2014), 843–51, 848, http://science.sciencemag.org/content /344/6186/843/tab-pdf.

131 **Reeves refers to the way college**: Reeves, *Dream Hoarders*, 86.

132 ***New York Times* columnist**: Frank Bruni, "Why College Rankings Are a Joke," *New York Times*, September 18, 2016, https://www.nytimes.com /2016/09/18/opinion/sunday/why-college-rankings-are-a-joke.html.

133 **"I love saying that"**: Freeman Hrabowski's comments come from an April 24, 2017, interview on WYPR's *Midday* with Tom Hall, https://www .listennotes.com/e/4fdd487bb3a74d51bf03f27cf728ed91/dr-freeman-hra bowski-on-education-civil-rights-and-baltimore-post-freddie-gray/?s=slug.

134 At UC San Diego, which five years: Detailed figures on Pell grants and their placement in American universities before 2013 are available from the Congressional Budget Office; see "The Federal Pell Grant Program: Recent Growth and Policy Options" (2013), https://www.cbo.gov/publication/44448. More recent data on Pell grant participation, endowment, and tuition figures are available from the 2017 College Access Index, *New York Times*, May 25, 2017, https://www.nytimes.com/interactive/2017/05/25/sunday-review/opi nion-pell-table.html.

135 As recently as 2003: Princeton's financial aid statistics are in David Leonhardt, "Princeton—Yes, Princeton—Takes On the Class Divide," *New York Times*, May 30, 2017, https://www.nytimes.com/2017/05/30/opinion/prince ton-takes-on-class-divide.html.

135 As the columnist David Leonhardt writes: David Leonhardt, "The Assault on Colleges—and the American Dream," *New York Times*, May 28, 2017, https://www.nytimes.com/2017/05/25/opinion/sunday/the-assault-on-colleges -and-the-american-dream.html.

136 well-meaning proposals like that: Katherine S. Newman and Hella Winston, *Reskilling America: Learning to Labor in the Twenty-First Century* (New York: Metropolitan, 2016).

Diversity in Higher Ed

143 Such "undermatching" of qualified students: Paul Fain, "Poverty and Merit," *Inside Higher Ed*, January 12, 2016, https://www.insidehighered .com/news/2016/01/12/high-achieving-low-income-students-remain-rare -most-selective-colleges.

143 In the words of the report: The 2016 Jack Kent Cooke Foundation study on low-income students' access to top institutions is Jennifer Giancola and Richard D. Kahlenberg, "True Merit: Ensuring Our Best Students Have Access to Our Best Colleges and Universities," http://www.jkcf.org/assets /1/7/JKCF_True_Merit_Report.pdf, 6.

144 As Caroline Hoxby, the Stanford economist: Caroline Hoxby's comments come from a March 16, 2015, interview with Don Gonyea on NPR's *How Learning Happens*; see the transcript at https://www.npr.org/templates/tran script/transcript.php?storyId=393339590. See also a paper authored by Hoxby and Christopher Avery, "The Missing 'One-Offs': The Hidden Supply of High-Achieving Low-Income Students," published by the Brookings Institution in 2013, https://www.brookings.edu/wp-content/uploads/2016/07/2013a _hoxby.pdf.

144 As Bruce Poch, then dean: Bruce Poch is quoted in Conor Friedersdorf, "Rural Kids and Elite Colleges," *Atlantic*, July 29, 2010, https://www.theatlan tic.com/national/archive/2010/07/rural-kids-and-elite-colleges/60591.

144 **Emily Steele, a senior at Fleming**: Emily Steele is quoted in Laura Pappano, "Voices from Rural America on Why (or Why Not) to Go to College," *New York Times*, February 5, 2017, https://www.nytimes.com/2017/01/31/education/edlife/voices-from-rural-america-on-why-or-why-not-go-to-college.html.

144 **A study by two sociologists**: Thomas Espenshade and Alexandria Walton Radford, *No Longer Separate, Not Yet Equal: Race and Class in Elite College Admission and Campus Life* (Princeton, NJ: Princeton University Press, 2009).

144 **"it was the reverse"**: Ross Douthat, "The Roots of White Anxiety," *New York Times*, July 19, 2010, http://www.nytimes.com/2010/07/19/opinion/19douthat.html.

145 **A poll conducted by the website**: For the 2017 survey conducted by *Inside Higher Ed* and Gallup, see Scott Jaschik and Doug Lederman, "2017 Survey of College and University Admissions Directors," https://www.insidehighered.com/booklet/2017-survey-college-and-university-admissions-directors.

From Inequality to Divisiveness

146 **The interview was with a Nicole Humphrey**: Nicole Humphrey's interview with Kelly McEvers aired on NPR's *All Things Considered* on May 10, 2017; see the transcript, "Section 8 Vouchers Help the Poor—but Only If Housing Is Available," at https://www.npr.org/templates/transcript/transcript.php?storyId=527660512.

147 **As the *Times* later reported**: John Eligon, Yamiche Alcindor, and Agustin Armendariz, "Tax Credits to House Poor Reinforce Racial Divisions," *New York Times*, July 3, 2017, https://www.nytimes.com/2017/07/02/us/federal-housing-assistance-urban-racial-divides.html.

148 **not, as we may like to assume**: Reeves, *Dream Hoarders*, 179.

148 **As the law professor Lee Anne Fennell**: Lee Anne Fennell, "Homes Rule," *Yale Law Journal* 112, no. 3 (December 2002), 617–44, 635.

148 **Reeves puts this in a nutshell**: Reeves, *Dream Hoarders*, 105, 27, 28.

149 **In his searing dissent**: See Thurgood Marshall's dissent, "*Regents of the University of California v. Bakke* (1978)," in *Thurgood Marshall*, 347–55, 352. The impact of the failure of the Supreme Court to protect education was discussed by Renee Montagne on NPR's *Morning Edition*; see the transcript, "Why America's Schools Have a Money Problem," at https://www.npr.org/templates/transcript/transcript.php?storyId=474256366.

The Revenge of the Middle Class

150 **Schaff hopes his political engagement**: Mike Schaff is quoted in Arlie Russell Hochschild, *Strangers in Their Own Land: Anger and Mourning on the American Right* (New York: New Press, 2016), 145 and 108.

151 **But as the moral psychologist**: Haidt's observations are in *The Righteous Mind: Why Good People Are Divided by Politics and Religion* (New York: Pantheon, 2012), xiv.

151 **In Hochschild's recounting**: Hochschild, *Strangers in Their Own Land*, 18.

152 **A 2011 Brookings Institution study**: For the 2011 Brookings study, see Elizabeth Kneebone, Carey Nadeau, and Alan Berube, "The Re-Emergence of Concentrated Poverty: Metropolitan Trends in the 2000s," https://www .brookings.edu/wp-content/uploads/2016/06/1103_poverty_kneebone_na deau_berube.pdf.

152 **As J. D. Vance reports on Middletown**: J. D. Vance, *Hillbilly Elegy: A Memoir of a Family and Culture in Crisis* (New York: HarperCollins, 2016), 50.

152 **In the words of local high school**: Jennifer McGuffey is quoted in Vance, *Hillbilly Elegy*, 55.

153 **Despite the words of its third**: For the University of Michigan motto and the educators' critiques of its inaccessibility, see Benjamin Wermund, "In Trump Country, a University Confronts Its Skeptics," *Politico*, November 9, 2017, https://www.politico.com/story/2017/11/09/university-of-michigan -admissions-low-income-244420.

153 **As one economist has written**: Steven Rosefielde, *Trump's Populist America* (Hackensack, NJ: World Scientific, 2017), xvii–xviii and 74.

154 **our military is made up of kids**: For figures on the demographic makeup of the U.S. armed forces, see the Department of Defense's report, "2015 Demographics: Profile of the Military Community," http://download.mili taryonesource.mil/12038/MOS/Reports/2015-Demographics-Report.pdf.

154 **The military, as Bill Bishop reports**: The DoD study is quoted in Bishop and Cushing, *The Big Sort*, 137.

155 **"Barack Obama strikes at the heart"**: Vance, *Hillbilly Elegy*, 191.

156 **Richard Rorty once argued**: For Rorty's ethnocentrism, see "On Ethnocentrism: A Reply to Clifford Geertz," *Michigan Quarterly Review* 25, no. 3 (Autumn 1986), 525–34, reprinted in *Objectivity, Relativism, and Truth* (1991), vol. 1 of his *Philosophical Papers* (New York: Cambridge University Press, 1991), 203–10.

156 **Instead, Rorty argued, we should**: For the concept of circles of loyalty, see Richard Rorty, *Contingency, Irony, and Solidarity* (Cambridge, UK: Cambridge University Press, 1989); and Richard Rorty, "Justice as Larger Loyalty," *Ethical Perspectives* 4, no. 3 (1997), 139–51, anthologized in *The Rorty Reader*, eds. Christopher J. Voparil and Richard J. Bernstein (Chichester, UK: Wiley-Blackwell, 2010), 433–43.

III. Community

Learning to Think

161 Murray is the coauthor of highly: Charles Murray presents theories linking IQ to race in *The Bell Curve: Intelligence and Class Structure in American Life* (New York: Free Press, 1994), coauthored with Richard J. Herrnstein. For some early critiques, see Bernie Devlin, Stephen E. Fienberg, Daniel P. Resnick, and Kathryn Roeder, eds., *Intelligence, Genes, and Success: Scientists Respond to* The Bell Curve (New York: Springer-Verlag, 1997).

162 As ranked by the *Princeton Review*: Reed College is listed first on the *Princeton Review*'s 2017 ranking of "Most Liberal Students," https://www .princetonreview.com/college-rankings?rankings=most-liberal-students.

162 As the group's leaders explained: The message from RAR is quoted in Chris Bodenner, "The Surprising Revolt at the Most Liberal College in the Country," *Atlantic*, November 2, 2017, https://www.theatlantic.com /education/archive/2017/11/the-surprising-revolt-at-reed/544682.

162 "In the face of intimidation": Lucía Martínez Valdivia, "Professors Like Me Can't Stay Silent About This Extremist Moment on Campuses," *Washington Post*, October 27, 2017, https://www.washingtonpost.com/opinions /professors-like-me-cant-stay-silent-about-this-extremist-moment-on-campuses/2017/10/27/fd7aded2-b9b0-11e7-9e58-e6288544af98_story .html?utm_term=.4eb857f4a859.

163 As one student put it, trying: The exchange between the two student activists is quoted in Bodenner, "The Surprising Revolt."

163 Yiannopoulos encouraged the crowd: Milo Yiannopoulos and Fred Smith Jr. are quoted in Eli Rosenberg, "A Graduation Speaker Raises Ire Before Taking the Podium," *New York Times*, May 27, 2017, https://www .nytimes.com/2017/05/26/nyregion/linda-sarsour-cuny-speech-protests .html.

164 As Martínez Valdivia put it: Martínez Valdivia, "Professors Like Me Can't Stay Silent."

166 As Erika Christakis notes: Christakis, "Americans Have Given Up on Public Schools." Christakis discusses a September 2017 survey by the Annenberg Public Policy Center; see "Americans are Poorly Informed about Basic Constitutional Provisions," https://www.annenbergpublicpolicycenter.org /americans-are-poorly-informed-about-basic-constitutional-provisions.

The Walrus and the Carpenter

168 some lines from Lewis Carroll's: "The Walrus and the Carpenter" appears in chapter 4 of *Through the Looking-Glass*; see Martin Gardner's revised edition, *More Annotated Alice: Alice's Adventures in Wonderland and Through* *the Looking-Glass and What Alice Found There* (New York: Random House, 1990), 218–22, 220.

169 The French sociologist Pierre Bourdieu: Pierre Bourdieu discusses "social capital" in "The Forms of Capital," first published in John Richardson, ed., *Handbook of Theory and Research for the Sociology of Education* (Westport, CT: Greenwood, 1985), 241–58, 242.

169–70 The column recounted him taking: David Brooks, "How We Are Ruining America," *New York Times*, July 11, 2017, https://www.nytimes.com/2017/07/11/opinion/how-we-are-ruining-america.html.

170 One week later he explicitly drew: David Brooks, "Getting Radical About Inequality," *New York Times*, July 18, 2017, https://www.nytimes.com/2017/07/18/opinion/inequality-pierre-bourdieu.html.

170 As he wrote almost seventy: Maynard Mack's article, "Directed Studies: Yale's Important New Contribution to Undergraduate Education," appeared in the May 1949 issue of the *Yale Alumni Magazine* and is quoted in Justin Zaremby's history of the program, *Directed Studies and the Evolution of American General Education*, published by the Whitney Humanities Center at Yale in 2006, https://directedstudies.yale.edu/sites/default/files/files/directed_studies_history.pdf.

170 what Roosevelt Montás, who directs: Roosevelt Montás is quoted in an article in the July-August 2017 issue of the *Yale Alumni Magazine*; see Molly Worthen, "Who Needs the Great Books?," https://yalealumnimagazine.com/articles/4528-who-needs-the-great-books.

171 As the *New Yorker* staff writer: David Denby, *Great Books: My Adventures with Homer, Rousseau, Woolf, and Other Indestructible Writers of the Western World*, 2nd ed. (New York: Simon & Schuster, 2005), 3.

171 As Danielle Allen has forcefully argued: Danielle Allen, *Our Declaration: A Reading of the Declaration of Independence in Defense of Equality* (New York: Liveright, 2014), 188.

171–72 The committee responsible for the choice: Loyola's mission to foster consideration for the oppressed is expressed in its Strategic Plan for 2017–2022, http://www.loyola.edu/about/strategic-plan; the Plan is quoted on the Common Text homepage, http://www.loyola.edu/department/messina/common-text.

172 According to Randall: David Randall is quoted in Dana Goldstein, "Summer Reading Books: The Ties That Bind Colleges," *New York Times*, July 1, 2017, https://www.nytimes.com/2017/07/01/us/college-summer-reading.html. Randall's most recent recommendations for common-text programs, published by the National Association of Scholars in May 2017, include Jane Austen's *Persuasion* but no works of Aristotle; see "Beach Books: 2016–2017: What Do Universities Want Students to Read Outside Class?," https://www.nas.org/images/documents/beach_books/NAS_beachBooks2016_full.pdf.

173 **Davis, writing about him**: Joshua Davis, *Spare Parts: Four Undocumented Teenagers, One Ugly Robot, and the Battle for the American Dream* (New York: Farrar, Straus and Giroux, 2014), 35–36.

174 **virtually all of those who continue**: A PPRI survey in February 2017 revealed that Republicans are now more likely to assert that white citizens faced "a lot of discrimination" than make the claim about any other race; see Robert P. Jones, Daniel Cox, Betsy Cooper, and Rachel Lienesch, "Majority of Americans Oppose Transgender Bathroom Restrictions," http://www.prri.org/research/lgbt-transgender-bathroom-discrimination-religious-liberty.

175 **As the philosopher Adam Smith**: See chapters 1.1.1.3 and 1.1.1.9 in Adam Smith, *Theory of Moral Sentiments*, 10, 11.

Education and Fellow Feeling

177 **They also emphasize that**: Goldstein, "Summer Reading Books."

177 **"under physical and moral oppression"**: Thomas Jefferson to Professor Charles Bellini, September 30, 1785, in *Letters Written While in Europe, 1784–1789* (1903), vol. 5 of *The Writings of Thomas Jefferson*, ed. Andrew A. Lipscomb (Washington, D.C.: Thomas Jefferson Memorial Association, 1903), 151–54, 152. This and the following letters of Jefferson are treated in John Ferling, *Jefferson and Hamilton: The Rivalry That Forged a Nation* (New York: Bloomsbury Press, 2013), 166.

177 **"several stages of degradation"**: See Thomas Jefferson's observations on a draft of Jean-Nicholas Démeunier's entry "États Unis" for the *Encyclopédie methodique*, "Jefferson's Observations on Démeunier's Manuscript, 22 June," in *1786: Continued* (1954), vol. 10 of *The Papers of Thomas Jefferson*, gen. ed. Julian P. Boyd (Princeton, NJ: Princeton University Press, 1950–), 30–61, 52.

177 **"ignorance and prejudices"**: Thomas Jefferson to Professor George Wythe, August 13, 1786, in *1786: Continued*, 243–45, 244.

178 **his version of civil society**: John Locke, *Letter Concerning Toleration*, trans. William Popple, ed. Mark Goldie, http://oll.libertyfund.org/titles/locke-a-letter-concerning-toleration-and-other-writings.

180 **This is what the First Amendment**: Citations of the Bill of Rights follow Neil H. Cogan's edition, *The Complete Bill of Rights: The Drafts, Debates, Sources, and Origins* (New York: Oxford University Press, 1997).

180 **a letter to Yale University's provost**: Pauli Murray is quoted in Peter Salovey, "Free Speech, Personified," *New York Times*, November 27, 2017, https://www.nytimes.com/2017/11/26/opinion/free-speech-yale-civil-rights.html.

181 **As Barack Obama put it**: For Barack Obama's June 4, 2009, address at Cairo University, see *Barack Obama: 2009* (2010), vol. 1 of the *Public Papers of the Presidents of the United States: Barack Obama* (Washington, D.C.: National Archives and Records Administration, 2010–), 760–68, 766.

Democracy and the Liberal Arts

182 **The young confederation's secretary**: John Jay to George Washington, June 27, 1786, in *April 1786–January 1787* (1995), vol. 4 of *The Papers of George Washington: Confederate Series*, eds. William Wright Abbot and Dorothy Twohig (Charlottesville: University of Virginia, 1983–), 130–32, 131. These and other letters from the period are treated in Ferling, *Jefferson and Hamilton*, 4.

182 **Washington's reply offered**: George Washington to John Jay, August 15, 1786, in *April 1786–January 1787*, 212–13, 212.

182 **"the good sense of the people"**: Thomas Jefferson to Colonel Edward Carrington, January 16, 1787, in *Letters Written While in Europe, 1784–1790* (1903), vol. 6 of *The Writings of Thomas Jefferson*, 55–59, 57.

182 **"enjoys a precious degree"**: Thomas Jefferson to James Madison, January 30, 1787, in *Letters Written While in Europe, 1784–1790*, 63–73, 65.

182 **"the more discerning part of the Community"**: George Washington to John Jay, March 10, 1787, in *February–December 1787* (1997), vol. 5 of *The Papers of George Washington*, 79–80, 80.

182 **"measures the best calculated"**: George Washington to John Jay, August 15, 1786, 212.

183 **his efforts ran up against the resistance**: Garrett Ward Sheldon, *The Political Philosophy of Thomas Jefferson* (Baltimore: Johns Hopkins University Press, 1991), 65.

183 **Jefferson's most famous attempt**: See Bill 79, "A Bill for the More General Diffusion of Knowledge," in *1777 to 18 June 1779, Including the Revisal of the Laws, 1776–1786* (1950), vol. 2 of *The Papers of Thomas Jefferson*, 526–35, 526–27.

184 **"mutually pledge to each other"**: Citations of the Declaration of Independence follow the transcription of the Timothy Matlack parchment by the National Archives, https://www.archives.gov/founding-docs/declaration-transcript. For a history of the document and reproductions of drafts and variant manuscripts, see Julian P. Boyd, ed., *The Declaration of Independence: The Evolution of the Text* (Washington, D.C.: Library of Congress, 1943). In April 2017, Danielle Allen and Emily Sneff of Harvard's Declaration Resources Project announced their identification of a second parchment in West Sussex, UK, dated to the late 1780s; see "The Sussex Declaration," Delcaration Resources Project, https://declaration.fas.harvard.edu/resources/sussex-dec.

185 **Ticknor, who eventually accepted**: George Ticknor to Thomas Jefferson, April 23, 1816, in *1 September 1815 to 30 April 1816* (2012), vol. 9 of *The Papers of Thomas Jefferson: Retirement Series*, ed. J. Jefferson Looney (Princeton, NJ: Princeton University Press, 2004–), 696–99, 698. On Ticknor's educational experience abroad, see Louis Menand, Paul Reitter, and Chad Wellmon, eds., *The Rise of the Research University: A Sourcebook* (Chicago:

University of Chicago Press, 2017). See also Leslie Bohon's 2014 article for the *William & Mary Educational Review*, "Accidental Agent of Change: George Ticknor's Study Abroad in 1815 Germany," https://publish.wm.edu/cgi/viewcontent.cgi?article=1020&context=wmer.

186 **dedicated himself to the study**: Jefferson's own education is discussed in Ferling, *Jefferson and Hamilton*, 13.

186 **"liberality of sentiment"**: James Keir, *Account of the Life and Writings of Thomas Day, Esq.* (London: John Stockdale, 1791), 30.

186 **As he later wrote**: Thomas Jefferson to Charles Yancey, January 6, 1816, in *1 September 1815 to 30 April 1816* (2012), vol. 9 of *The Papers of Thomas Jefferson: Retirement Series*, 328–31, 331.

186 **In that letter Banneker challenged**: Benjamin Banneker to Thomas Jefferson, August 19, 1791, in *6 August 1791 to 31 December 1791*, ed. Charles T. Cullen (1986), vol. 22 of *The Papers of Thomas Jefferson*, 49–54, 50.

Media Literacy

187 **The Czech novelist Milan Kundera**: "Man Thinks, God Laughs," Kundera's acceptance speech for the 1985 Jerusalem Prize for Literature, was printed in the *New York Review of Books* in June 1985 and published as "Jerusalem Address: The Novel and Europe," part 7 in *The Art of the Novel*, trans. Linda Asher (New York: Grove Press, 1988), 155–165, 164–65.

188 **By the sixteenth century**: Anthony Grafton and Lisa Jardine, *From Humanism to the Humanities: Education and the Liberal Arts in Fifteenth- and Sixteenth-Century Europe* (Cambridge, MA: Harvard University Press, 1986), 125.

189 **As the historians Anthony Grafton**: Grafton and Jardine, *From Humanism to the Humanities*, 137.

190 **in the words of the Oxford historian**: James McConica is quoted in Grafton and Jardine, *From Humanism to the Humanities*, 141.

190 **what twentieth-century critics and teachers**: F. R. Leavis, *The Living Principle: "English" as a Discipline of Thought* (New York: Oxford University Press, 1975), 13.

190 **Such training would be**: Grafton and Jardine, *From Humanism to the Humanities*, 138.

190 **Specifically, he was convinced**: Grafton and Jardine, *From Humanism to the Humanities*, 145, 144.

190 **As Erasmus writes about his model**: Desiderius Erasmus is quoted in Grafton and Jardine, *From Humanism to the Humanities*, 147.

191 **in the words of Laura Boldrini**: Laura Boldrini is quoted in Jason Horowitz, "Taught in Italy: Reading, Math and Fake News," *New York Times*, October 19, 2017, https://www.nytimes.com/2017/10/18/world/europe/italy-fake-news.html.

191 **In an early essay penned**: Martin Luther King Jr.'s essay "The Purpose of Education" was published in the January-February 1947 issue of the Morehouse *Maroon Tiger*; it is reprinted in *Called to Serve: January 1929–June 1951* (1992), eds. Ralph E. Luker and Penny A. Russell, vol. 1 of *The Papers of Martin Luther King, Jr.*, gen. ed. Clayborne Carson (1992–2014), 123–24, 124.

192 **"Writers and thinkers need skills"**: Allen, *Our Declaration*, 149.

192 **This is what Daron Acemoglu**: See the 2014 paper by Daron Acemoglu and James A. Robinson, "The Rise and Fall of General Laws of Capitalism," 1, http://gabriel-zucman.eu/files/teaching/AcemogluRobinson14.pdf; and *Capital in the Twenty-First Century*, trans. Arthur Goldhammer (Cambridge, MA: Belknap Press, 2014).

192 **Allen adds, commenting**: Danielle Allen, *Education and Equality* (Chicago: University of Chicago Press, 2016), 32.

193 **In 2010, a report**: The 2010 report on civics proficiency was prepared by the National Assessment of Educational Progress for the National Center for Education Statistics; see "The Nation's Report Card: Civics 2010," https://nces.ed.gov/nationsreportcard/pdf/main2010/2011466.pdf.

193 **The Campaign for the Civic Mission**: Six strategies for energizing civics instruction are treated at length in a 2012 report by the Campaign for the Civic Mission of Schools, "Guardian of Democracy," http://civicmission.s3.amazonaws.com/118/fo/5/171/1/Guardian-of-Democracy-report.pdf.

193 **"factual knowledge about government"**: Alex Lin, "Citizenship Education in American Schools and Its Role in Developing Civic Engagement: A Review of the Research," *Educational Review*, 67, no. 1 (2015), 35–63, 38.

193 **This is what Allen proposes**: Allen, *Education and Equality*, 43–45.

Jefferson's Words

194 **a letter signed by more than 450**: The e-mail from UVA faculty and students is quoted in Karin Kapsidelis, "U.Va. Faculty, Students Ask Sullivan Not to Quote Jefferson," *Richmond Times-Dispatch*, November 14, 2016, http://www.richmond.com/news/virginia/u-va-faculty-students-ask-sullivan-not-to-quote-jefferson/article_cbb2f84f-edc6-56b6-9fcc-059ee8123d28.html.

195 **In her response to the letter**: Teresa Sullivan's e-mail is quoted in Kate Bellows, "Professors Ask Sullivan to Stop Quoting Jefferson," *Cavalier Daily*, November 13, 2016, http://www.cavalierdaily.com/article/2016/11/professors-ask-sullivan-to-stop-quoting-jefferson.

195 **Some of the marchers raised**: The neo-Nazi chants are reported in Elizabeth Chuck, "Holocaust Survivor on Charlottesville: 'White Supremacists Are Finding Another Voice,'" *NBC News*, August 14, 2017, https://www.nbcnews.com/news/us-news/holocaust-survivor-charlottesville-white-supremacists-are-finding-another-voice-n792461.

196 **There were "very fine people"**: "The President's Words On Hatred and History," *New York Times*, August 16, 2017, https://www.nytimes.com /2017/08/15/us/politics/trump-press-conference-transcript.html.

198 **Alexander Stephens, the vice president**: Alexander Stephens's "Cornerstone Address" is published as appendix B in Jon L. Wakelyn, ed., *Southern Pamphlets on Secession, November 1860–April 1861* (Chapel Hill: University of North Carolina Press, 1996), 402–12, 406.

198 **in a passage from Jefferson's original**: Thomas Jefferson's "Rough Draft of the Declaration of Independence" is document 5 in Boyd, ed., *The Declaration of Independence*, 51–54, 53.

199 **As Allen puts it regarding**: Allen, *Our Declaration*, 245.

200 **in Abraham Lincoln's words**: The five variants of Abraham Lincoln's Gettysburg Address all contain the promise of "a new birth of freedom"; see the appendix to Sean Conant, ed., *The Gettysburg Address: Perspectives on Lincoln's Greatest Speech* (New York: Oxford University Press, 2015), 321–32.

201 **This has led to the predominance**: David Brooks's "America: The Redeemer Nation" appeared in the November 24, 2017, edition of the *New York Times*, https://www.nytimes.com/2017/11/23/opinion/america-the-redeemer -nation.html.

201 **Lincoln used his characteristic**: For Lincoln's second inaugural address, see Harold Holzer and Thomas A. Horrocks, eds., *The Annotated Lincoln* (Cambridge, MA: Belknap Press, 2016), 563–66, 565, 564.

202 **For Brooks, the Second Inaugural**: Brooks, "America: The Redeemer Nation."

What Are People For?

204 **Over the last quarter of a century**: For data on the wage and debt increase for college graduates, see Shahien Nasiripour and Nicky Forster, "3 Charts That Show Just How Dire the Student Debt Crisis Has Become," *Huffington Post*, February 3, 2016, https://www.huffingtonpost.com/entry/3-charts-stu dent-debt-crisis_us_56b0e9d0e4b0a1b96203d369.

204 **students who show a balanced curriculum**: Data suggesting that a graduate with a STEM/humanities double major makes about five thousand dollars more can be found in Christos Makridis, "Does It Pay to Get a Double-Major in College?" *PBS NewsHour*, March 30, 2017, https://www .pbs.org/newshour/economy/pay-get-double-major-college.

204 **In University of Warwick economist**: Robert Skidelsky, "Basic Income Revisited," *Project Syndicate*, June 23, 2016, https://www.project-syndicate .org/commentary/unconditional-basic-income-revisited-by-robert-skidelsky -2016-06. On basic minimum income proposals, see most recently Philippe Van Parijs and Yannick Vanderborght, *Basic Income: A Radical Proposal for*

a Free Society and a Sane Economy (Cambridge, MA: Harvard University Press, 2017).

205 **While Cash refocused her practice**: Hilarie Cash is quoted in Johann Hari, *Lost Connections: Uncovering the Real Causes of Depression—and the Unexpected Solutions* (New York: Bloomsbury, 2018), 88.

206 **"While placing more and more"**: Ruth Whippman, "Happiness Is Other People," *New York Times*, October 29, 2017, https://www.nytimes.com/2017/10/27/opinion/sunday/happiness-is-other-people.html.

206 **As Johann Hari puts it**: Hari, *Lost Connections*, 82.

207 **Recently Les Moonves, the chairman**: At a conference in February 2016, Les Moonves of CBS remarked that Donald Trump "may not be good for America" but is "damn good for CBS"; see Paul Bond, "Leslie Moonves on Donald Trump: 'It May Not Be Good for America, but It's Damn Good for CBS,'" *Hollywood Reporter*, February 29, 2016, https://www.hollywoodreporter.com/news/leslie-moonves-donald-trump-may-87 1464.

207 **He claimed that the "thresholds"**: Mark Granovetter, "Threshold Models of Collective Behavior," *American Journal of Sociology* 83, no. 6 (May 1978), 1420–43.

208 **What Gladwell writes of the two-decade-long**: Malcolm Gladwell, "Thresholds of Violence," *New Yorker*, October 19, 2015, https://www.newyorker.com/magazine/2015/10/19/thresholds-of-violence.

208 **As David Brooks puts it**: David Brooks, "How to Engage a Fanatic," *New York Times*, October 24, 2017, https://www.nytimes.com/2017/10/23/opinion/engaging-fanatics.html.

209 **As Andrew Hussey has put it:** Andrew Hussey is quoted in George Packer, "The Other France," *New Yorker*, August 31, 2015, https://www.newyorker.com/magazine/2015/08/31/the-other-france.

Growing Community

209 **As Michael Higgins, president**: Higgins is quoted in Joe Humphreys, "Teach Philosophy to Heal Our 'Post-Truth' Society, Says President Higgins," *Irish Times*, November 19, 2016, https://www.irishtimes.com/news/education/teach-philosophy-to-heal-our-post-truth-society-says-president-higgins-1.2875247.

210 **As he put it**: See section 1:6.6 of Newman, *The Idea of a University*, 103.

210 **in the words of Bryan Doerries**: See the "Overview" for Theatre of War Productions at http://theaterofwar.com/projects/theater-of-war/overview.

212 **As journalist Gregory Warner tells**: Mohamed Barud is featured on a September 11, 2017, episode of Gregory Warner's podcast *Rough Translation*,

"Anna in Somalia," produced by Jess Jiang, MP3 audio, 31:42, https://www.npr.org/podcasts/510324/rough-translation.

212 **the fact that fewer that 7 percent**: On the educational attainment of members of the U.S. armed forces, see "2015 Demographics: Profile of the Military Community."

213 **Recalling what he saw**: Barack Obama is quoted in Ed Hornick, "Obama Highlights Plan for National Service," *CNN* July 2, 2008, http://www.cnn.com/2008/POLITICS/07/02/obama.service.

213 **As he wrote in a widely cited article**: Stanley McChrystal, "You Don't Have to Wear a Military Uniform to Serve Your Country," *Atlantic*, July 20, 2016, https://www.theatlantic.com/politics/archive/2016/07/you-dont-have-to-wear-a-military-uniform-to-serve-your-country/491765.

213 **with then senator John Ashcroft**: John Ashcroft is quoted in Richard Stengel, "A Time to Serve," *Time*, August 30, 2017, 2, http://content.time.com/time/specials/2007/article/0,28804,1657256_1657317_1657570-1,00.html.

214 **calling on Americans**: In an announcement about airline travel sixteen days after 9/11, George W. Bush urged viewers to visit "America's great destination spots"; he is quoted in "Bush on Airline Safety Measures," *Washington Post*, September 27, 2001, http://www.washingtonpost.com/wp-srv/nation/specials/attacked/transcripts/bush_092701.html. On this advice and the "broader pattern of encouraging financial irresponsibility," see Justin Fox, "Telling Us to Go Shopping," *Time*, January 19, 2009, http://content.time.com/time/specials/packages/article/0,28804,1872229_1872230_1872236,00.html.

214 **as one commentator has put it**: Stengel, "A Time to Serve," 2.

215 **The area is 97 percent**: Statistics on Sandtown-Winchester can be found in a 2011 report by the Baltimore City Health Department, "2011 Neighborhood Health Profile: Sandtown-Winchester/Harlem Park," https://health.baltimorecity.gov/sites/default/files/47%20Sandtown.pdf.

216 **created about a decade ago**: Marin Alsop's letter about the mission of OrchKids is available on the Baltimore Symphony Orchestra website, https://www.bsomusic.org/education-community/young-musicians/orchkids/letter-from-marin.aspx. See also the OrchKids site at http://www.bsomusic.org/education-community/young-musicians/orchkids.aspx.

The Idea of America

218 **quoting Dante's assertion**: Unbeknownst to most, they are quoting John F. Kennedy, not Dante. JFK's misquotation is cataloged by the John F. Kennedy Presidential Museum and Library at https://www.jfklibrary.org/Research/Research-Aids/Ready-Reference/JFK-Fast-Facts/Dante.aspx.

219 **Garrison Keillor rips into congressman:** Garrison Keillor, "Thank You, Trump Voters, for This Wonderful Joke," *Washington Post,* December 6, 2016, https://www.washingtonpost.com/opinions/thank-you-trump-voters -for-this-wonderful-joke/2016/12/06/235877ae-bbe2-11e6-91ee-1adddfe36 cbe_story.html?utm_term=.c33b45ee7322.

219 **When Mark Lilla, calling:** Lilla, *The Once and Future Liberal,* 133, 129.

219 **David Brooks, a conservative:** David Brooks, "How Cool Works in America Today," *New York Times,* July 25, 2017, https://www.nytimes .com/2017/07/25/opinion/how-cool-works-in-america-today.html.

219 **Lilla cites Lincoln's dictum:** Abraham Lincoln is quoted in Lilla, *The Once and Future Liberal,* 5.

220 **Van Jones has said it best:** Van Jones, *Beyond the Messy Truth: How We Came Apart, How We Come Together* (New York: Ballantine Books, 2017), 44.

220 **Political philosopher Yuval Levin:** Yuval Levin, "Taking the Long Way: Disciplines of the Soul Are the Basis of a Liberal Society," *First Things,* October 2014, https://www.firstthings.com/article/2014/10/taking-the -long-way.

221 **Van Jones, an observant:** Jones, *Beyond the Messy Truth,* 29.

221 **As Levin puts it:** Levin, "Taking the Long Way."

221 **David Brooks succinctly summarizes:** David Brooks, "Our Elites Still Don't Get It," *New York Times,* November 17, 2017, https://www.nytimes .com/2017/11/16/opinion/elites-taxes-republicans-congress.html.

222 **journalist Molly Worthen quoted:** Molly Worthen, "How to Escape From Roy Moore's Evangelicalism," *New York Times,* November 17, 2017, https://www.nytimes.com/2017/11/17/opinion/sunday/escape-roy-moores -evangelicalism.html.

224 **Unlike that Colossus:** "The New Colossus," in Emma Lazarus, *Selected Poems,* ed. John Hollander (New York: Library of America, 2005), 58.

224 **As Danielle Allen writes:** Allen, *Our Declaration,* 23.

Index

A Note on the Author

William Egginton is the Decker Professor in the Humanities and director of the Alexander Grass Humanities Institute at the Johns Hopkins University. His highly praised books include *How the World Became a Stage*, *The Theater of Truth*, *The Philosopher's Desire*, and *The Man Who Invented Fiction*. He regularly writes for the *New York Times*' online forum The Stone, the *LA Review of Books*, and Stanford University's *Arcade*. Egginton lives in Baltimore, Maryland, with his family.